The Handbook of Cricket

The Handbook of Cricket

KEITH ANDREW

PELHAM BOOKS

To Joyce, my wife and my best friend.

PELHAM BOOKS

Published by the Penguin Group
27 Wrights Lane, London W8 5TZ, England
Viking Penguin Inc., 375 Hudson Street, New
York, New York 10014, USA
Penguin Books Australia Ltd, Ringwood, Victoria,
Australia
Penguin Books Canada Ltd, 10 Alcorn Avenue
Toronto, Ontario, Canada M4V 3B2
Penguin Books (NZ) Ltd, 182–190 Wairau Road,
Auckland 10, New Zealand

Penguin Books Ltd, Registered Offices:
Harmondsworth, Middlesex, England

First published 1989
Revised edition 1995

Printed in Singapore
Typeset by Wyvern Typesetting Ltd, Bristol

A CIP catalogue record for this book is available from
the British Library

ISBN 0 7207 1893 7

Acknowledgements

I should like to thank the following: MCC, for permission to print the Laws of Cricket (1980 Code); NCA, for encouragement in all my writings, from which I have quoted (with NCA's permission as appropriate); Stephen Green, the MCC Curator, for kindly ensuring that I have not unwittingly changed the history of cricket! Tony Pullinger, David Walsh and Bob Cherry, not to mention one or two anonymous contributors, for willingly giving me information on their particular organisations within cricket; John Gray and John Reader for their contributions on the skills of bat and ball manufacture; and Joyce Andrew, for her tolerance with the author at all times and her patience in transcribing the manuscript.

Historical photographs—MCC and Sport and General Press.
Test match and special photography—Patrick Eagar.
Coaching photographs—Keith Andrew (Richard Hadlee sequence—John Cope).
Illustrations and diagrams—David Gifford.
Designed by Penny Mills.

Contents

CONTENTS

FOREWORD by
Sir Colin Cowdrey

In this wide-ranging book, Keith Andew draws upon the experience of a lifetime in cricket, having become an England wicket-keeper of real class, a National Coach and now the Chief Executive and Director of Coaching of the National Cricket Association. In writing this foreword I am delighted to remind you of how fine a cricketer he has been.

Keith was born and lived his early years in Lancashire. He was blessed with a good eye for a ball and a sharpness of mind which, I suspect, usually saw him at the top of his class. He graduated in Mechanical Engineering at the Manchester College of Technology and in later years became a lecturer on the subject.

Both he and Frank Tyson found their way blocked in Lancashire and qualified by residence for Northamptonshire, making their debut against the Australians in 1953. Keith burst upon the scene in 1954, attracting the selectors' attention immediately. A number of wicket-keeping sages were alerted to cast a discreet eye over him, Herbert Strudwick, Leslie Ames and George Duckworth as the principal observers. They were so impressed with him that he was to win the second wicket-keeper place, partnering Godfrey Evans, on Leonard Hutton's MCC team to Australia in 1954–5. It was a remarkable achievement after so few first-class matches. Practically unknown in May, he was destined to play his first Test match at Brisbane in November – my first Test match too.

At Northamptonshire, he was confronted with the stiffest possible examination, coping with Frank Tyson, as fast a bowler as the game has seen, and to the other extreme, reading the mysteries of chinaman and googly bowler George Tribe. Very quick on his feet, he moved deftly, especially when standing up to the wicket, and impressed everyone with the most marvellous pair of hands. All bowling came alike to him, no flap, no noise, no fuss and never in a hurry. If Godfrey Evans had not been at the height of his powers and five more years of running in him, I am sure that Keith would have won a regular England place and kept it for a long time.

It is on tour that cricketers really come to know one another well and it was my good luck to have Keith as a good friend and travelling companion on that first tour to Australia. He was dedicated to his wicket-keeping art, always superbly fit and meticulous in his attention to detail. He was a good listener and a shrewd observer with an impish sense of fun. He was particularly sharp at identifying the strengths and weaknesses of the opposition.

I do not doubt that the events of those early days did much to shape Keith's understanding and feel for the game, which is so well expressed in all his writings, and particularly in this book. In Chapter One, there is nostalgia for the history and personalities of the game. This is followed immediately by incisive technical comment on the skills and coaching of cricket. I particularly like the heading 'Attitudes' to cricket, wherein Keith suggests that a simple distillation of success is as good a way as any to reach conclusions on how the game may be played. In other words, without being dogmatic, there are many different ways to the top! Also, the very comprehensive 'Structure of Cricket' will be a revelation.

I commend this book to every thinking cricketer and suggest that it be a priority in the school library and on the bookshelf of every coach.

Colin Cowdrey

AUTHOR'S INTRODUCTION

This is the second of two introductions I have written to this book. Let me explain. My first effort was written before I put pen to paper on the book itself; my second was written on completion and some considerable time later. The book format is more or less as planned, but when I came actually to write the words I felt that somehow I needed to change their emphasis, as against my original intentions of writing for the already committed cricket lover. Without over simplifying any part of the subject I have tried to introduce an element that may interest a wider range of readers, the whole family in fact.

Colin Cowdrey has very kindly written a foreword to the book. I first met Colin when I played for Northants against Kent in 1954. I had never before seen anyone with so much 'time' to play every stroke. Even Frank Tyson did not seem so fast when Colin was at the wicket. I was privileged to play for England in his first Test match at Brisbane that same year. A record number of Test matches later, after an immense and continuing contribution to cricket, Colin Cowdrey is no different—a really nice man and a credit to the game.

Chapter One comprises a potted history of cricket and a few thoughts on the great players through the years, with a few facts and figures that might come in handy. I believe that the history and the records of the very best players are an integral, even an essential part of the understanding and enjoyment of the game, whereas in most other sports they do not seem to generate quite the same relative interest.

Having hopefully captured some of the flavour of cricket in the first chapter, I have next looked in some depth at the skills and techniques of playing cricket and the methods of training cricketers, mainly through coaching. I do not subscribe to the view that cricket is a simple game but I have attempted to make this section as straightforward as possible without being dogmatic. Most of the instruction, both in words and in the form of drawings and photographs is simply a distillation of the methods used by many of the best players in the world over a period of time. It is true there are exceptional players and coaches who successfully develop so-called unorthodox methods, but whilst they are in the minority there is no reason why they should conform to a particular pattern if nature rules otherwise. What suits one may not suit another. Success is the yardstick.

After what may be termed the technical sections of the book, I have put together a chapter on the structure of cricket, briefly defining the role played by the amazing number of major cricket organisations. The gathering of this information has been a revelation. I am sure that readers will be as surprised as I was at the active involvement and following that the game has. Neither in this have I mentioned the media who play an immense if not a purely cricket role. At the very least a lot of the mystifying initials now in use will be given some identity, whether it be NCA, TCCB, MCC, ACU or the host of others.

The subject of Chapter Five is 'cricket's necessities', that is the equipment and grounds which, with time, have achieved a place in the game, appreciated most by its ardent followers.

Next, I have taken time off and really

indulged myself in selecting favourite books and places where I have enjoyed cricket. I hope you get a fraction of the pleasure from my choices as I have had in making them.

Last but certainly not least I have taken a look at umpiring, scoring and the Laws of Cricket—a book in themselves. There is enough meat here to keep any erstwhile student of the game occupied well into the early hours. Maybe the reader, having acquired the knowledge, will be tempted to participate and become an umpire or a scorer, leading to a lifetime of warm companionship with the most friendly group of people and an unsurpassed view of the game.

So, I have completed this *Handbook of Cricket*. I hope every member of the family will find the book stimulating, enjoyable and useful.

Keith Andrew
Lord's Cricket Ground
1988

CHAPTER ONE

The History and Great Men of Cricket

If you have a love for the game of cricket, whether you are a player, an ex player, or simply an onlooker, many will be the pleasures in your life. Maybe you have the special pleasure of being a parent, whose son is just about the best batsman that ever was! Maybe you are one of the guardians of our game—an umpire or scorer. You could be one of a growing band of enthusiasts with a commitment to coaching young cricketers. Perhaps you just enjoy reading the sports pages in summer, sometimes crossing sporting swords with your mates in the local pub. No matter what your link with the game, you can be certain that sometime, somewhere, its environment and its traditions will catch up with you and give you a taste of bygone summer days. A taste very likely to turn into an appetite, even an addiction for cricket and its long and fascinating history.

For those of you who do succumb to the call to share a kindred feeling for cricket's past there are everlasting benefits, not least of which is the welcome to an international camaraderie whose members are almost duty-bound to participate, either as speaker or listener, in any 'in-depth' cricketing conversation—anywhere. No place is sacred: committee room, dressing-room, president's balcony, members' lounge, even in the 'standing room only' sections of any meeting place. Thankfully, having put the cricketing world, not to mention the world at large, right on many occasions, together with others of a similar ilk, I am a long-standing member of that fraternity. How else would I be writing this book? But membership is not easy to come by, nor is membership entirely concerned with cricket discussion. Experience of cricket history is an essential qualification—let me tell you how I gained some of mine. . . .

In my privileged position as a worker inside the Grace Gates of the famous Lord's Cricket Ground, I am of necessity required to pass through the Long Room, that cricket-

THE LONG ROOM—Pen and ink drawing by K. Fletcher, 1949.

ing holy of holies. Thousands of others have done so before me, but perhaps not all at such odd hours as on a Tuesday morning when the sun is rising, or at eleven o'clock at night in the middle of December.

I really feel that I earned my spurs one Hallowe'en when working very late in my pavilion office on the top floor. As I came down the darkened stairs, feeling for the outside door, I realised I was in fact in the Long Room and someone was talking in very strange tones. I listened with pounding heart to the voice of a man named Nyren relating cricketing stories from another age. Crouching under the massive table, in spite of my shivers of fright, I think I saw the ghost of Silver Billy Beldham going out to bat, and as the door reopened, W.G. himself thundered past, in not the best of moods, on his way to the dressing-room above. I got the feeling that he had been given out LBW! I shall also confide in you that on a cold winter's night in the year of the Centenary Test match I swear I heard the noise of cricket boots tumbling down the stairs. This time it was a team of Australians. They were congratulating two men, I think named Victor and Warwick, apparently on the innings they had played the day before. I knew they were Australians, as above the noise made by the boots on the stairs I also heard a comment, in a strong Australian accent, referring to the parentage of an English cricketer called MacLaren. Since then I understand it to be a term of endearment, used by Aussies when describing blueblooded Englishmen in general.

So I 'experienced' cricket history and became a 'member of the club'. What fun it is discussing the past with friends and comparing cricket's different eras, and even though my haunts have changed more towards the library than the pavilion these days, I am not averse to visiting places where the very best ghosts appear from time to time. Therefore, forgive me please, if in the short journey into history that lies ahead, I show something of a bias towards my 'special' friends. All addicts do, and after all they were more than just good players—they really were cricketers.

My closeness to the MCC Library with its unique collection of writings has been something of a barrier to me in recording some of the more significant occurrences in cricket history. I am sure the reader will appreciate the temptations for any cricketer, especially with little experience as a researcher, to be something of a grasshopper, trying to take in everything that was ever written on the game and its personalities, in the shortest possible time. Little did I know what treasures there were under my very nose. Little did I know what pleasures there could be in reliving history through the works of its marvellous chroniclers. One thing the many extra hours of reading have given me is another dimension to my enthusiasm for coaching. Already, by relating newly acquired historical knowledge to young players I seem to have kindled an extra interest in many of them.

Let us start at the very beginning. . . .

The Early Days

Apparently and understandably the beginnings of cricket are shrouded in mystery. From early translations it seems that as long ago as the thirteenth century a form of cricket was played in parts of Kent under the name 'creag'. The Reverend James Pycroft in *The Cricket Field* (1851) identified 'club ball' as the name which stood for cricket in the thirteenth century. 'Club ball', 'creag', or whatever, it seems reasonable to assume that a form of cricket had begun, although there is little evidence of cricket progressing further over the next two to three hundred years. The first definite written reference to cricket was discovered in a manuscript dated 16 January 1598, now in the possession of the

Mayor and Corporation of Guildford: 'When he was a scholler in the free school of Guildeford, he and several of his fellowes did runne and play there at cricket and other plaies.'

At this time and through the years of Oliver Cromwell, cricket or 'krickett' as it was then described, was played, but under some restriction in the sense that it had become a pastime linked with betting sports, such as wrestling and bear-baiting. In Ireland at one time it was banned altogether.

However, following the Restoration of 1660, as the reign of Charles II progressed, cricket became more popular, and by the early eighteenth century it was being played in a number of southern counties; in particular, Kent, Surrey, Sussex and Hampshire and to a lesser degree Essex, Hertfordshire, Bucks, Oxon and Berkshire. Cricket could be said to have been established and growing at this stage, although mainly in the London area.

Cricket first earned Royal patronage in 1723, when Frederick, the Prince of Wales and son of King George II, became an enthusiast, promoting many matches around London. His passion for the game and his considerable involvement did much to popularise cricket with the nobility of the day. In fact, a considerable number of eighteenth-century cricketers were of great social distinction.

In 1744 the first Code of Laws was drawn up by the then very well-established London Club who played on the famous Artillery Ground. Surrey cricket became a force to rival Kent having supplied many players to the London Club.

In the 1770s two of cricket's legendary characters were becoming recognised by their cricketing deeds. Edward Stevens or 'Lumpy', as he became known throughout the cricket world, was one of the most famous bowlers of the time. He was renowned for his accuracy and on one memorable occasion in 1775, when playing against the great Hambledon Club, he delivered three balls that went 'through' the wicket (at that time only two stumps surmounted by one bail) without disturbing the bail. Hambledon won the match in the end, amongst some controversy, but the accuracy of Lumpy Stevens resulted in the third stump being added to the wicket in a very short space of time.

The other character was Thomas 'Shock' White, a batsman of some renown in Surrey, who once appeared to bat against Hambledon with a bat as wide as the stumps. As a matter of some urgency his bat was shaved with a knife and a law was introduced, limiting the width of a bat to four and a quarter inches. This law stands today.

William Beldham was born at Wrecclesham, near Farnham, Surrey, on 5 February 1766. One of cricket's legendary figures, he was known as 'Silver Billy' because of the early silvering of his hair. He was reckoned to be the best batsman of his day and played for Surrey and later Hambledon. A tremendous hitter, he was the first man to consistently 'go down the wicket', or 'give it a rush', i.e., hit the ball on the full toss. He died aged ninety-six years, and it is believed that he was the father of over thirty children, which says little for his cricket prowess but certainly suggests he was a man of some stamina.

In the late eighteenth century, after over fifty years of Royal patronage, no one was more enthusiastic than another Prince of Wales, the eldest son of George III, later to become George IV. It was written of him in 1790 as 'making a party of cricket almost every day'.

With the patronage of the Royal Family over such a period, cricket had attained a position in the English way of life that it was never to lose. The formation of the MCC (Marylebone Cricket Club) in 1787 was undoubtedly a result of cricket's popularity amongst the nobility and their links with the

The LAWS of the NOBLE GAME of CRICKET,
as Established at the Star and Garter Pall-Mall by a Committee of Noblemen & Gentlemen.

THE BALL.
Must not weigh less than five Ounces and a half, nor more than five Ounces and three Quarters.
It cannot be changed during the Game, but with Consent of both Parties.

THE BAT.
Must not exceed Four Inches and One Quarter in the Widest Part.

THE STUMPS.
Must be Twenty two Inches long.
N: It is lately settled to use three Stumps instead of two to each Wicket, the Bail the same Length as above.

THE BOWLING CREASE.
Must be parallel with the Stumps Three Feet in Length, with a Return Crease.

THE POPPING CREASE.
Must be Three Feet Ten Inches from the Wickets and the Wickets must be opposite to each other at the Distance of Twenty two Yards.

THE PARTY, which goes from home.
Shall have the choice of the Innings, and the pitching of the Wickets, which shall be pitched within Thirty Yards of a Centre fixed by the Adversaries.
When the Parties meet at a Third Place, the Bowlers shall toss up for the pitching of the First Wicket, and the Choice of going in.

THE BOWLER.
Must deliver the Ball with one Foot behind the Bowling Crease, and within the Return Crease, and shall bowl four Balls before he changes Wickets, which he shall do but once in the same Innings.
He may order the Player at his Wicket to stand on which side of it he pleases.

THE STRIKER. is out,
If the Ball is bowled off, or the Stump bowled out of the Ground —
Or if the Ball from a stroke over or under his Bat or upon his Hands (but not Wrists,) is held before it touches the Ground, though it be hugged to the Body of the Catcher —
Or if in striking, both his Feet are over the Popping Crease, and his Wicket is put down, except his Bat is grounded within it —
Or if he runs out of his Ground to hinder a Catch —
Or if the Ball is struck up, and he wilfully strikes it again —
Or if in running a Notch the Wicket is struck down by a Throw, or with the Ball in Hand before his Foot, Hand or Bat is grounded over the Popping Crease, but if the Bail is off, a Stump must be struck out of the Ground by the Ball —
Or if the Striker touches or takes up the Ball before it has lain still, unless at the Request of the Opposite Party —
Or if the Striker puts his Legs before the Wicket, with a Design to stop the Ball, and actually prevent the Ball from hitting the Wicket by it —
If the Players have crossed each other, he that runs for the Wicket that is put down is out, if they are not crossed, he that has left the Wicket that is put down is out.
When the Ball has been in the Bowlers or Wicket Keepers Hands, the Strikers need not keep within their Ground, till the Umpire has called Play, but if the Player goes out of his Ground with an Intent to run before the Ball is delivered, the Bowler may put him out.
When the Ball is struck up in the Running Ground between the Wickets, it is lawful for the Strikers to hinder its being catched, but they must neither strike at, nor touch the Ball with their Hands.
If the Ball is struck up, the Striker may guard his Wicket either with his Bat or his Body.
In Single Wicket Matches, if the Striker moves out of the Ground to strike at the Ball he shall be allowed no Notch for such Stroke.

The WICKET KEEPER.
Shall stand at a reasonable Distance behind the Wicket, and shall not move till the Ball is out of the Bowlers Hand, and shall not by any Noise incommode the Striker, and if his Hands, Knees, Foot or Head be over or before the Wicket, though the Ball touch it, it shall not be out.

THE UMPIRES.
Shall allow Two Minutes for each Man to come in, and Fifteen Minutes between each Innings, when the Umpire shall call Play, the Party refusing to play, shall lose the Match.
They are the sole Judges of fair and unfair Play, and all Disputes shall be determined by them.
When a Striker is hurt, he shall be allow another to come in and the Person hurt shall have his Innings in any Part of that Innings.
They are not to order a Player out unless appealed to by the Adversaries. — But if the Bowlers Foot is not behind the Bowling Crease within the Return Crease when he delivers the Ball, the Umpire unasked must call No Ball.
If the Strikers run a short Notch the Umpires must call No Notch.

BETS.
If the Notches of one Player are laid against another, the Bet depends on both Innings, unless otherwise specified.
If one Party beats the other in one Innings, the Notches in the First Innings shall determine the Bet.
But if the other Party goes in a second Time, then the Bet must be determined by the Numbers on the Score.

THE END

Court. Names such as the Hon. Charles Lennox, later to become the Duke of Richmond, an intimate friend of the King, and Lennox's friend Lord Winchelsea figure prominently at this time. In fact, the principal founder of MCC was Lord Winchelsea who, as a leading member of the White Conduit Club, originally a tavern, had the initiative to both persuade disillusioned members of that club to form the MCC whilst also prompting one Thomas Lord, a retainer of the White Conduit club, to search for another suitable ground on which a newly-formed Club might play cricket. Lord was a resourceful man and very soon obtained, at a very reasonable cost from the Duke of Dorset, another great cricket enthusiast, a twenty-one year lease on ten acres of ground in the parish of Marylebone. Dorset Fields was the first of three grounds that Lord procured for the newly-formed MCC. So, Lord's Cricket Ground and MCC became one and the same, as it is today at St John's Wood, the third of Thomas Lord's three grounds. The second ground at North Bank was occupied for only a very short time, filling in for MCC after it left Dorset Fields in 1810, till 1814 when the first MCC match was played on the present site.

Hambledon

For some thirty, even forty years during the latter part of the eighteenth century the little Hampshire village of Hambledon experienced what can only be described as a cricket phenomenon. In this time the Hambledon Club attracted the greatest players of the day to its ranks and did battle against the finest teams in the country on the bleakest of fields known as Broadhalfpenny Down. How on earth did this small village, similar no doubt to hundreds of others throughout the land,

(*Opposite*) THE LAWS—Published 1 September 1785.

play such an important role in the development of the game?

The complete answer of course can never really be known but every indication is that good fortune went hand in hand with coincidence and the result was Hambledon. Good fortune came through the person of a great cricketer of the times, Richard Newland, who played for England and the fashionable Sussex Club of Slindon, noted for its aristocratic patrons. He was a particularly fine batsman and in 1744 achieved fame as Captain of both his club and his country. Not only was Richard Newland a fine cricketer and a charming man but he was also a very capable coach, it seems. Before leaving Slindon to practise surgery in Chichester he was responsible for passing on to his nephew Richard Nyren, not only his love for cricket but also many of his skills in the game. Coincidence then took over, and in 1763 Richard Nyren, by now a redoubtable left arm bowler, became landlord of The Bat and Ball Inn overlooking Broadhalfpenny Down, very close to the village of Hambledon. Was it then surprising that the Hambledon Club blossomed? Perhaps not, as so often when industry, enthusiasm and a feeling for cricket are encapsulated in one man, an environment of camaraderie is created in which all the facets of the game thrive.

Very soon Slindon's place in cricket was taken over by Hambledon, as the best players wanted to join this progressive club, to play against the most celebrated teams in the land. In fact, it is recorded that in 1772 Hambledon convincingly beat a twenty-two of England and not for the last time. Later, in 1793, they beat an England eleven by an innings and over a hundred runs.

Many were the famous names that played for the club in those days. Apart from Richard Nyren, there was his son John, himself a fine cricketer, and by whom much of the Hambledon history was recorded. Some of the others who left their mark were William Hogflesh, James Aylward, William Barber and the wicket-keeper Tom Sueter. Rating a special mention in any discourse on Hambledon is the famous John Small who, it is believed, was the batsman on the memorable occasion already mentioned, when Lumpy Stevens, playing for the Five of Kent against the Five of Hambledon in a single wicket match, bowled the ball three times through the wicket without disturbing the bail. This must have been a rare event, however, as John Small had a great reputation as a batsman. He became the greatest exponent of 'straight bat' play, as an answer to the 'length' bowling that was developing at the time. To say that John Small was an all-rounder is not quite true, but his talents were many. He was one of the early bat-makers and also an expert ball-maker. Outside his house he hung a sign proclaiming:

> Here lives John Small
> Makes bat and ball,
> Pitch a Wicket, Play at Cricket
> With any man in England

Whilst Hambledon's batsmen of note were many, it was the excellence and variety of the bowling that really gave them such success and captured the public's imagination. In the early days on Broadhalfpenny Down, Thomas Brett was the fastest and the best. In later years when Hambledon played on Windmill Down, David Harris, who was born in Elvetsham, Hampshire, in 1754, was the greatest of them all. He first played for Hambledon in 1782 and developed such accuracy and variation in spin and pace that a whole new batting technique, almost as we know it today, had to be developed to cope with his bowling.

It is fascinating to read the accounts of this remarkable period, recorded by four influential men in the world of cricket. The first was John Nyren, in collaboration to a greater

JOHN NYREN (1764–1837).

rather than a lesser degree, it is suspected, with a known man of letters, one Charles Cowden Clarke. They produced such classics as *The Young Cricketer's Tutor* (1833) and later *Cricketers of my Time*. Both these titles were more recently reissued (London, 1974) with an introduction by John Arlott. In 1851, the Reverend James Pycroft in his classic book, *The Cricket Field*, is indebted to his remarkable interviews with William (Silver Billy) Beldham, then in his eighties, who apparently was able to give an account of cricket as he had known it, in some detail.

How marvellous it is, that even today we can in our mind's eye visualise those men of Hambledon with their velvet caps and sky

HAMBLEDON—The Bat and Ball Inn.

blue coats, their knee breeches and buckled shoes, striding across Broadhalfpenny Down as the sun set over The Bat and Ball Inn and 'mine host' Richard Nyren drew foaming tankards of ale to celebrate Hambledon and a special chapter in cricket history.

After Hambledon

The formation of the MCC in 1787, and the development of Lord's Cricket Ground, first at Dorset Fields and later at St John's Wood, considerably accelerated the growth of cricket in England in the early nineteenth century. Towards the turn of the century Hambledon had returned in some degree to its rural inheritance, as its many wealthy patrons were tempted into the now fashionable London cricket scene. As the century progressed, London and its adjacent counties became more and more the centre of cricket from which wandering professional XIs spread, fostering an appetite for the game throughout the country. These teams usually contained some of the best cricketers in England and, with good management, proved to be successful in every way. County cricket was becoming more established, with MCC drawing up a set of rules for county qualification in the 1860s.

Many more fine players were being produced by the county clubs because they were led by men of enthusiasm and vision. Constant changes were taking place as the game captured the public's imagination more than ever before. The betting of large sums of money, which had been a part of cricket since the earliest games of the eighteenth century, continued unabated until bookies were banned at Lord's in 1817 following an 'incident' when a well-known Surrey professional, William Lambert, was accused of 'selling' a match.

After a hundred years, large wagers between contesting sides, not to mention the volume of side bets by spectators, gradually became less evident as a result of MCC's stand. Yet, it was probably as a result of gambling that cricket had made such progress in the eighteenth century. Most big match posters highlighted the amounts at stake, with such sums as five hundred and a thousand guineas-a-side being common-place, an astonishing amount of money when converted and compared with today's currency. Nevertheless, it is unlikely that the bigger matches would have taken place, neither would they have drawn crowds, without the wealthy patrons indulging their gambling instincts in the way they did. Nor would the professional cricketers have emerged in such quantity or quality. As always, more often than not the wealthiest employers engaged the best players. John Nyren recalls that very few matches at Hambledon were played for less than five hundred guineas-a-side. However, as the marriage between MCC and Lord's Cricket Ground blossomed, so the high stakes gradually disappeared, as did the very high fees paid to many of the professionals. The wandering teams with their entrepreneurial managers, still 'put on a good show' but their appearances were reduced as the competition between counties became more intense and their crowds became greater.

In this period of great change and progress, as one would expect, there were those whose contributions were outstanding. Some left their mark simply through their performances on the field, but more often than not the truly brilliant characters that emerged were not only good players but flamboyant personalities in every sense of the word. The Reverend Lord Frederick Beauclerk, Vicar of St Albans, was not only the most gifted amateur cricketer of his generation, he was also an aristocrat of significance—a great grandson of Charles II. His calling had no effect on his attitude to gambling however, and he would often boast of the vast sums of money he made by betting—and not always on cricket. In those days cock-fighting and horse-racing were also a temptation to those with money to spend. Neither was Lord Frederick the most even tempered of men. In fact, it was as a result of his frustration with the well-known and very successful professional, William Lambert (mentioned earlier) that he lost a famous, if ill-tempered, challenge match in 1810. Coincidentally, seven years later, Lambert was banned from playing again at Lord's, having, it is said, 'sold' a match at Nottingham early in that season. Lord Frederick was very much involved in MCC at this time and was responsible for conducting a campaign against the evils of betting on 'fixed' matches. What characters and what a story there must have been wrapped in the history of those years of intrigue.

The following report was given in *John Bull* (a popular newspaper of the time) on Sunday, 31 July 1825: 'About one o'clock on Friday morning a fire broke out in the pavilion in Lord's Cricket Ground, and, from its being built of wood, it burnt with such fury that the whole was reduced to a heap of ruins before it was possible for fire engines to render any assistance. . . .'

This stark report introduces our next man of cricket, William Ward, who was born at Islington, London, on 4 July 1787, the year in which the first Lord's came into being. William Ward was one of the finest of batsmen

(*Above*) NICHOLAS WANOSTROCHT ('Felix').

(*Right*) ALFRED MYNN (1807–61).

and for over one hundred years held the record for the highest score made on the present ground: 278 for MCC against Norfolk in 1825. This score was made with a bat weighing 4lb which, whilst considerably lighter than the 5lb 5oz bats used in the early Hambledon days, was still heavier than even the 'Jumbos' of today which weigh just over 3lb. (Sir Donald Bradman, one of cricket's master batsmen used a bat weighing 2lb 3oz.) More importantly, William Ward was the man who saved Lord's after the fire of 1825. He bought the ground in trust for MCC from Thomas Lord in 1825 who, with retirement imminent and facing the disastrous effects of the fire, felt compelled to offer it to the highest bidder. In fact it was due to be purchased by a builder for development when Ward stepped in. What a debt cricket and MCC owe to him. But I wonder how many MCC members will have heard of William Ward.

Nicholas Wanostrocht was a man of many talents. A fine cricketer, he played in the great Kent side of the 1830s under the name Felix, an alias. Felix was a schoolmaster and an artist of distinction. His water-colour portraits of the immortal Alfred Mynn and that other great Kent cricketer Fuller Pilch are MCC treasures, still to be seen at Lord's. Another of the talents of Felix was that of inventor. Of lasting fame was his invention of the first bowling machine. In addition, he was an author and something of a coach, as his classic book, *Felix on the Bat*, shows us. A true all-rounder, with a bubbling personality that endeared him to all, Felix was a very special man of cricket. The reason he became Felix rather than Nicholas was simply that he thought his dignity as a schoolmaster may well have suffered in the eyes of his boys' parents, had they known of his profession in cricket. Times have changed indeed!

Now to the man who made the greatest of all impressions on the public up to the advent of W.G. Grace. Alfred Mynn—the 'Lion of Kent'—was born in 1807 and became the first really great all-rounder. He was a huge man, weighing some twenty stone, and like many of his girth, he had a 'larger than life' personality, always ready to laugh but still a man of gentleness and sensitivity. When Alfred Mynn died in 1861 he was already a legend. His memory was preserved forever through the poet William Jeffrey Prowse who wrote:

With his tall and stately presence, with his
  nobly moulded form
His broad hand was ever open, his brave
  heart was ever warm.
All were proud of him, all loved him. As
  the changing seasons pass,
As our Kentish champion lies asleeping
  underneath Kentish grass,
Proudly, sadly, we will name him—to
  forget him were a sin:
Lightly lie the turf upon thee, kind and
  manly Alfred Mynn.

To make up the famous trio with Felix and Alfred Mynn was the Norfolk batsman Fuller Pilch. His stylish front-foot techniques made him one of England's most successful batsman for twenty years and more. A quiet thoughtful man, Fuller Pilch became an umpire at the end of his playing career, with a fondness for giving batsmen not out LBW—no matter what the bowler thought!

Of all the characters that influenced the development of cricket during the first half of the nineteenth century none must have created a greater impact than William Clarke, the first professional cricketer/entrepreneur. Born in 1798 at Nottingham, William Clarke, with great foresight and not a little business acumen, founded his highly successful touring team under the banner of 'The All England XI'. His marriage to a widow who kept the Trent Bridge Inn at Nottingham was a fortuitous partnership that prospered. The pair quickly developed the riverside land into the excellent ground we know today. With this base at Nottingham, he organised matches there and progressively throughout the country. He gathered the best players to play for his England XI. William Clarke himself was a good all-round cricketer with a phenomenal record over his forty years of playing in every corner of England. In the early 1850s, however, Clarke's dominance of the entrepreneurial cricket scene began to show signs of cracking. His payment of the best players became questionable as he lost his impartiality. There was a feeling that his 'share of the cake' was becoming increasingly exorbitant. By 1854 his team had split up, and a new team, under the name of the United England XI, took its place.

The new team was managed by Dean and Wisden (the founders of the *Cricketers' Almanack*). William Clarke died in 1856, but in spite of his financial manoeuvrings there can be no doubt that his initiative had instigated progress in the game, which would not otherwise have occurred.

In these post Hambledon days, probably more changes took place than at any other time in the history of cricket. One big change was the legalising of round-arm bowling by

(*Opposite*) MATCH POSTER, 1847.

A GRAND MATCH

WILL BE PLAYED IN

LORD'S GROUND,

MARYLEBONE,

On Monday, JULY 19th, 1847, & following Day,

The Gentlemen against the Players.

PLAYERS.

Gentlemen	Players,
Sir F. BATHURST	BOX
N. FELIX, Esq.	CLARK
A. HAYGARTH, Esq.	DEAN
A. M. HOARE, Esq.	GUY
R. T. KING, Esq.	HILLYER
J. LEE, Esq.	LILLYWHITE
A. MYNN, Esq.	MARTINGALE
W. NICHOLSON, Esq.	PILCH
O. C. PELL, Esq.	W. PILCH
G. YONGE, Esq.	PARR
C. G. WATSON, Esq.	SEWELL

MATCHES TO COME.

Monday, July 26th, at Lord's, a Grand Match in honour of A. Mynn, Esq. Kent against all England.

Wednesday, July 28th, Thursday, July 29th, Friday, July 30th, & Saturday, July 31st, the Annual Matches between the Gentlemen of Harrow, Eton, and Winchester.

DARK's newly-invented Leg Guards.

Also his TUBULAR and other INDIA-RUBBER GLOVES, SPIKED SOLES FOR CRICKET SHOES, CRICKET BALLS, the LAWS OF CRICKET, (as authorized by the Marylebone Club) and DENISON's CRICKETER'S COMPANION, to be had of R. Dark, at the Tennis Court.

R. D being the Manufacturer of all the various articles which are here enumerated, and therefore assured as to the excellence of the quality of the different materials with which they are constructed, can with the greatest confidence recommend them to the cricketing world.

Cricket Bats and Stumps to be had of M. Dark, at the Manufactory on the Ground.

Admittance 6d..... ...Stabling on the Ground......Ordinary at 3 o'clock.

Morgan Printer, 38, Church-st, adjoining the Theatre,

the MCC in 1828, followed by the full legalising of over-arm bowling in 1864.

The Years of Grace

I first played cricket at Lord's in 1951 for the Combined Services XI. I shall always remember that occasion, or should I say incident, when I had the ignominy of having my off-stump removed after three balls. A member, the only one left in the Long Room as I passed through, made no comment! He simply looked at me through a large eyeglass.

In the intervening years, as a player, worker, spectator, like many before me I have been acutely conscious of the unique atmosphere, the traditions, the sounds, even the smells of the place. Perhaps more than any one thing has been the overriding feeling of being somehow in a 'presence'. As soon as the heavy ponderous 'Grace Gates' swing slowly open the feeling is there. How strange it is that one man can have influenced a place so much—but this man has; not simply because of his supreme ability as the 'Champion Cricketer' but also because of his larger than life personality, that left its mark on England perhaps as much as any one character has done in a lifetime.

W.G. Grace was born on the 18 July 1848 in the village of Downend in Gloucestershire. He was the fourth son in a family of five sons and four daughters born to Henry and Martha Grace. All but one of the five sons became doctors like their father. Sadly, the youngest, Fred (G.F.), died shortly before obtaining his degree. Of the five sons, Edward Mills, E.M., (six years older than W.G.) became a truly magnificent cricketer in his own right, and G.F. appeared to be following his two brothers before his untimely death at the age of thirty. The eldest son Henry was quite a good local cricketer but not in the class of his three brothers. Alfred, the second son, was also

not a bad cricketer, but achieved more of a reputation locally as an amateur boxer. Their father, Dr Henry Mills Grace, was, as one would expect, a great cricket enthusiast himself and even with a busy practice he still managed to organise and play in many games in Gloucestershire and the surrounding counties. He was very keen on hunting throughout his life and it may be that this was the reason why his wife Martha became the guiding light on the family cricket scene and on W.G. in particular.

She was, it seems, a very special lady, having acquired a remarkable knowledge of cricket techniques. So much so, that she was not averse to putting it to good use when her boys warranted it. She was a determined person, physically strong, respected by all and worshipped inside her family. One suspects that her knowledge of cricket stems from her brother Alfred Pocock who was also W.G.'s guide and mentor in his formative cricket years. Recognising the superb natural ability of E.M. with his tendency to play the most outrageous cross-bat shots, Uncle Pocock, as he was known, instilled the principles of straight bat play in the young W.G. at an early age. We now know how well it paid off! W.G. himself let it be widely known that his success at cricket was as much due to his own hard work and sound instruction by Uncle Pocock and his mother, as to any natural ability. In his remarkable book *Cricket*, published in 1891, he states, 'I should like to say that good batsmen are born not made; but my long experience comes up before me, and tells me that it is not so. There are gifts of eye and wrist which nearly all good batsmen possess in greater or lesser degree, that enables them to play certain strokes with great effect; but, to acquire all-round proficiency I am strongly convinced that constant practice and sound coaching have all to do with it. I try to remember

(*Opposite*) W.G. Grace (1848–1915).

the time when I first handled a bat and I can recall nothing but the advice that was drilled into me—stand well up to the wicket; keep your left shoulder well forward; practise constantly and put your whole heart into it.'

What refreshing words of encouragement for us all and what a compliment to his upbringing in cricket. There are many many stories of the Grace family and it was indeed a great day for cricket when Dr Henry Mills Grace met Martha Pocock. One of the Doctor's very important decisions was that on the birth of his eldest son he decided to install a cricket wicket in the back garden. W.G. was to follow his father's lead when he acquired his own house. This is not unlike the story of one M.C. Cowdrey, whose father and who later himself did the same thing with similar effect.

A wonderful story of Mrs Martha Grace comes from her decision to write to the manager of the wandering All England XI, George Parr, extolling not only the abilities of her son E.M. Grace, but gravely advising him that she had a younger son who would do even better, as he had a sounder defence. This most treasured of letters still exists today in the safe keeping of MCC.

I am afraid I cannot advise the mothers of today's young cricketers to write to the Chairman of Selectors expecting similar success, although I have no doubt it has been tried. So, the remarkable and unique career of W.G. was nurtured. In the warmth of his family he was brought up to respect life and his part in it. He knew what hard work was and more importantly practised what he preached. His enormous strength and stamina, that stood him in such good stead, grew from a caring home where love, compassion and discipline went hand in hand. Martha Grace died in 1884. Rightly her memory is preserved and permanently recorded in *Wisden*'s Births and Deaths of Cricketers.

W.G.'s first-class career began in 1865 and finished forty-three years later in 1908. In this time he played 1,388 innings and scored 54,896 runs at an average of 39.55. He also took 2,864 wickets at 17.97 each. W.G. made his first first-class century—224 against Surrey—in 1866 and thirty-eight years later made his last. In all he made 131 first-class centuries. Of course, he played in hundreds of lesser games so it is hard to imagine just how many runs, wickets and catches he made in total. When one thinks of the hardships of travelling endured by cricketers in those early days, the pure stamina and good health required to maintain his continuity of excellence must have been incredible. Add to this the fact that in between times he practised as a doctor in Bristol and as a young man had established a reputation as an athlete at a very high level.

It may be said by some that since Grace there have been better players, better batsmen and better bowlers, even better all-rounders, but no one can say there has been a better cricketer. W.G. Grace influenced the most significant developments in cricket at a time when cricket needed to change. The conditions under which he played, particularly with regard to wickets in his early days, have left his batting feats unsurpassed, even by Bradman and Hobbs, with whom it is hardly fair to make a comparison as their best days were so far removed from his.

In avidly reading histories of this great Victorian, I, like everyone else, can only be enormously impressed by his volume of cricketing success. Much more than this however, has been the impression of the man. From the pens of all the marvellous scribes I have read there is a consistency of description that makes me feel I almost know him. I have an image of an immensely strong man, an authoritarian, roguishly humorous, but serious enough when it was necessary to show kindness and compassion, even softness, that must have been bred in him hrough the warmth of his family. These are ill phrases that come to mind after reading ibout W.G. I have no doubt that they are not far adrift. Neither do the historians record iny unpleasantness of spirit in the great man. If anything there is an overwhelming youthfulness that apparently never left him. Such s the man whose name is perpetuated on the memorial gates at Lord's with the inscription:

To the Memory of William Gilbert Grace,
The Great Cricketer
1848–1915
These gates were
erected by the MCC
and other friends and admirers.

As we look back over the years of Grace, his phenomenal record and immense personality can easily allow one to think only of him, very often to the detriment of many other fine cricketers and occasions. Being the game it is, however, cricket transcends players and places, memorable occasions

and glorious feats—and so it should. Therein lies its eternal fascination. In many ways W.G. Grace himself could not have been born at a better time. His genius acted as a catalyst to the eventful years. The wandering XIs of William Clarke and George Parr had stimulated the playing of cricket in every corner of the country. Even in other lands the game was growing as the emigrants from England pitched their wickets in virgin cricket soils.

1859 saw the very first tour abroad by an English team. Strangely enough it was to Canada, where the first game was played against Montreal. Later Philadelphia became the centre of American cricket and produced a number of good teams in spite of the Civil War in 1861. The war had its effect however, and cricket never had the chance to rival

1859, THE FIRST EVER OVERSEAS TOUR—A team drawn from members of the All England and United England XIs toured the United States and Canada under the joint captaincy of GEORGE PARR and JOHN WISDEN.

baseball again in America.

Instead, Australia took cricket to its heart. The new settlers in the country had already experienced its increasing popularity in England and bearing in mind what was going on in America, in 1861 Australia welcomed the first English touring team. W.G. Grace himself took a team there in 1873/4.

In 1877 the first 'Test' match between England and Australia was played on the famous Melbourne Cricket Ground, later the scene of some of the most epic encounters between the two countries. Australia won this first Test match by 45 runs. Charles Bannerman of New South Wales achieved cricket immortality by scoring the first Test match century. He made 165, a remarkable innings in that none of his colleagues made more than 20 in either innings of the match.

In 1868 Australia had toured England for the first time, when an English cricketer called Charles Lawrence had brought over a team of Aboriginals. The first Test match to be played in England took place at The Oval in 1880. On this occasion England triumphed by 5 wickets. Significantly, Fred Spofforth, Australia's 'demon' bowler, could not play in that match but he did play in the Oval match of 1882, when England wanting 85 to win were all out for 77 in the most exciting of finishes. Spofforth took 7 for 44 and rightly was made what we would call these days the Man of the Match.

The day after the match *The Sporting Times* published the famous obituary notice of English cricket, it read:

'In affectionate memory of English Cricket which died at The Oval on the 29th August 1882. Deeply lamented by a large circle of sorrowing friends and acquaintances. R.I.P. N.B. The body will be cremated and the Ashes taken to Australia.'

THE ASHES.

To set the seal on the legend of the Ashes, the story is related that following the 1882/3 series of Test matches in Australia (won by England), some Melbourne ladies burned a bail, sealed it in an urn and presented it to the England Captain. Ivo Bligh, later married one of the ladies. He became Lord Darnley and on his death in 1927 bequeathed the Ashes to MCC. Henceforth, in every Test match series between England and Australia 'The Ashes' have been at stake, although, no matter who wins them, they are always retained at Lord's.

So the scene was set for what must be the most unique and long lasting sporting rivalry at international level. One might only conjecture as to how the history of cricket—even the history of the world—might have progressed had not the American Civil War been responsible for sending the enterprising cricketers of England in other directions, particularly to Australia.

Back to England and the revolution of cricket, as it exploded in the heavily populated areas of the Midlands and the North.

The Nottinghamshire Club, formed in 1841, was the centre of the revolution in these areas and the county had a very successful time right through to the turn of the century, with the exception of a period following the demise of William Clarke. From the 1860s through to the end of the nineteenth century they won or shared the championship fifteen times. They had many fine players with perhaps two, Alfred Shaw and Richard Daft, being outstanding.

Alfred Shaw was without question one of the greatest slow medium bowlers in cricket history, with a record of over 2,000 wickets at just over 12 runs each. His accuracy was legendary, with more than half his overs in twenty-seven seasons being 'maidens'. An astonishing record even in a time of four-ball overs. It is said that Richard Daft for over twenty years was, apart from W.G. Grace, the best all round batsman in the country, a great accolade for any cricketer.

Also from Nottingham was Arthur Shrewsbury who successfully captained England in Australia and made 59 centuries in first-class cricket, ten of which were double. He was a fine player on all wickets and drew an historic remark from W.G., who, when asked who he wanted to select first in his England team, said: 'Give me Arthur.'

Lancashire and Yorkshire cricket also became well established, county clubs being formed in 1864 and 1863 respectively. Lancashire rivalled Notts in their early days and won the championship in 1881, sharing with Notts in 1882. Two families, the Rowleys and the Hornbys, were most dominant in the progress of the club. A.N. (Monkey) Hornby made an immense contribution as Captain for eleven seasons and President for twenty-three years. Known by all as 'the Boss', he was partnered at the wicket by R.G. Barlow and they were immortalised in the following poem by Francis Thompson.

My Hornby and My Barlow

It is little I repair to the matches of the
    Southron folk,
Though my own red roses there may
    blow;
It is little I repair to the matches of the
    Southron folk,
Though the red roses crest the caps, I
    know;
For the field is full of shades as I near
    the shadowy coast,
And a ghostly batsman plays to the
    bowling of a ghost,
And I look through my tears on a
    soundless clapping host
As the run-stealers flicker to and fro—
    To and fro —
O my Hornby and my Barlow long ago!

Lancashire had Hornby, and Notts had progressed through the earlier influence of William Clarke and George Parr. Yorkshire, with players such as Ulyett and Peel, were not far behind, and later under the inspiring leadership of Lord Hawke they truly came into their own. He was a great disciplinarian but set achievable standards for all his players. Under his captaincy Yorkshire won eight championships.

The Golden Age
(1895–1914)

As the twentieth century dawned, cricket was established as *the* national game, supported at national and county level by large crowds. Of the seventeen counties that now contest the County Championships all but two, Northamptonshire and Glamorgan, had still to join. This they did in 1905 and 1921 respectively. The Minor Counties Association was formed in 1895 to represent counties other than 'first-class', the term originally defined by MCC and now by the TCCB (the Test and County Cricket Board). Club and league cricket had also grown to feed the counties, and the 'Golden Age' was indeed an appropriate term, that could be applied to cricket throughout the country.

The public schools had earlier invested in cricket by establishing the game as an integral part of their educational strategy (what a pity that the same policy is not in all schools today). With this attitude, it followed that the best conditions were obtained for playing the game in these schools. By further astutely employing the best professional coaches they ensured the quality of amateur cricket for fifty years and more, both in a playing and administrative capacity. A simple study of a *Who's Who* in cricket today more than confirms these comments. In fact the policy quickly became evident as the amateurs married skill to their inherited mantles of leadership.

Cricket reflected an age of optimism in Great Britain at its greatest, the wars it was to know as yet undreamed of.

In the wings, if not exactly on the stage, the magic names of the Golden Age were beginning to assemble. 'Plum' (P.F.) Warner of Middlesex, Charles (C.B.) Fry and Prince Ranjitsinhji of Sussex. From Surrey there was Tom Hayward, to be followed by Jack Hobbs, Archie (A.C.) McClaren, Johnny Briggs and J.T. Tyldesley from Lancashire; and across the Pennines in Yorkshire, following the inspiration of Lord Hawke, were Wilfred Rhodes, George Hirst and Scholfield Haigh and one of cricket's most gifted and aristocratic of men, the Hon. F.S. Jackson. Gilbert Jessop (the Croucher) of Gloucestershire followed W.G. and became the most devastating hitter ever seen until perhaps Ian Botham nearly a hundred years later. The Foster family from Worcester made their impact and their most gifted son, R.E. Foster, was classed as an equal of the many great batsmen in his short time in cricket. Of the counties that played the most marvellous cricket at this time, Kent are well represented by Frank Woolley and Colin Blythe who rivalled Wilfred Rhodes as the greatest of all slow left-arm bowlers.

Frank Woolley's first game of his long career was played in 1906. He went on to score nearly 60,000 runs in first-class cricket not to mention his 2,000 wickets at under 20 runs a wicket. Maybe these figures, allied to the graceful and majestic manner in which they were compiled, make a case for him to be classified as cricket's greatest all-rounder.

S.F. Barnes from Staffordshire was selected to play for England in Australia in 1901 by Archie MacLaren whilst he was a league professional. Sydney Barnes who played most of his cricket in the leagues, was acknowledged by many to be the most complete bowler of them all with an astonishing record in Test cricket of 189 wickets at 16.43 runs per wicket. He was noted for the variety of deliveries he could bowl, but his most lethal was the true leg-cutter, in his case apparently a fast leg-break, only paralleled in comparatively recent times by Alec Bedser.

B.J.T. Bosanquet, a very useful all-round cricketer, was famous as the inventor of 'the googly' or 'Bosie', that is, the delivery bowled with a leg-break action that is in fact an off-break. He learned the technique whilst experimenting with spinning a billiard ball. Some writers give the impression that Bosanquet was something of a 'flash in the pan' in so far as his bowling was concerned but he took over 600 first-class wickets at 23.80 runs per wicket before retiring in 1905.

Following on the heels of these developments in spin came the realisation of the possibilities of 'seam' bowling, that is, obtaining lateral deviation from the pitch by delivering the ball in such a way as to land it on a vertical seam. The next logical step that followed this type of bowling was 'swerve' or 'swing' as we now call it. Purely by constantly releasing the ball with the seam vertical, it became increasingly evident that in certain atmospheric conditions the ball would swing one way or another. Cricket was becoming more complex—but more interesting—and it continued, as it always will, to produce those with the dedication and enthusiasm to develop its skills.

Besides those I have mentioned there are many others—Tom Richardson, Bobby Abel, George Lohmann and Herbert Strudwick of Surrey; fast bowler, opening batsman, all-rounder and wicket-keeper respectively. Great players and great characters. A special wicket-keeper of the day was A.A. Lilley of Warwickshire and England. The most graceful of batsmen, Reggie Spooner has not been mentioned, as Lancastrians will be quick to point out, but where does the list end?

What about the players from overseas, whose contribution to the Golden Age was no less? Perhaps the greatest was the immortal Victor Trumper who played for the State of New South Wales and Australia for nearly twenty years and died aged thirty-seven. As a man he was revered for his grace and courtesy to everyone. As a batsman he was a great artist. The accounts of many of his great innings are in themselves masterpieces of cricket writing and deserving tributes to the man.

Monty Noble was another of Australia's great cricketers who played in forty-two Tests between 1899 and 1909. He became one of the most successful of Australia's captains. Another New South Welshman was Charles McCartney, nick-named 'the Governor-General' for his audacious style. His days of glory came in the latter half of his career. South Australian Clem Hill had a distinguished career without having the flair of Trumper or the power of Macartney. Another South Australian we cannot forget is George Giffen, a man whose record allows him to stand alongside the best all-rounders. In his career he took over 1,000 wickets and had a great influence on the game in Australia.

At the turn of the century, Queensland and Western Australia were not involved in the Sheffield Shield Competition. Victoria made up the trio of states that produced teams of Test standard and contested the handsome trophy presented by the Earl of Sheffield on a tour in 1891. Centring on the famous Melbourne Cricket Ground, Victoria boasted some marvellous players in continual rivalry with New South Wales. Warwick Armstrong was probably the greatest cricketer from Victoria. A huge man, he had a magnificent record in cricket, captaining Australia ten times without defeat. He made 45 centuries in his career, six of which were in Test matches. He also took over 800 wickets at less than 20 runs per wicket. He appeared to be very much in the mould of W.G. Grace, and more recently

GEORGE BELDHAM'S historic photograph of the immortal VICTOR TRUMPER—G. W. Beldham (1868–1937) was the first great cricket photographer making hundreds of now treasured plates of famous players of the 1900s.

Freddie Brown—rather awe-inspiring on the outside but with a kindly twinkle in his eye.

Hugh Trumble is not generally remembered as one of the greatest cricketers, but in Australian and particularly Victorian eyes, and just as importantly 'in the book', he was. For the record he took 929 wickets at 18.5 runs each and of these 141 were against England—a record achievement. He became a most popular Secretary of the Melbourne Cricket Club for twenty-seven years from 1911 to 1938.

Amongst the many significant occurrences in the first decade of the twentieth century was the emergence of South Africa as a cricketing nation. Almost certainly a great part of their early success was due to one R.O. Schwartz having close ties with England's B.J.T. Bosanquet. Whilst at school with Bosanquet and later as a contemporary at Oxford and then Middlesex, Schwartz learned to bowl the googly so successfully that on a tour of England in 1904 he took over 90 wickets at 14 runs each. Even more important than his own skill was his teaching of fellow South Africans Vogler and Faulkner, who justified the ability of their teacher by taking 65 of 85 England wickets in the Tests of 1907. Allied to the skills of their master wrist-spin bowlers, two or three other fine cricketers contributed to establishing

South African cricket in international terms. Along with his bowling skills, Aubrey Faulkner developed his batting and became a very high-class all-rounder. Later he retired to England and was recognised as one of cricket's finest ever coaches. Percy Sherwell was a fine wicket-keeper batsman of those days, but the exceptional batsman, well-fitted to be a part of the Golden Age, was Herbie Taylor, described by those who saw both play as almost an equal of Victor Trumper himself.

Between the Wars

The twenty years between the terrible wars of 1914–18 and 1939–45 consolidated the playing of cricket in England and in many Commonwealth countries. In particular West Indies, New Zealand and India were to produce teams which whilst collectively not highly successful, contained individuals of brilliance in all the skills of the game. From 1922, for nineteen consecutive seasons English northern teams (Yorkshire in particular with twelve wins) dominated the County Championship. Good players were many and great players more than a few—and not all confined to the most successful clubs. There was a feeling that whilst times were not prosperous for the average family, county cricket was an institution of solidity and hope. The players, whether amateur or professional were very much part of a special English way of life that must have seemed eternal. Cricket was a happy game and in the main its players were men of character and integrity who, compared with today, played into comparatively old age. One has the feeling that these older players had a very worthwhile and steadying influence on the game, giving it an aura that would never be recaptured.

Jack Hobbs, later Sir Jack, of Surrey and England, together with his England opening partner, the Yorkshireman Herbert Sut-cliffe, epitomised all that was good in English cricket between the wars, not only in the volume of their performances but by the manner in which they achieved success. Jack Hobbs retired in 1934 aged fifty-one, having scored 61,237 runs in first-class cricket at an average of 50.65. He made 197 first-class centuries (98 of these after his fortieth birthday) and in Test matches made 15 centuries whilst averaging 56.94. He took part in twenty-three century opening partnerships for England, fifteen with Herbert Sutcliffe and eight with Wilfred Rhodes. He was more than respected by all who knew him and without question to those he was 'the Master'. Sir John Berry Hobbs extended the Golden Age in his contribution to cricket.

Herbert Sutcliffe opened the batting for Yorkshire for thirty years, scored over 50,000 runs in first-class cricket and averaged 60.73 for England in eighty-four innings. As much as anyone he was responsible for improving and setting standards for the professional cricketer in every respect—in manner, appearance and behaviour. He was at his best on the big occasions.

As we know there were many fine players in this period between the wars, but in the early 1920s it should be realised that as many as a hundred cricketers that might have expected to play in county and Test cricket were tragically killed in action or disabled. This resulted in many of the stalwarts from earlier times extending their careers and preparing the way for the game to recover from the ravages of war.

Frank Woolley and Wilfred Rhodes were the two most outstanding players at this time, but soon the unforgettable Patsy Hendren arrived on the scene to score 57,611 runs in a thirty-year career with Middlesex. He scored 170 first-class centuries, averaging over 50. He played 83 innings for England in 51 Tests, scoring 3,525 runs at an average of 47.63. It was not only his great ability that made him much loved and respected. His irrepressible

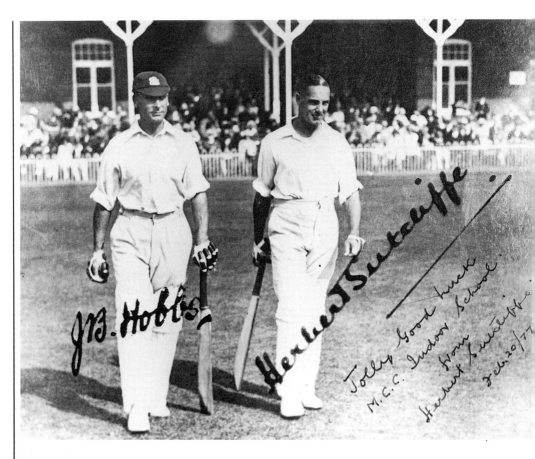

JACK HOBBS and HERBERT SUTCLIFFE.

humour and optimism was legendary and his contribution to the game he loved is immeasurable. One of the many stories of Patsy Hendren relates to the 1929/30 MCC tour of the West Indies, through which it is said that the left-arm wrist-spinner's off-break (bowled with a leg-spinning action) became known as a 'Chinaman'. When playing in one of the matches he was bowled out by Ellis Achong, a West Indian of Chinese extraction, who normally bowled slow left-arm orthodox spinners. Patsy already having scored a lot of runs, Achong experimented with a left-handed wrist-spinner as against his normal finger-spin. By chance the delivery deceived the great man and bowled

him out. On returning to the pavilion Patsy's first words were: 'Fancy being bowled out by a Chinaman.' Since then the left-hander's off-break (to the right-handed batsman, that is) has been known as a 'Chinaman'.

Almost an opposite to Patsy Hendren, but nevertheless blessed with a fair sense of Yorkshire humour and a kindliness of spirit, was Maurice Leyland. He played forty-one Tests between 1928 and 1937, averaging 46 with 9 centuries. A powerful hitter, he was always the man for a crisis, playing his finest innings for England and Yorkshire when his team were in trouble.

Ernest Tyldesley, brother of the great J.T. Tyldesley, was a Lancastrian of the most equable temperament. A craftsman of the highest class. Without the touch of genius that at times characterised J.T.'s batting, Ernest Tyldesley will always be considered one of Lancashire's great batsmen. For some reason although he averaged 55 in 20 innings for England he played only fourteen Tests.

Whilst Ernest Tyldesley played for Lancashire from 1909 to 1936, at the other end of England another greatly loved character plied his trade for Hampshire. Philip Mead emerged four years before Ernest but finished in the same year, 1936. He made 153 centuries in his career and played seventeen times for England. He has been eulogised by John Arlott, that great recorder and enjoyer of cricketing life, a Hampshire man himself.

The first of the great bowlers to arrive on the scene after the 1914–18 war was Maurice Tate. In his career with Sussex and England he took 2,784 wickets at 18.16 each, a phenomenal record. Almost in passing he scored 1,000 runs in twelve appearances. He had a magnificent action and varied his pace cleverly without ever being a genuine fast-bowler. He was a strong man with a single philosophy on the game in that he gave of his best all the time—and his best was to make him the finest bowler of his type ever, perhaps with the great Alec Bedser of later years running him a close second.

Leslie Ames played for Kent from 1926 to 1951. Since those days he has been Secretary and Manager, and is now President. He first played for England in 1929. Compared with his famous contemporaries and other famous players from different eras he has had far less recognition as the great cricketer he undoubtedly was. In first-class cricket L.E.G. Ames scored 37,248 runs at an average of 43.51 including 102 centuries. He also took 1,113 victims behind the stumps which included 415 stumpings. He played forty-seven times for England.

Now I come to a pause in my writings on the best English players of the 1920s and 30s to pay a tribute to the man who in his own way made as much of an impact on the game between the wars as did W.G. Grace in the latter part of the nineteenth century. I refer of course to 'The Don', Sir Donald Bradman, the greatest run-getter of all time, who, on average, made a century every third time he went to the wicket in first-class cricket. Had he scored one more boundary in his career he would have averaged an incredible 100 per innings. In twenty years he made 117 centuries, 29 of them in Test matches. He once made 452 not-out and six times exceeded 300, not to mention 37 double centuries. The mind does indeed boggle at the immensity of his performances.

In a few words I am sure that it would be pointless to attempt to fully describe either the man or the player. This has already been done many times by the most distinguished writers. However, one of my oldest friends is an Australian cricketer himself—Jock Livingston of Northamptonshire and New South Wales. Jock has, to his own delight, been a life-long friend of Sir Donald, so it has been a privilege for me to hear Jock speak of the man who has influenced him and for whom he had so much respect.

Donald George Bradman was born at Cootamundra, New South Wales, but lived as a boy at Bowral, a little township nearly a hundred miles from Sydney. He showed an immense talent for ball games and had a natural athleticism that was certain to take him quickly into the Sydney cricket scene and Australian Grade cricket. He played for New South Wales when he was nineteen and in his first Sheffield Shield match scored 118. The following year he played his first Test match at Brisbane without distinction, but in the Third Test match—his second—at Melbourne he made 79 and 112. From then on he never looked back and more than dominated world batting for twenty years, as statistics clearly show. He became a national institution which understandably isolated him to some degree from many of his contemporaries.

'THE DON'—A famous photograph of SIR DONALD BRADMAN. BILLY GRIFFITHS of Sussex and England is the wicket-keeper, later to become Secretary of MCC.

What made 'The Don' the great cricketer that he was? Jock Livingston tells me that any form of challenge to him needed to be taken up in full; he gave it not only his physical best but an almost awesome, unrelenting concentration on the detail required to accomplish his aims. He radiated a quiet, almost cold confidence without any form of brashness that disarmed all but the strongest of his opponents. It is said that his methods were somewhat unorthodox but one suspects this might stem from the pure audacity of his stroke-play. True, his grip was that of a short rather than a tall batsman, with the 'vees' formed by thumb and forefinger located towards the splice of the bat rather than the edge, but it was the astonishing speed of his footwork that was really the key to his success. He was always looking to position himself perfectly for the stroke he wanted to play and very seldom was he caught out of position.

Don Bradman played his last Test match in 1948. Ironically he was bowled out for 0 by Eric Hollies, which somehow was as it should be in cricket.

In these decades of run-getting and the ascendancy of batsmen it is perhaps worth noting one or two significant changes in the laws of the game. For example, in 1927 the ball was reduced in size and in 1931 the wickets were increased in size. Both changes seemed to make little difference as the batting surface was constantly improved, but in 1937 an alteration to the LBW law certainly affected batting techniques. No longer would

WALTER HAMMOND—England's finest batsman of
his time. The wicket-keeper is W. A. (BERT)
OLDFIELD, another all-time 'great'.

a batsman be allowed to 'pad away' any ball
pitching outside the off-stump if it was likely
to hit the wicket. That is, the law was introduced whereby if, in the umpire's opinion a
ball pitching outside the batsman's off-stump
would hit the wicket, providing the ball was
intercepted by the batsman's person
between wicket and wicket, the umpire could
give the batsman out. Hitherto the ball *had*
to pitch between wicket and wicket for an
LBW decision to be made.

Whilst the Bradman era was just beginning
in 1928, Walter Reginald Hammond, one of
England's greatest cricketers was also making his early mark on the MCC tour of South
Africa. In 1927 he had already scored 1,000

runs in May for Gloucestershire, finishing
with an aggregate of 2,969 and averaging 69.
He played his first Test match on that tour
and went on to create his own marvellous
career, parallel to and in many ways as a
batsman almost the equal of the incredible
Australian.

Wally Hammond scored 50,551 runs in his
first-class career averaging 56.10. He made
167 centuries, twenty-two of them in Test
matches. He also took 732 wickets and held
819 catches. He is another of that immortal
group from which the greatest all-rounder
could, in theory, be selected.

Bodyline

In recent times, to cater for the insatiable
appetite of television viewers, the 1932/3
MCC tour of Australia was brought to life—

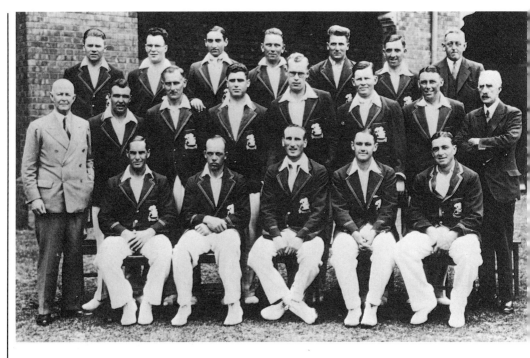

MCC TEAM TO AUSTRALIA, 1932–33.

an overstatement if ever there was one. Nevertheless, the cricket tour from which the Australian Press coined the term 'bodyline' had all the drama demanded of the modern 'soap opera'. An explanation of this extraordinary series of cricket matches is probably contained by now in at least a million words. It behoves me therefore to produce at least a view of those historic days of cricket when the emotions of a nation were exposed and transmitted across the world. Such were the traditional feelings engendered when it was felt that the ethics of cricket were not being observed—how times have changed!

The first telegram from the Australian Board of Control to MCC was sent on the 18 January 1933. It read: 'Bodyline bowling has assumed such proportions as to menace the best interests of the game, making protection of the body by the batsman the main consideration. This is causing intensely bitter feelings between the players as well as injury.

In our opinion it is unsportsmanlike. Unless stopped at once it is likely to upset the friendly relations existing between Australia and England.'

Douglas Robert Jardine was a man of courage and great determination. He was aloof, autocratic, shrewd and, it seems, a believer in winning, no matter what the cost. On his appointment as Captain of the team to tour Australia he was already aware of the strength of the Australian batting, lead by Bradman, having toured Australia in Chapman's team of 1928/9. What thoughts must have passed through his mind at this time we will never know, but almost certainly his plan of campaign was already decided, although I am sure its outcome can hardly have been foreseen.

Of course, as a man of some resolve his prime consideration must have been to devise a plan to restrict Bradman if nothing else, as there seemed no other way of achieving any success in Australia. An assessment of England's strengths and possibilities came

28

from Arthur Carr, Nottinghamshire's Captain who knew as well as anyone of the skills of Harold Larwood and Bill Voce, the men most likely to put any bowling plan into action. To a limited degree they had tried a form of leg-theory previously but not with any concentrated attention to the field placing. After discussions with Arthur Carr there was no doubt, in retrospect, that Jardine was convinced that Larwood and Voce were the men with the skills to put his plan into action. Harold Larwood was in his prime, the fastest and, just as important, the most accurate English fast bowler ever, a real professional of his day who would obey his captain, come what may. The younger Bill Voce had almost the same credentials, with the advantage of being left-handed, presenting a different line of attack. So the plans were laid quietly but carefully and held in reserve until the team were in Australia. G.O. (Gubby) Allen, (now Sir George) the Middlesex amateur and a fast bowler of real pace who would have added to the batsmen's difficulties by bowling leg-theory (or bodyline, as it was

'BODYLINE'—LARWOOD fells OLDFIELD in the third Test match, Adelaide 1933.

later called) refused point-blank when asked by Jardine to follow the new tactics. It is a commentary on the times that such a situation should have occurred.

The First Test match was played in Sydney. Bradman did not play. England won by 10 wickets. Larwood and Voce took 16 of the 20 Australian wickets that fell. Larwood at various times in the match had eight fielders in the leg-side.

In effect, bodyline was practised by using bowlers of exceptional pace and accuracy with two cordons of fielders on the leg-side. Backing the close catchers were as many as three outfielders square and behind square to catch the mis-hit hook stroke. The line of attack was slanted towards the leg-stump, with the more than occasional short-pitched and very short-pitched (bouncer) delivery. The batsman was left with few alternatives. He could either duck and let the ball sail over his head. Alternatively, he could try to hook, taking the chance of a mis-hit going to the leg-side fielders on the boundary. Sometimes he could fend the ball away at chest-height, with every likelihood of being caught by the close leg-side catchers. It was a poor way to play the game and still is. It was, however,

successful for Jardine, if winning is success and the end justifies the means, but in a very short time, especially after the West Indians had used the same methods against England on their return, it was abandoned by common consent. Neither Jardine nor Larwood continued for very long in the game on their return to England. Ironically and with some bitterness after his treatment by the authorities in England, Larwood retired into obscurity and after the war emigrated to a quiet life in Australia.

The Australians throughout the series expressed resentment of the tactics employed against them, but to their credit and in particular to that of their captain Bill Woodfull, they never retaliated. Don Bradman's average was almost halved. Bert Oldfield, Australia's great wicket-keeper, was badly hurt by a bouncer in the Adelaide Test. Stan McCabe played his great innings of 187 in the First Test, whilst seven of his partners only made 90 runs between them. Also in the team was another of cricket's great run accumulators, the genial Bill Ponsford, whose bat in normal days appeared wider than anyone else's, it was said. In the bodyline series he was totally eclipsed by Larwood.

There were others too, who played in this series and whose mark in cricket should not go unrecognised in these pages. Clarrie Grimmett was one of the greatest of Australia's great wrist-spinners. He played from 1925–36 and took then a record number of 216 Test wickets. He was small but with all the subtle variations in flight, pace and spin. It is said that it was Grimmett who invented the lethal but very difficult method of delivery known nowadays as 'the flipper'. What a pity it is that he is not bowling in world cricket today. Then comes Bill O'Reilly, 'Tiger' as he was nicknamed. Very soon his aggressive bowling made its mark. He was the very opposite of Grimmett being over six feet tall and pulling the ball down with some pace for a leg-spin bowler. With Grimmett they formed by far the finest combination of wrist-spinners there has ever or is ever likely to be. He took 774 wickets at 16.60 in first-class cricket. Of these, 144 were taken in Tests with an average of 22.4 runs per wicket. Truly remarkable figures for a leg-spinner on the wickets he must have bowled on.

On the English domestic scene, the County Championship was in the hands of the northern clubs. Unbelievably, Lancashire won the last of their championships to date in 1934, but Yorkshire under the outstanding leadership of Brian Sellars, a man born in Lincolnshire but truly cast in a forthright Yorkshire mould, won the championships of 1937, '38 and '39.

Little did anyone realise then that Hedley Verity, the delightful man who in the years from 1930 had inherited the mantle of Rhodes as England's slow left-arm bowler, was never to return as a result of the war that was becoming increasingly likely. Even so, fame was to strike at another Yorkshire batsman in the person of Len Hutton, who in the course of following his illustrious predecessor Herbert Sutcliffe, scored the then world-record Test score of 364 at The Oval in 1938 against Australia. Significantly, another young batsman, Denis Compton of Middlesex was making his mark about the same time. They both played against Australia in the Test matches of 1938 and both scored centuries against the West Indies in 1939 whilst in their early twenties.

What of others? I have mentioned most of the great English and Australian cricketers and one or two South Africans, but in the developing years of the West Indies and to a lesser degree India and New Zealand they also produced marvellous entertainers and players of the highest quality. A name which immediately comes to mind is Learie Costantine who became a most respected West Indian politician and was honoured by the

Queen with the title Lord Baron of Maraval and Nelson after becoming the West Indian High Commissioner for Trinidad and Tobago. If ever one word could sum up the all-round ability of one player, that word must be 'mercurial' when describing Learie Constantine on the cricket field. Figures sometimes lie when lined up against a player's deeds. In the case of this great West Indian in every sense—they do.

In all the years before the 1939–45 war there was only one West Indian batsman who could be ranked with the very best and he was George Headley, very often referred to, I suggest unnecessarily, as 'the Black Bradman'. In fact Headley had his own style and in this respect was the forerunner of such players as Worrell, Weekes, Sobers and Nurse. Playing on the excellent West Indies batting wickets these players developed the essentially West Indian technique of hitting the ball 'on the up'. This technique, which may be described as a delayed-action drive, enabled the good-length ball to be hit along the ground with great power. Being a stroke requiring supreme confidence, on indifferent wickets it can easily become a 'getting out stroke'. George Headley's position as a great batsman in cricket history can be realised through the fact that in only twenty-two Test matches he made over 2,000 runs whilst averaging 60.83 and making 10 centuries.

England first toured New Zealand in 1864. Sixty-three years later New Zealand toured England. As a very young and thinly populated country it is understandable that cricket developed only slowly in New Zealand. English teams visited the country only as an appendage to their Australian tour. Nevertheless, New Zealand was and is a country of sport, and cricket did take its hold there with the help of its Australian neighbours and its own inborn enthusiasm. Some marvellous performances from the leading international players of the day also helped to interest the younger generations in

cricket. Walter Hammond, for example, made consecutive Test scores of 227 and 336 not out on the 1938 tour in what were memorable occasions before New Zealand cricket truly came into its own. Of the many fine players that made their marks in the early days however, only one was truly outstanding on the international stage. C.S. Dempster, in only fifteen Test innings, all against England, scored 723 runs at an average of 65.72.

India before the war was in a similar position in international cricket to New Zealand, although obviously with a greater depth of organisation and number of players. Two outstanding players were Lala Amarnath and Vijay Merchant. Amarnath was a fine all-rounder in every sense of the word and did much for Indian cricket in its earliest international days. Vijay Merchant might be termed as the father of Indian batting. He was the outstanding batsman of his generation, once making 359 not out for Bombay in a state match. His influence on Indian cricket was also considerable in the field of administration.

Post-War Years

The time immediately after the Second World War must have been a delightful period in which to play cricket. What a wonderful feeling, to have lived through those dark years and to once again run freely on the lovely cricket grounds of the world in friendly competition, with the anticipation of great Test matches ahead, played between the heroes we knew and heroes we had yet to create. Would the County Championship still provide the breakfast table with the fascination it always had? Would Yorkshire continue their domination of the championship? Who would better Len Hutton's 364? Would it be the greatest batsman of the times 'The Don', or would it be Denis Compton, our 'Brylcream Boy', the cricketer, footballer and the champion of every young sportsman in England? The stage was set with all to play for.

Almost as soon as the war was over the Victory Tests were played: five first-class but unofficial 'Tests' between the AIF (Australian Imperial Forces) and England. The spirit between the teams was as one can only imagine. Those who witnessed the games (three at Lord's, one each at Old Trafford and Bramall Lane) speak of them as special, never to be forgotten memories.

Every type of bowler bowled, every temperament of batsman batted. Hutton and Washbrook continued their opening partnership that promised so well before the war. Hammond was still Hammond. Bill Edrich was without his partner Denis Compton but Gubby Allen was there, as was Jack Robertson whose career with Middlesex was to be an example of all that is best in the true sportsman. I imagine him to be another Jack Hobbs in his demeanour and attitude towards the game.

On the Australian side as always there were outstanding cricketers; but discerning on-lookers, not to mention those that played against them, recognised more than just ability in one or two of the team. The Captain, Lindsay Hassett, was a batsman of real quality complemented by an impish sense of humour that could only auger well for the Test matches of the future. The dashing, handsome Keith Miller with two magnificent centuries at Lord's promised not only to rival Denis Compton on the field but also off it.

India were the first official team to tour England after the war. It was an undistinguished series marred by bad weather, but on the credit side was the introduction into the England team of Alec Bedser, whom with Maurice Tate from pre-war days might be said to be incomparable as medium-fast opening bowlers of courage and stamina, not to say results.

Alec Bedser took 1,924 wickets in first-class cricket at 20.41 runs per wicket and in Test matches took 236 wickets at 24.89. He was Chairman of the England Selectors for over twenty years.

As the 1946 season closed, there was a special air of anticipation for the Australian tour of 1946/7, which in fact was soon tempered by the obvious inadequacies of the England pace attack. Australia in this part of the game had more than a head start, Alec Bedser being the only pace bowler of real quality in the English side. The series confirmed what had been suspected the year before. Australia were gathering a team of all talents. A great opening attack in Lindwall and Miller was followed by a variety of all-round talent in Loxton, Johnston, Tochack and McCool. With the brilliance of Don Tallon behind the stumps and the batting line-up of Arthur Morris, Bill Brown, Sidney Barnes and Bradman himself, Australia were more than a match for an England still to recover from losing some of its pre-war stalwarts. There were compensations however in the solid batting of Hutton and Washbrook and the virtuosity of Compton, who with Arthur Morris of Australia produced a hundred in each innings of the Test match at Adelaide. Another English bonus was the emergence of Godfrey Evans, destined to become one of the greatest of all English wicket-keepers. He was a 'keeper far removed from the classic styles of Oldfield, Tallon and Ames. In a way he could have been a super reincarnation of the effervescent Lancastrian George Duckworth from pre-war days. When Godfrey Evans was behind the wicket batsmen felt oppressed. He was a coiled spring of energy, going after anything that looked like a catch whilst exhorting bowlers and fielders alike to extra effort. Godfrey was a record-breaking wicket-keeper. At the end of his career he had dismissed 219 batsmen in Tests.

The strength of Australian cricket at this

THE GREAT GODFREY—The most mercurial of all wicket-keepers.

Robertson 12 each. Len Hutton and Cyril Washbrook had 11 each and Winston Place of Lancashire made 10.

1948 saw Australia coming to England with what has been said was their best side ever. To the experienced players of 1946/7 was added the name of Neil Harvey who scored a century in his first Test match at Leeds, the match that Australia won by scoring over 400 in the fourth innings. Without taking anything away from the Australians however, it should be mentioned that in the 1948 Test matches a new ball became available every 55 overs. A great advantage, well exploited by Bradman. Don Bradman, as Captain, achieved his great ambition by leading his team throughout a tour of England, unbeaten. The first time such a feat had been achieved. It has been said that the 1948 Australians were the best touring team ever but as we all know it is impossible to really compare the different eras. Nevertheless, the team contained six of the greatest cricketers ever to play together in one team— Bradman, Harvey, Morris, Hassett, Miller and Lindwall. We have already spoken of Bradman the great run-getter, but in Neil Harvey was a player who eventually retired in 1962 as the second leading run-getter in Australian cricket. In seventy-nine Tests he made 21 centuries and 6,149 runs at an average of 48.41. A deceivingly slight figure, Harvey was the supreme artist and as fine a 'timer' of the ball as surely there ever has been. Everything he did seemed easy and his fielding in all positions was of the highest class. He was as modest as he was talented and like many of his kind left the most abiding memories.

Not far behind Harvey was Arthur Morris whose charming, almost diffident personality belied a temperament of steel. He too produced some memorable innings for Australia. Almost an opposite was Lindsay Hassett, delightfully humorous and again a marvellous inventive cricketer. Between them these

time can be realised by the fact that Bruce Dooland and George Tribe, two of the finest of wrist-spinners, played only a total of five Test matches for Australia between them. Their later performances in English county cricket only strengthens this view.

1947 in England was a vintage year; South Africa were the visitors and played attractive cricket throughout a golden summer. Alan Melville was Captain and crowned his career with four consecutive Test hundreds. It was a batting year, with Middlesex the team to watch, as Denis Compton, Bill Edrich and to a lesser degree Jack Robertson, plundered all the bowlers who came up against them. The record aggregate for the total runs scored by one player in a season was broken by both Compton and Edrich with 3,816 and 3,539 respectively. Centuries were in abundance. Compton had 18, Edrich and

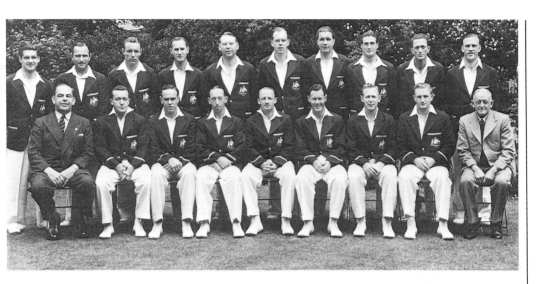

(*Above*) AUSTRALIAN TOURING TEAM TO UK, 1948.

(*Opposite*) BILL EDRICH and DENIS COMPTON—
Legends on and off the field.

two very personable Australians scored over 6,000 Test runs including 22 centuries.

If in going back over all my cricketing days I had to pick a hero, of the two that spring to mind, Keith Miller just takes pride of place in front of Denis Compton. He was the complete sportsman and not only on the field. I can say no more than if I was born again I would not mind being just like him and opening the bowling with Ray Lindwall, as he seems a good man, too. Keith Miller played in fifty-five Tests and took 170 wickets at 22.97 each. He also made 7 centuries whilst averaging 36.97. Ray Lindwall played in 61 Tests taking 228 wickets at 23.03. A tremendous record for any fast bowler—but Lindwall was not any fast bowler, he was the first of a new post-war breed. Supremely fit, with a classical action and perhaps more variation than any previous bowler of his type.

Denis Charles Scott Compton was the genuine *Boy's Own* idol who played cricket and football for England. He was a natural ball player, born with a genius for improvi-sation and timing. He was attractive in personality and appearance, with an indefinable charm that made him the most popular sportsman of his day—and not only with men and boys. Part of his charm lay in his own fallibility, sometimes shown in a total lack of concentration that would have been an annoying trait in anyone else. In his cricket, it was very often shown by his running between wickets, which, even on his good days was problematical. He was probably the worst ever runner between wickets for a top-class batsman, but to his credit, more often than not he was the man to be run out rather than his partner. An exception to this occurred when he ran out his brother Leslie (also a Middlesex cricketer, and Arsenal and England footballer) for 0 in his Benefit match—it could only have happened to Denis. In his career Compton scored 38,942 runs at an average of 51.85 with 122 centuries. In Test matches he made 17 centuries and in 131 innings averaged 50.06.

It is fitting that the name of Bill Edrich should be linked with that of Denis Compton. They partnered each other often enough at the wicket. Bill was in many ways the perfect foil for Denis. He was almost an opposite in style and application. Whereas

Denis was an artist and improviser, Bill's game was based on determination and courage. He was by no means graceful but he was a fighter who never surrendered his wicket. As one would expect he was at his best in a crisis, as was proved by his distinguished war record. When the war was over his adventurous and dangerous experiences had given him the desire to make up for lost time. This he did as much as anyone could and he was loved for it by his army of admirers. Bill Edrich scored 36,965 runs for Middlesex at 42.39 with 86 centuries. In Test cricket in sixty-three innings he made 6 centuries and averaged 40.

1949 ended with some satisfaction all round. A good team came to England from New Zealand but whilst the next decade promised much, the Fifties did in fact mirror the times. It was a period of uncertainty as new ideas were hatched but did not at the time progress. It was a crossroads in cricket, a period when new names were to make the headlines and great names were to fade away. Some cricket historians have almost written off the Fifties as a grim time, a time of attrition rather than adventure, and to some degree there was a period, perhaps of necessity, when the game was looking for direction.

Nevertheless, even in the search for direction there were many days of delight. The early Fifties saw the visit to England of a West Indian side that was not only a joy to watch but a winning joy. The mantle of George Headley had descended not on one batsman but on three. Frank Worrell, Clyde Walcott and Everton Weekes, the three Ws as they became known, presented a variety of entertaining batting styles that had never before been seen in one team. Two spin bowlers, Sonny Ramadhin and Alf Valentine created havoc amongst batsmen in 1950, and beyond. Both were aged nineteen, with little experience of first-class cricket when first selected. They were mainly responsible for the West Indies winning their first Test in

England at Lord's in 1951 and then going on to win the series. A joyful West Indian calypso was composed after the Lord's Test, honouring their victory—it started: 'Cricket lovely cricket, at Lord's where I saw it,' and ended 'With those two little pals of mine, Ramadhin and Valentine.'

The 1951/2 tour of Australia was captained by F.R. (Freddie) Brown, a big man in every sense of the word. He was a born leader, with the courage and talent to lead from the front and win against the odds. In the Melbourne Test, England won, probably through inspired captaincy, if not because of Bedser's marvellous bowling and Reg Simpson's memorable innings of 156 not-out. This was Australia's first defeat in twenty-six consecutive Test matches.

In 1952, in the Test matches against India, Leonard Hutton was appointed the first ever professional Captain of England. The Ashes were won in England in 1953, and retained in the 1954/5 series in Australia. This for the first time in over thirty years. Len Hutton was knighted in 1956 for his services to cricket. For over twenty years he had been the platform from which England and Yorkshire had campaigned successfully more often than not. During the war an accident had resulted in one of his arms becoming shorter than the other but it seemed to make little, if any, difference to his performances, all of which were measured and very professional. He might have been labelled taciturn by his contemporaries but for his very dry sense of humour, often revealed in the most unlikely circumstances through a guarded twinkling in the bluest of eyes, eyes that missed little on a cricket field or anywhere else, I suspect. He was the classic opening batsman eschewing few risks; the

(*Opposite, above*) ENGLAND TEAM *v.* AUSTRALIA AT LORD'S, 1953.

(*Opposite, below*) BRISBANE, 1954—GEORGE DUCKWORTH, THE AUTHOR and GODFREY EVANS.

epitomy of a Yorkshireman in spirit and application and as a captain was shrewd enough to remember the past, in that he was very much aware of which tactics won matches. Sir Leonard Hutton made 40,140 runs in his first-class career at an average of 55.51. He played in seventy-nine Test matches, averaging 56.67. In all he made 129 centuries, 19 of which were in Test matches. In 1938 at The Oval, in the Test match against Australia he made the then record score of 364.

Whilst Len Hutton had many opening partners in his career, Cyril Washbrook of Lancashire was the man who shared the most

(*Opposite*) SIR LEONARD HUTTON—Yorkshireman in application and spirit.

(*Below*) JIM LAKER in action during his record-breaking performance at Old Trafford in 1956—19 wickets in the match—a lesson in itself for any aspiring off-spin bowler.

defiant partnerships with him in the difficult days after the war. Cyril Washbrook's name is synonymous with Lancashire cricket. He played over a period of twenty-six years and in 1987 was still a major influence in the club. A tough uncompromising man with great pride in his Lancashire heritage. Cyril Washbrook scored 34,101 runs in first-class cricket at an average of 42.67 including 76 centuries.

In 1950 Surrey started their astonishing run of success by sharing the County Championship and then by winning it for an unprecedented seven years from 1952–8. In these years the formula for success was as always a balanced team with confident and consistent batting, top-class pace and spin bowling and great catching close to the wicket. Surrey had the lot, including an ideal captain in Stuart Surridge.

Peter May, the young Cambridge University batsman, looked like fulfilling all that had been forecast for him, and Ken Barrington was emerging; but in truth the side was so rich in bowling that few counties could make enough runs to have a chance of winning. The pace bowlers were Alec Bedser and Peter Loader, backed by Surridge if necessary; but it was through Jim Laker and Tony Lock that the *coup de grâce* was so often given to so many teams. They were probably the finest combination of spin bowlers ever to play together for one county, if not one country.

In the Old Trafford Test of 1956, Jim Laker took 10 for 53 in the first innings and 9 for 57 in the second innings. He was probably the best off-spin bowler ever. In first-class cricket he took 1,944 wickets at 18.44 each and in Test cricket took 193 wickets at 21.44 in forty-three Test matches. He also achieved four hat tricks. One has the feeling that he should have played for England more often. As in most good partnerships, the partners complement rather than merge. This was the case with Laker and Lock. Tony Lock was the extrovert to the more serious

The ENGLAND TEAM gathers around FREDDIE TRUEMAN who has just taken his 300th Test wicket. When asked how he felt, he said 'tired'!

and reserved Laker. When Laker took a wicket it seemed a matter of course—almost inevitable. When Lock took a wicket it was a result of his extortion of the batsman, sometimes the umpire, even the ball. A Lock wicket was a triumph of enthusiasm crossed with belligerence—and yet off the field he was the opposition's greatest friend.

Tony Lock was controversial enough to leave Surrey and start a new career, first with Leicestershire and then with Western Australia—a place that seemed made for him. In fact, in a comparatively short career in Australia he became the most successful slow left-arm bowler to play there. In first-

class cricket Lock took an astonishing 2,844 wickets at 19.23 and in Test matches 174 wickets at 25.58.

Of the many other players of quality who truly made their marks in the 1950s were two extra special batsmen in Peter May and Colin Cowdrey. May the sword, Cowdrey the rapier. Along with the elegance of Tom Graveney and later the daunting solidity of Ken Barrington, England were well served.

'Well served' may also apply to England's pace bowling with the immortal Freddie Trueman becoming a legend in his own time, taking 307 Test match wickets in the process. Freddie Trueman was another product of his Yorkshire environment, and proud of it. A man of immense stamina and optimism, his bowling was never the 'faster than fast' that it was labelled by some of his more biased admirers. In fact, Frederick Sewards True-man had more than a streak of shrewdness in him and was one of the most subtle and accurate of all fast bowlers, although it must be said—he always looked fast! In all first-class cricket, the original 'Fiery Fred' took 2,304 wickets at 18.29 and as any Yorkshire-man would say: "Nuff said'.

Once again the other half of the partner-ship was almost an exact opposite. Brian Statham was smooth when Trueman was rough, he was quiet when Fred was loud. When most fast bowlers would be bowling a bouncer, 'George' as he was affectionately known by his close associates, bowled a yorker. Statham was to Lancashire what Trueman was to Yorkshire. For England he was more than a foil, but in spite of his supreme accuracy and equable tempera-ment, at Test level he was perhaps just behind Fred in the list of great bowlers.

Of the others there are two, one of whom made history and the other who did not but might have done.

Frank Tyson went to Australia with Len Hutton's team in 1954/5 as a 'shot in the dark' to say the least. Everyone in England (including Len Hutton, fortunately) knew he was fast, but his performance in county cricket was nothing out of the ordinary. On this 1954/5 tour, the young Lancastrian, raw and fresh from Durham University cricket, must have bowled as fast as anyone had ever done in the history of the game—of that everyone who saw him, including myself, was certain, and it is still irrefutable.

Re-adjusting his run-up after the dis-astrous First Test, he demolished the cream of Australian batting in the Second and Third Tests and was nicknamed Typhoon Tyson from then on. He was a meteor in cricket, shooting across the scene, leaving a brief but exciting trail whilst looking to maintain a level of fitness to bowl faster than anyone had ever done before. It was possible, but only for the shortest time. Frank retired in 1959 to

Melbourne, the scene of his greatest triumph, where as coach and commentator for many years he has added much to his already memorable name.

Les Jackson, a miner from Derbyshire, was one who might have done but did not. One wonders why, because at the time if you had asked any opening batsman in the country who was the bowler they most feared in county cricket, almost invariably the name Les Jackson would have been the first to be mentioned. Partnered by the renowned Cliff Gladwin, a Derbyshire professional if ever there was one, the pair made life very uncomfortable for the very best batsmen in the country on any wicket. Les Jackson took 1,733 first-class wickets at 17.36 runs per wicket. In the only two Test matches that he played he took 7 wickets at 22.14.

One could never categorise Johnny War-dle as anything but one of the best and a worthy successor to the breed of great York-shire slow left-arm bowlers. In Test cricket he was very successful but playing in the same era as Tony Lock he was bound to suffer in selection terms. His marvellous variations in technique, particularly his ability as a left-arm wrist-spinner were never fully utilised. He was a popular crowd entertainer but in the Yorkshire dressing-room did not fulfil the humorist role and seemed to be at odds with the committee. Sadly he left his native county before his time. Johnny Wardle took 1,842 wickets in first-class cricket at 18.95 runs per wicket. He played in twenty-eight Tests and took 102 wickets at 20.39.

Peter May captained England forty-one times in a period of six years from 1955. For many people he has been England's finest post-war batsman, although his premature retirement from first-class cricket may give him a minority vote in this ongoing argu-ment. Whatever position he occupies in cricket however, Peter May's batting style was as English as the game itself. Over six feet tall, elegant and composed, his driving on both sides of the wicket and particularly between mid-on and mid-wicket was classic and sometimes, belying his personality, even savage. There seemed to be a ruthless streak in his captaincy, maybe as a result of his apprenticeship under Sir Leonard Hutton. In sixty-six Test matches Peter May scored 4,537 runs at an average of 46.77 including 13 centuries. In all first-class cricket he made 85 centuries in 27,592 runs averaging 51.00.

In this period when May was Captain of England and Surrey it would be unlikely, in general terms, to talk about him without reference to his great contemporary Colin Cowdrey, even though Colin went on to play for many more years in first-class cricket. It is perhaps appropriate somehow that any comment on either should be in tandem.

Michael Colin Cowdrey, given the initials M.C.C. by his cricketing father, lived up to his early promise in no uncertain terms. His natural 'ball-sense' allied to good technique made him a great batsman in spite of what appeared on some occasions to be a doubt of his own ability. If ever a man looked to giving credit and encouragement to opposition and team-mate alike that man is Colin Cowdrey. When Cowdrey came to the wicket there was a feeling of respect around, just as much from him as to him. From the beginning of an innings he would caress the ball to the boundary without one really being aware that he was scoring. Suddenly you would realise that he had scored 40 or more. That is the hallmark of a great batsman and that was what he was, despite his modesty. Colin Cowdrey played in a record 114 Test matches scoring 76,624 runs whilst averaging 44.06 with 22 centuries. In all first-class cricket he made 42,719 runs at 42.89 with 107 centuries.

To complete this trio of great batsmen— and I make no apology for using the word 'great' so often in my references to many players in this book—there is Thomas William Graveney. Somehow I feel he is a Glou-

(*Above*) PETER MAY—Magnificent batsman in the Fifties; controversial selector of the Eighties.

(*Opposite*) COLIN COWDREY leaving the Pavilion at Lord's in the 1963 Test match against the West Indies. With his arm broken, Colin remained at the non-strikers end while David Allen withstood the last over from Wes Hall.

cestershire cricketer although he was born in Northumberland and played the last ten years of his career with Worcestershire.

Tom Graveney was the supreme stylist. He never seemed to hit the ball hard and yet it crashed into the boundary rails often enough. He was the 'super de luxe' cover driver and the master of all types of spin bowling. Tom's personality is a reflection of his batting or vice versa. He never has had a bad word to say about anyone—even as a commentator. He only looks for the good in the game and that is surely how it should be.

So to the end of the 1950s and the beginning of a new age in cricket. Over the fifteen years or so following the Second World War there had been many changes in rules and regulations, designed to stimulate 'brighter cricket' and attract both people and finance to the game. Many fine players from overseas

had been engaged by the counties, and in truth many were the exciting and enjoyable cricket matches played throughout the country. Unfortunately, or fortunately, depending upon your point of view, the exciting times in a three-day county match tended to be in the last few hours of the match—Tuesday and Friday afternoons in fact. Usually only a handful of spectators had the pleasure of seeing this cricket and so change was needed and change came. . . .

The Years of Change, 1960 Onwards

The years from 1960 seem but a short time when compared with the two hundred years and more I have so far charted. Yet, the volume of incident in this short time and the way it has been handled is a testimony to the strength of the game. 'Radical' could be the word to describe the whole period, as radical times they have been, in cricket terms. Limited-over cricket has been an emotive influence on a bigger scale than could ever have been imagined. Sponsorship and all its demands have also necessitated the most revolutionary changes in style of play, presentation and attitudes. It might even be said that cricket at the highest level has become the servant of the media—if the media be television.

The Packer revolution in the 1970s was certainly the catalyst in the trial of strength between the traditional cricket authorities and the media personalities, represented by Kerry Packer, the Australian television magnate. Packer won the day and gave his viewers what he wanted them to have or what they wanted, take your pick. He also gave his 'mercenaries', as some people called the players, what they wanted—money! Whether he gave cricket what it needed, time will tell.

Whatever, it somehow left an unusual taste in the mouth. The memory of watching Tony Greig (the South African who acted as recruiting agent for Packer) lead out the England side in the Centenary Test at Melbourne in 1977 whilst at the same time secretly trying to persuade them to join the Packer 'circus' does not let me think that cricket was the better for it—or was it? Standards do change, perhaps we had ours wrong!

However, let us start at the beginning and in the turmoil of the times, remember the great players, regardless of the rules they played under.

May, Cowdrey, Graveney and Barrington were the standard-bearers of batting in the Fifties and were still supreme in the Sixties. Trueman and Statham were probably past their best in the Sixties but still a force. If there was a man synonymous with this period it was Ted Dexter, 'Lord Ted' as he was known. Like Peter May he retired prematurely, but he left his mark, and a very good mark it was. He was the most gifted athlete and a batsman of great power and flair, capable of playing every stroke in the book. One was always left with the feeling that Ted Dexter's great gifts were not really valued by himself and so we never saw them as we might have done. Nevertheless, one could very definitely say that this talented man did not pass through the game, or anywhere else, unnoticed. Ted Dexter played in sixty-two Tests and scored 4,502 runs at 47.89. He made 9 Test centuries.

Ken Barrington was the professional's professional. In everything he did there was a concern for the game he loved and respected. When Ken went in to bat, whether it was for England or Surrey, in a Lord's Taverners' match or simply at the nets, he did his very best. He was always well turned-out. In the Seventies he became a father figure to the England touring teams, guiding them as coach and confidant in some very trying times. He died when he still had very much more to give in this role. I have heard him described as something of a sergeant-major but if he was, it was certainly a special one, as compassion was never far below the surface in his dealings with younger players. As a player he was very definite in his role. He played the game exactly as it stood—if defence was needed, so be it. His sense of responsibility, especially to England, never really let him give full rein to his vast range of stroke-play—but his record speaks for itself. He had a lovely sense of humour and was at his most amusing when imitating the legendary figures and in particular the famous Surrey and England bowler Alf Gover. Ken Barrington played in eighty-two Test matches, scoring 6,806 runs at an average of 58.67. In all first-class cricket he scored over 30,000 runs which included 76 centuries.

In the other Test playing countries the game was not undergoing the trauma that it was in England with its seventeen county clubs to support. Not being a professional game as such, domestic cricket was more

easily sustained financially. Consequently, change did not come so quickly, and whereas 1963 saw the first major sponsorships of one-day cricket in England, it was ten years and more before our major Test cricket opponents were required to consider the problems confronting England in the early Sixties.

At this time a memorable game took place in Australia. The first Test match of 1961/2 between Australia and West Indies ended in a tie. The first tie in Test match history. Appropriately, the two captains were Richie Benaud and Frank Worrell who in the series as a whole promoted and produced some of the most stimulating cricket ever seen. Both these captains and a number of their players rightly come into the category of the great— but as always, as much by the manner in which they played the game as the statistics they created.

Richie Benaud ranks as one of Australia's best and most successful captains, and not only in results. He was the ideal leader in that he led from the front in every department.

THE TIED TEST MATCH AT BRISBANE, 1960—A moment in cricket history!

RICHIE BENAUD—Marvellous Captain, leg-spin bowler and commentator.

(*Above*) SIR FRANK WORRELL, the immortal West Indian and one of the three Ws— WORRELL, WEEKES and WALCOTT, who became legends in their time.

(*Opposite*) LORD'S, 1962—The last Gents (above) *v.* Players (below) match. The first match was played in 1806 on Thomas Lord's first ground in Dorset Square.

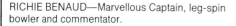

He was tactician and psychologist, great leg-spin bowler and majestic stroke-maker. I should imagine that playing cricket under Richie Benaud's captaincy was a very enjoyable experience, whether you were a shy newcomer or a well-tried campaigner. He practised what he preached in every sense. Only through an abnormal amount of practice did he become the great leg-spin bowler that he was. Richie Benaud played in sixty-three Test matches and took 248 wickets at 27.03.

Sir Frank Worrell was knighted in 1964 after his historic tour of England in 1963. Sadly this marvellous man died of leukaemia in 1966 at the age of forty-two. In every respect he was a magnetic personality who, through his mature and inspiring captaincy of

the West Indies, brought pride and success to the wayward talents of its players. He could and did 'walk with Kings—nor lose the common touch'*. He was one of three Ws with Everton Weekes and Clyde Walcott, whose batting artistry thrilled the world throughout the Fifties. He personified the lithe elegance of the West Indies and the warmth of its cricket. In fifty-one Tests he averaged 49.5 with 9 centuries.

The first of the historic events of the Sixties and Seventies occurred in 1962 when the last

* The quotation is from the poem 'If—' by Rudyard Kipling.

TED DEXTER, 1963—The Captain of Sussex holds aloft the Gillette Cup after winning the final of this first major limited overs competition in cricket history.

Gentlemen v. Players match was played at Lord's. In all there had been 248 matches in 157 years. I should think the stories behind these stark facts would rate a book in themselves. However, it may be of interest to know that in all matches the Gentlemen won 61, the Players won 117, and 69 were drawn. The match of 1883 was tied.

For some time the game had been something of a sham in its description, if not in its performance. A number of the Gentlemen could hardly be classified as amateurs. Nevertheless there is no doubt that there was and had been since its inception a special atmosphere surrounding the match. Over the years there had been many fine genuine amateur players who had brought much distinction, individuality and character to English county and Test cricket and it would indeed have been a lesser game without them.

1963 saw the first major sponsorship of limited over cricket, when Gillette, a name renowned for razor blades, attached itself to a trophy that has since become an equivalent in cricket terms, of the FA Cup in football. Being a knock-out competition, with the 'sudden death' aspect of the 'once only' chance of fame, much of the razzmatazz associated with cup football has come to cricket. The Gillette Cup, now the Nat-West Trophy, with other limited over competitions has been the saviour of County cricket as we know it. They have produced millions of pounds for cricket, with the original formula being continually varied to produce

THE ENGLAND TEAM *v.* WEST INDIES at OLD TRAFFORD, 1963.

other varieties of the limited over game that attract more and more sponsors and income. The message has spread in all directions, with cricket leagues and associations joining a bandwagon of opportunity to maintain and develop the club scene to a level never before experienced, even in the Golden Age or in the halcyon days between the wars. One-day Test matches are now commonplace and like football we now have a cricket World Cup, which in its short history has already produced magnificent individual performances and spectacular success in terms of showmanship, bringing the crowds back to watch a game full of excitement that will at least produce a result in one day.

Having described some of the benefits of limited over cricket, I must point out that this type of cricket also has its disadvantages, in that tactically the bowling is geared to restriction of stroke-play as a priority, rather than the taking of wickets. This strategy undoubtedly changes the nature of the game. For example, attacking field-placing is very seldom seen and consequently this applies also to attacking bowling. In the years since their inception, competitions between forty and sixty-five overs per side have taken place and it may be said that the more the overs per side are restricted, the less the values of the traditional game are seen. However, with the different requirements of the different types of spectators—and consequently sponsors— so the game is structured to cater for the maximum public support. Test match players of quality tend to be bred from the longer, traditional game. Certainly the arts of spin-bowling do not seem to be developed in limited-over cricket and this is one of its major drawbacks. Yet the experienced spin-bowler seems to have a degree of success when conditions are right in limited over games.

That limited over cricket is here to stay there can be no doubt. It has an important place in today's cricket and as such it needs to be considered in a positive rather than a negative way. One good thing that certainly comes from it is the necessity for batsmen of all attitudes to learn the art of stroke-making and to cultivate a will to hit the ball hard. Many players have already become that much better with this realisation.

Through these years of variety, when cricket matches have been designed to suit everyone's taste, there have been a few special players who could adapt to any of the changes. One of them was to make such a mark on cricket as to almost certainly qualify as the greatest cricketer of all time. That man is Garfield (now Sir Garfield) St Aubrun Sobers, born in Barbados, West Indies. He was the most complete of cricketers in that he was supreme in all the skills of batting, bowling and fielding. In addition, his personality, his grace of movement and his open-mindedness on matters other than cricket gave him an aura that could only be associated with greatness, whether it be as an athlete or in any other walk of life.

Whilst Sobers was a genuine all-rounder, left-handed in batting and bowling, his greatest strength was perhaps shown in the sheer brilliance and range of his stroke-play. A measure of the pleasure he gave may be imagined through the adjectives that have been used to describe it. His driving power was *awesome*, his cutting *savage*, and on the only occasion that Trueman bowled him a bouncer in the West Indies, the riposte was *vicious* enough to persuade even Fred not to try one again. Playing for the Rest of the World XI in Australia in 1971/2, he made 254

runs in what was described by Sir Donald Bradman as the finest innings he had ever seen. Praise indeed! In this innings he 'murdered' Dennis Lillee, himself the finest of bowlers and the best fast bowler of the day. Sobers' batting feats were legendary. At the age of twenty-one he made the world record score of 365 not out against Pakistan. In 1968 when playing for Nottinghamshire against Glamorgan, he hit 6 sixes off a six-ball over by Malcolm Nash.

His bowling was a captain's delight in that he was a genuine left-arm extra-fast bowler who could swing the ball both ways. If the conditions were right he could bowl slow left-arm, either in the orthodox manner or as a wrist-spinner. He had success in all three styles. As a short-leg fielder he has had few equals and I believe that on the odd occasion he has kept wicket impeccably.

Once, in 1960 when practising in the nets in Trinidad just before the final Test of that series, Tommy Greenhough of Lancashire and I were besieged with literally hundreds of boys who wanted to practise with us. Whilst a few of them were allowed to bowl the rest clustered round the net. When the practice was over we walked towards the pavilion followed by what was quite a crowd. On turning round, we saw the remarkable sight of at least half the youngsters walking along with the distinctive left-arm swing and pronounced 'leaning forward' stroll of Sir Garfield Sobers—such is real fame!

Sir Garfield Sobers scored 28,315 runs in first-class cricket at an average of 54.87 including 86 centuries. He took 1,043 wickets and 407 catches. He played in ninety-three Test matches and made 8,032 runs at 57.78 including 22 centuries. He took 235 wickets and 109 catches. It should be mentioned that he has played cricket in many other matches all over the world including long spells of

(*Opposite*) SIR GARFIELD SOBERS—One of the world's greatest ever cricketers.

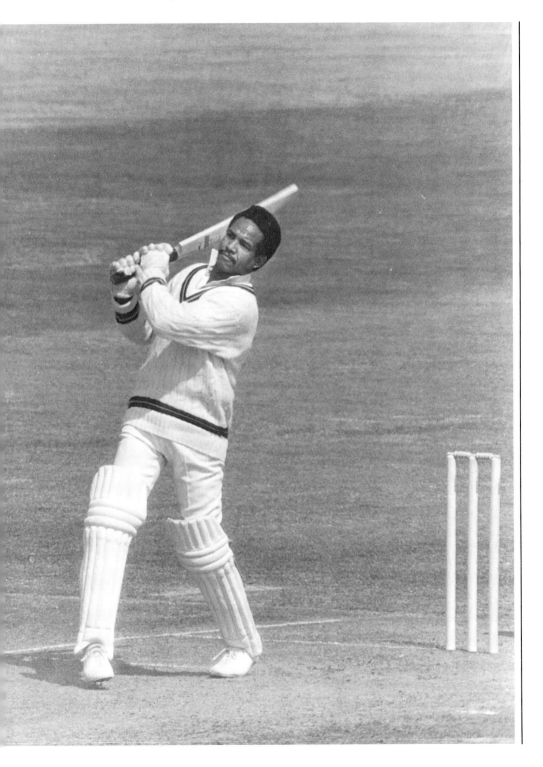

league cricket in England. His standards never dropped no matter where he played.

Of the influx into the UK in these years there were other magnificent West Indian cricketers. Although without the all-round talents of Sobers, they were nevertheless very fine players in their own right. One thinks of Rohan Kanhai, a magnificent stroke-player from Guyana who made 15 Test centuries and played with great distinction for Warwickshire. So much so that he scored 85 centuries in first-class cricket. Wesley Hall was another who made an outstanding contribution to West Indian cricket. A Barbadian fast bowler is always fast. With his long and dramatic run-up, 'Wes', one of the most popular West Indians, produced bursts of Tyson-like speed for a short time in the Sixties. Another fine bowler was record-breaking Lance Gibbs from Guyana who took 312 wickets in Test cricket and likeKanhai had much success with Warwickshire. He was one of the few bowlers to achieve success through subtle flight and variations of pace whilst regularly bowling on good, hard wickets.

In the autumn of 1968 one of the most controversial periods in cricket history began. It was to be known as 'the D'Oliveira Affair'. Basil D'Oliveira, a black South African, had come to England to play cricket in the Central Lancashire league, but with the hope of playing first-class cricket if he could make the grade. It was soon evident that he could. After being engaged by Worcestershire and playing with great success he qualified and played for England, again very successfully. At the end of the 1968 English season the controversy began. Would D'Oliveira be selected for the South African tour or not? Remember, the apartheid laws of South Africa were now being violently opposed by many countries and the anti-apartheid movement was growing rapidly. As it happened, D'Oliveira had lost some form after a comparatively unsuccessful

West Indies tour and as the last Test match against Australia was due to be played at The Oval without him, it seemed that he would not be selected to tour South Africa after all, although it was probably his greatest wish. Fate then really took a hand. Roger Prideaux of Northamptonshire, having been selected for the last Test match at The Oval (his second), withdrew from the side—although he played in the corresponding county match for Northamptonshire commencing on the Saturday of the Test match. The selectors then brought in D'Oliveira who, after being dropped several times, made 158 in the first innings.

Amidst much conjecture the tour selectors met and with the whole country now expecting D'Oliveira to be selected they opted instead for Tom Cartwright, who was the better bowler of the two all-rounders. With much conjecture taking place in various corners of the world, the final twist occurred when Tom Cartwright withdrew from the touring team that had been selected. Whom did the selectors choose to replace him? No prizes for guessing—Basil D'Oliveira!

This decision proved unacceptable to the South African authorities, who by this time had named D'Oliveira a 'political football'. Further controversy raged and the tour was cancelled. Later, as the problems of apartheid remained, the British Government were instrumental in prohibiting the 1970 South African tour of England. So the last Test match between England and South Africa had been played in 1965.

In the previous years some tremendous players had emerged from a South African system supported to a great degree by English county cricketers/coaches who had travelled in considerable numbers to the various South African boarding schools to teach during the English winters.

Whilst it is difficult to fully assess the place of players in the lists of ability when they have played little, if any Test cricket in these years, there are a few South Africans to whom everyone with a knowledge of the game would give the highest recognition. Eddie Barlow is well known in England for his all-round skills and dynamic leadership. Barry Richards in his time with Hampshire was recognised as a batsman of world class. There are others, including Mike Procter, a delightful man and another world-class performer. As an all-rounder, he was in the mould of Gary Sobers. Outstanding amongst outstanding South Africans however, was the man whom many say could have been recognised as the best batsman of them all—Graeme Pollock. One magical day in 1970 he and Garfield Sobers batted together, making 88 runs in one hour against England for the Rest of the World XI. Ironic, tragic, what can be said?

John Snow of Sussex was a fine fast bowler, who virtually 'held the fort' for England in the late Sixties and early Seventies until Bob Willis came on the scene. On his good days he was one of the best, but great fast bowling success usually comes from being one of a pair, as history shows. Nevertheless, John Snow in forty-seven Test matches took 209 wickets for England at 26.66 each. In first-class cricket he exceeded 1,000 wickets at 22.72 each.

In the late Sixties and early Seventies England had mixed success with a variety of captains—Ted Dexter, Mike Smith, Colin Cowdrey, Brian Close, Ray Illingworth, Mike Denness and Tony Greig. The man who might have been the best of all England's captains nearly did not captain England at all. D.B. Close, throughout his long career, was surrounded by controversy, and true to form after displaying his great flair for captaincy in seven Test matches in 1966/7, he was dropped, as a disciplinary measure for time-wasting when captaining Yorkshire against Warwickshire. A heavy penalty, or so it appeared from afar.

Brian Close is not a complex man as some would think, but being the greatest of great triers, bred not to lose at all costs, his very nature has caused him to fly in the face of reality. He is a tough intimidating character on the field, but I have found him to be a most warm-natured, likeable man off it. I first played with him when we both did National Service in the early Fifties. He had already become England's youngest Test player at the age of eighteen. His figures belie his ability yet do justice to his service to English cricket.

Brian Close played twenty-two Test matches, scoring 887 runs at an average of 25.97. In all first-class cricket between 1949 and 1977 he scored 34,824 runs at 33.29 including 52 centuries. He took 1,166 wickets at 26.41 and 808 catches. As a genuine all-rounder, he also made one stumping.

It seems more than appropriate that Brian Close and Raymond Illingworth should be linked together in anything to do with cricket. Both are Yorkshiremen and both are alike in their approach to playing cricket, although their methods are different. Whereas Brian Close was the fearless 'up lads and at 'em' captain, Raymond Illingworth was shrewd and subtle with an incisive cricket brain and, in my experience, the most able tactician of any captain, although I suspect he would have a fascinating contest with Mike Brearley.

Playing cricket against Yorkshire with Brian Close, Fred Trueman, Johnny Wardle and Ray Illingworth in the side was a difficult but fascinating experience. If your team were lucky enough to have won the match against them, exhilaration was not the word! ('Lucky' was their word, but not mine!) Ray Illingworth played almost as long as Brian Close. He scored 23,977 runs in first-class cricket at 28.40 with 22 centuries. He also took 2,031 wickets at 19.93 and made 432 catches. In sixty-one Tests he scored 1,836 runs at 23.24 and took 122 wickets at 31.20—a surprising statistic.

If ever there was a player for the big occasion it was Tony Greig. In fifty-eight Test matches he averaged 40.43 and took 141 wickets at 32.20. In first-class cricket he made 16,660 runs at 31.19 and took 856 wickets at 28.85. He was an aggressive all-round cricketer who, although a South African, captained England fourteen times. It was after he captained England in the Centenary Test match at Melbourne in 1977 that he was found to have been recruiting players to join the Kerry Packer World Series cricket. The English cricket authorities considered this a betrayal of trust, and although he played again for England he was relieved of the captaincy. Tony Greig was a major influence in the 'Packer Affair' and following his involvement he very soon retired to Australia to progress his business life. History will look at Tony Greig's influence on cricket and make its own judgement. It may be that he could have achieved his ambitions by following a different path—but however cricket may view Greig's role in cricket, one thing history has again made plain is that the game is very much bigger than the players, the administrators and anybody else—and always will be!

In brief, in the mid-Seventies Australian cricket was in excellent shape, winning Test matches, attracting large crowds and making excellent profits. There were many good players, some of whom were world class— Dennis Lillee, Rodney Marsh, the two Chappell brothers and possibly Jeff Thompson. Throughout the world the commercialism of sport was getting into its stride and in some sports other than cricket, star performers were making a lot of money. In Australia, where sports stars received the acclaim that pop stars received in other parts of the world, a formula for revolution was being created: a successful game, glamorous and talented performers and the ambitious commercial interests of the media moguls.

One mogul in particular had the power,

the money, the interest in cricket and moreover the desire to put a 'package' together that would give him the opportunity to dominate the Australian cricket scene on television. From the records it seems that to begin with, Kerry Packer, with huge financial backing, wanted exclusive rights to film the Australian Test match cricket. As it happened, the Australian Cricket Board felt that they could not give exclusive rights to the Packer Channel 9 television against the state-owned Australian Broadcasting Commission. From then on, a combination of Kerry Packer's frustration at not being able to realise his aims for Channel 9 and the power of his money, led, not only Australian cricket but also world cricket, into a period of controversy and chaos, the results of which will not truly be known for many many years to come.

Without the exclusive rights to televise international cricket in Australia, Packer decided that he would 'buy' the world's best players and set up his own series of televised cricket matches between them. He recruited leading Australian players, in particular the captains of the Australian states, lead by Greg Chappell. Richie Benaud was involved and Tony Greig, then England Captain was persuaded to act as a main recruiting agent for the rest of the cricket world. The Centenary Test match at Melbourne proved useful to Greig and his allies and in a comparatively short time thirty-five of the world's leading players had been signed to play in a series of matches organised on behalf of Packer by JP Sport, a company experienced in sports promotions.

Unable to agree on many of the new developments, the Packer organisation fought the established cricket authorities who tried to ban players from their regular

(*Opposite*) KERRY PACKER and TONY GRIEG leave the court on the first day of the case now known as 'The Packer Affair'.

selection as Test match players. In a court case lasting seven weeks in England, the Packer side won, giving them an immense influence on cricket, whilst costing the cricket authorities approximately £250,000, mainly paid for by the TCCB. Obviously, these few words by no means describe the great trauma of the times, the antagonism between former friends and the feeling of the established cricket authorities that they had been deceived in a most underhand way quite outside the ethics of the game. Tony Greig, the South African Captain of England and collaborator in this secretive plan was reviled by the English press—and in a very short time was relieved of both the England and the Sussex captaincy. He commented that this was no more than he expected and further stated that his actions were, in his opinion, for the betterment of world cricket. . . .

Exactly two years from the date that the Packer Affair commenced, the Australian Cricket Board gave Packer exclusive TV rights for three years. Just over a month later the former antagonists signed a ten-year agreement of co-operation. ICC (International Cricket Council) approved the agreement in June 1979 and 'everything in the garden was rosy', or so it appeared. Let us hope the changes that this extraordinary period wrought on the game, will be for its good. If they are, nothing is lost and much gained, but never again can the game of cricket be associated with that old-fashioned word—*trust*, and in that there is an irretrievable loss.

The great Australians of the Seventies were a very lively foursome from any point of view.

Dennis Lillee was one of the greatest fast bowlers in history. Like Trueman, he graduated from a one-pace, hostile fast bowler to become an artist in his field, reminiscent of his predecessor Ray Lindwall. Lillee had all the attributes required for the job—strength, stamina, height, a magnificent action and a balanced aggression that enabled him to maximise his skills of swing and subtle change of pace. He was dedicated to keeping himself at peak physical fitness and it was this attitude that enabled him to get over injuries that would have restricted, even stopped a lesser man. In seventy Tests he took 355 wickets at 23.92 each.

There are those who say Greg Chappell is the best Australian batsman since the war, which in itself indicates the quality of this quiet Australian. Quiet, but as a captain, a man with firm opinions to match his ability as a player. He gives an impression of aloofness, but this may be because of his upright yet graceful style. He plays every stroke in the book and is perhaps the finest ever exponent of the on-drive, one of cricket's most difficult strokes. In eighty-seven Tests he has scored 7,110 runs at an average of 53.86 including 24 centuries.

Ian Chappell, the eldest of three Chappell brothers, was also a fine Captain of Australia. He inspired the rest of his very tough team, leading from the front in word and deed. He was a courageous batsman, at his best when the odds were against him. His forceful manner belies a man of great sincerity. He played in seventy-five Tests, scoring 5,345 runs at an average of 42.42, including 14 centuries.

From inauspicious beginnings, Rodney Marsh became one of the finest wicket-keepers, standing back to the fast bowlers, to ever play for Australia. This is praise indeed when one thinks of Oldfield, Tallon, Grout and Langley, all magnificent Australian wicket-keepers.

If ever there was a cricketing desperado, at least in appearance, Rod Marsh was that man. With his baggy Australian cap set low over deep brown eyes and a Mexican style moustache, he somehow intimidated the batsman in front of him. With a 'gunfighter's gait' and gloved hands that appeared to be constantly hovering over low-slung holsters, 'Hot Rod', as he was sometimes called, really put the seal on the 'Chappell gang'. For the record he took 804 catches and 65 stumpings in all matches (869 dismissals).

On the England side, in perhaps most of the Test matches played between England and Australia in this period, was another great wicket-keeper, Alan Knott. Alan followed in the footsteps of the famous Kent wicket-keepers, Leslie Ames and Godfrey Evans. His agility, superb hands and brilliant anticipation, both standing up to and back from the wicket put him in a special place in the wicket-keeping list of greats. An unorthodox but effective batting style was the bane of captains when he came in to bat at number seven. Alan Knott played in ninety-five Tests and scored 4,389 runs at an average of 32.75 which included 5 centuries. In all first-class matches he dismissed 1,340 batsmen, 133 of whom were stumped.

It seems quite normal for the name of Underwood to follow that of Knott. The words 'c Knott b Underwood' must have appeared in the Kent and England score sheets on numerous occasions. Apart from their supreme ability, two nicer men you could not imagine. Derek Underwood, nick-named 'Deadly' by his contemporaries, was the most lethal of left-arm (nearly slow) bowlers on a turning wicket. He was also the most accurate on all wickets and if I had to pick a World XI, I would be tempted to select Derek at his best. He has taken 2,465 wickets in first-class cricket at 20.28 each, including 297 in Test matches at an average of 25.84.

Another English cricketer in this particular group of players is a man who, like his namesake, was above all a fighter, whose wicket was prized by the world's best bowlers. John Edrich was one of the unique band of batsmen to make over 100 centuries in first-class cricket, all of them battled for. He scored 39,790 runs in first-class cricket at an average of 45.47 including 103 centuries.

DEREK UNDERWOOD in the delivery stride—A model for any young spin bowler.

In Test matches he made 12 centuries, including one triple (310 not out), at an average of 43.54.

Who else could we mention in our roll of fame? What about Freddie Titmus, a great Middlesex character and off-spin bowler *par excellence*; the only man of modern times to play first-class cricket in five decades from 1949 to 1983. He took 153 Test wickets in fifty-three Test matches.

Alongside Freddie I must remind you of two delightful cricketers who graced the game for many years not that long ago. They both established records that may never be surpassed: Bob Taylor of England and Bobby Simpson of Australia, wicket-keeper and slip fielder, probably the safest catchers of a cricket ball in history; one with and one without gloves. R.B. Simpson captained Australia and played in sixty-two Test matches, scoring 10 centuries whilst averaging 46.81. His record number of catches for Australia (mainly at slip) was 110. Bob Taylor, coming late into Test cricket because of the all-round brilliance of Alan Knott, still made his mark, not only for having the safest hands in the business but simply for being a nice guy. Bob Taylor holds the world record for the number of dismissals in first-class cricket: 1,528.

Looking overseas again, does the most subtle of Indian slow left-arm bowlers compare to our string of English greats? Yes, I believe Bishan Bedi does, at least his contemporaries think so. What an attractive sight Bishan was on the field with his different coloured turbans brightening some of cricket's most depressing days. In sixty-seven Tests Bishan Bedi took 266 wickets at 28.71 each, a record for India.

Pakistan are increasingly producing batsmen of the very highest quality, and in Mushtaq Mohammed, brother of Hanif and one of five cricketing brothers, they have the youngest Test player ever. Mushtaq played his first Test match for Pakistan at the age of fifteen years 124 days. He is also the youngest to score a Test century at seventeen years eighty-two days. The third and perhaps most enduring record is that he played his first first-class game aged thirteen years forty-one days. Somehow I cannot see any of these records being bettered.

Zaheer of Pakistan was a batsman of great ability who played with distinction for Gloucestershire, as did Glenn Turner for New

BISHAN BEDI—Flight, spin—delight.

Zealand and Worcestershire. Both were in the '100 centuries in first-class cricket' class, Zaheer with 107 and Glenn Turner with 103

So to the Eighties and one of cricket's most exciting decades. Test matches are more keenly contested than ever before as enormous cash and material incentives are offered to the players and very often those they represent. Limited over cricket is an essential diet of any summer at all levels of play. On television, cricket is dramatised beyond belief at times, as techniques of production, some of them inspired by the Packer cameras, bring every possible controversy into our living rooms. Very fast, short-pitched bowling has become a feature of play as helmeted batsmen, the gladiators of the game, duck and weave the excess of intimidatory bowling. Where it will all lead I cannot begin to think, but within the controversies created by a sports-hungry following, a number of great players shine through and give the cricket-loving public some very memorable days. Botham, Lloyd, Hadlee, Imran, Richards, Miandad, Marshall, Holding, Greenidge, Brearley, Gower, Gavaskar, Boycott, Gouch and Gatting: these are some of the great players of the era about whom so many words have already been written. In the same league younger players whose talents have yet to fully develop are Martin Crowe, the mercurial Javed Miandad and, perhaps the most outstanding talent of them all, Graeme Hick from Zimbabwe, almost certain to be a sensation for England in the Nineties.

Of all the men who may be called legends in cricket there are a very special few whose personality and performances have taken them into realms of their own. Of today's players Ian Botham is the Colossus of cricket. On his good days and there are many, he bats like every boy and man in the

BENSON AND HEDGES FINAL AT LORD'S, 1982—NOTTINGHAMSHIRE v. SOMERSET. The crowds gather for the presentation; an indication of the popularity of the one-day game.

(*Above*) CLIVE LLOYD, speaking at the Guildhall Bi-Centenary Dinner, 1987.

(*Opposite*) BRIAN LARA, the record breaker.

land dreams of doing. He hits the ball as it has never been hit before—at least that is how it appears, as in nearly every stroke he plays he gives the impression of brute strength, hiding to a large degree his very sound technique. Whilst his bowling on occasions can appear innocuous, as soon as he makes a breakthrough, the 'chips go down' and every post becomes a winner, as he exhorts himself to take a wicket every ball. From a casual 'hands on knees' position when standing closer than he really should at slip he catches 'pigeons' with the reflexes of a cat. Ian Botham is 'one of the boys' and they think he is great. Like many men of his kind he can suddenly reveal a disarming modesty seconds after appearing to be the most immodest man on earth. He is the crowd-puller supreme. With some Ian

Botham is unpopular, but for me he is and always will be good-hearted cricketer.

J.M. Brearley is another fascinating man, of great intellectual stature and quiet determination. I cannot remember an innings of his, but I can certainly remember his presence on the field. I always had the feeling that no matter how bad things were for England, as long as Mike Brearley was Captain everything would come right—and so it did. Brearley captained England in thirty-one Tests, eighteen of which were won and only four lost. His modest record of 1,442 runs at an average of 22.88 in 39 Test Matches only emphasizes his ability as a captain.

Of the other great cricketers of the eighties, Viv Richards was probably the best batsman, with Gordon Greenidge, a West Indian who learned his cricket in England, a good second in my opinion. Clive Lloyd was to the West Indies what Mike Brearley was to England, even if his credentials were very different. Clive was, of course, a great

61

(Above) BOYCOTT—A great batsman.

batsman in his own right and, as a young man, one of the best cover fielders ever. His natural modesty only added to his credentials for captaining his highly talented West Indian team. Clive Lloyd scored 7,515 runs at an average of 46.68 in 110 Test Matches. For the record, Mike Brearley and Clive Lloyd never played against each other in Test Cricket, which in some quarters takes something from Mike Brearley's remarkable record as a captain.

Sunil Gavaskar, truly the modern master batsman, retired from Test cricket in 1987 and his phenomenal record is worth noting. He played in 125 Test matches, scoring 10,122 runs at an average 51.12. His record number of Test centuries is 34. Geoffrey Boycott of Yorkshire and England is to this country what Gavaskar is to India. His controversial career has been the subject of discussion in print, on film and in pubs and clubs throughout the world. If the words 'complete dedication' can be applied to any man in cricket, Boycott is that man. He has unquestionably given the most single-minded attention to the subject of batting, if not the art of batting, in the history of the game. Many batsmen in the game's history have been able to concentrate during an innings and occasionally make big scores. The difference between the others and Geoffrey Boycott is that, whilst the others concentrated on batting whilst batting, it seems that Geoffrey has concentrated on batting as a part of his life. He has lived by the saying that 'practice makes perfect' and, in doing so, by his own very high standards, has developed a defensive technique that is unlikely to be surpassed. I do not know Geoffrey Boycott that well, but what I do know of him, I respect. He has received an enormous amount of criticism, probably unjustly. Like most Yorkshiremen he says what he thinks and his word is his bond. I hope he is allowed to make his contribution to cricket off the field. Others of his generation have that privilege with far less to give. In 108 Test matches Boycott scored 8,114 runs at an average of 47.78 with 22 centuries. In first-class cricket (at the end of 1986) he had made 48,426 runs at an average of 56.83 with 151 centuries and 238 fifties.

From the eighties to the nineties, a decade of satellites and sponsorship, of coloured clothing, Sunday Test Matches and corporate crowds. Significantly, the public's appetite for television cricket has resulted in a contract between television and cricket amounting to an incredible £50,000,000. Where is it all going to end? Was it only twenty-five years ago that my old friend Ken Turner, Secretary of Northamptonshire County Cricket Club, ran discos and pop concerts in the indoor school at the County Ground to help keep the Club alive! Yes, it was, and in this spirit of nostalgia it behoves me to comment briefly and list the remarkable Test Match statistics of seven great cricketers, now retired, who made an enormous impact on the game in recent years. In alphabetical order (I leave the order of greatness to the reader) they are as follows:

ALLAN BORDER (Australia)

AB, the epitome of the tough Australian cricketer in his baggy green cap; always his team's inspiration as he battled his way to an all-time record number of Test Match appearances.

IAN BOTHAM (England)

'Beefy' as he is known by friend and foe alike and about whom I have written earlier in this book. A flamboyant personality; always ready to do battle against the odds, take on the establishment, bowl bouncers and hit sixes. His belligerence hides a warm personality and I should think he makes a good friend.

KAPIL DEV (India)

A mercurial all-rounder of film-star popularity in his own country. The last of the seven to retire, in November 1994, having just broken Sir Richard Hadlee's bowling record in Test Match cricket.

DAVID GOWER (England)

A favourite son of every cricket age group, from junior schoolboy to senior citizen. A left-handed virtuoso at the wicket and a cricketer whose style and pleasant demeanour will be remembered as long as cricket is played.

SIR RICHARD HADLEE (New Zealand)

A man who represents everything that is good about cricket and New Zealand cricket in particular. In horse racing terms, Nijinsky comes to mind; it is something to do with class.

IMRAN KHAN (Pakistan)

The pride of Pakistan, maybe one day they will make him President! His influence on cricket in Pakistan is incalculable. Truly a man of destiny and, in passing, a great all round cricketer.

VIV RICHARDS (West Indies)

Probably the batsman most feared by the opposition since the days of Bradman. An arrogant destroyer of every type of bowling on his day—and his day was often. A man with great pride in his West Indian heritage.

	Matches	Runs	Average	Wickets	Runs/ Wickets
Allan Border	156	11,174	50.56	—	
Ian Botham	102	5200	33.54	383	28.40
Kapil Dev	131	5248	31.05	434	29.64
David Gower	117	8231	44.25	—	—
Richard Hadlee	86	3124	27.16	431	22.29
Imran Khan	88	3807	37.69	362	22.81
Viv Richards	121	8540	50.24	—	—

It is said that figures do not lie and to some degree that is true of the great players, but only in so far as they do not tell the full story. This is the prerogative of those lucky enough to have actually seen them at their best, or perhaps to a lesser extent, have read the works of the brilliant scribes of the day, whose powers of description bring back the most wonderful memories.

And now from memories to anticipation—who will be the next generation of great cricketers? Curtly Ambrose must be a favourite, although he is perhaps beyond the anticipation stage. This towering West Indian has already taken over two hundred Test Wickets and hardly seems to have started. The same may be said about Pakistan's lethal opening bowlers, Wasim Akram and Waqar Younis. Already they have taken over 300 wickets between them at not much more than 20 runs per wicket. The word anticipation is perhaps more suited to Shane Warne, Australia's new golden boy of spin. An outstanding success on his first tour of England in 1992, he spins the ball like a top and has more than proved that wrist spin is far from dead as he takes his place in the long line of great Australian wrist spin bowlers. Of all the stars of the nineties, however, the most sensational is Brian Lara of Trinidad and the West Indies. He is already the holder of two remarkable records—the highest ever Test innings of 375 for West Indies against England in Antigua in early 1994 and only weeks later an unbelievable 501 not out for Warwickshire against Durham at Edgbaston. It is hard to imagine either of these records ever being surpassed, but having done it once who is to say that this amazingly gifted young man will not do it again!

From one generation to the next and, thankfully, as always, the game has come up trumps. Exciting teams and star players will come and go and, in spite of the political manoeuvrings that make up the dark side of cricket, we can look forward to the 21st century with much optimism. If there has been a blow for cricket freedom in time for the new dawn, it has, without doubt, been the return to the fold of South Africa, mainly through the dreams and inspiration of four men—Ali Bacher, Krish Mackerdhuj, Geoff Dakin and Govan Mbeki—not to mention the even wider dreams of Nelson Mandela and F.W. De Klerk, two truly great men of destiny. The whole story has still to be told, but one day it will be, and what a tribute that will be to cricket. It makes one think that the United Nations should come to Lord's for the next meeting of the International Cricket Council! South Africa were re-admitted to ICC on 10 July 1991, playing their first Test Match since March 1970 against India in November 1992.

So I come to the end of what has been a very enjoyable journey for me. I hope it has given you pleasure and briefly refreshed for some of you happy memories of days past and marvellous cricket. Was it really two hundred years ago when the Earl of Winchelsea and Charles Lennox commissioned Thomas Lord to find a ground on which they could play cricket with their friends? Does Dorset Square now stand where once was Dorset Fields?

What sort of a man was W.G. Grace? How would he have fared today? Of course we can only guess, but as we all know, the game will always be greater than the player, whoever he may be, and two hundred years is, after all, only a fragment in time, or a few pages in a book. . . .

CHAPTER TWO

The Skills of Cricket

This chapter is about 'how to play cricket'. It is intended mainly for players and coaches but it will, I hope, also give those that watch and listen to the game a deeper understanding of its skills and techniques, so that their enjoyment will be that much more. At all levels of cricket there are measures of success. Twenty runs in a junior school match can mean as much to a twelve year old as 100 runs might to a seasoned professional in a county match. But what is success? Is it how many runs you get, or the way you get them? Perhaps it is both, but real success is in the enjoyment of the game and the thought, not always shown in results even, that you are improving as a player. What a thrill it is when suddenly something clicks and instead of getting out at 10 or 20 you make 50! If you happen to be a bowler it is fairly certain that if an extra wicket is a result of new-found pace or extra spin, so your day, and maybe that of your team, will be made.

Even if success has not come with bat or ball, a better than average catch or a slick leg-side stumping can have just as much effect. Of course, there is nothing like a little success to stimulate enjoyment and cricket is no different from any other pastime in that respect. So, if success is to do with improving skills, how might we progress?

Firstly, it should be appreciated that every player is an individual, born with varying degrees of natural ability. There are those of great natural talent who seem to learn simply by watching others and adopting their ideas as required. Encouragement and opportunity are all that is needed by the gifted few—but the right type of encouragement is also important and opportunity is not necessarily as much an accident of birth as it might appear. A great deal of enthusiasm is needed by a number of people to create the right conditions for a cricket talent to develop. I can think of vast numbers of young athletes who will never go anywhere near a cricket ground or hit a cricket ball.

On the other side of the coin are those born without great flair but with the priceless quality of determination. These players contribute to the game just as much as the great individual entertainers—especially when it comes to winning matches.

The words 'technique' and 'coaching' when applied to cricket can have a very 'off-putting' effect on many people in the game, especially those who are gifted or those who are used to dealing only with the gifted players. Simplicity and natural ability are all-important, they say, defying the fact that cricket is a complicated game. Naturally, it is important to convey advice in the simplest way possible but this is the job of the coach anyway and an indication of why coaching has become a skill, if not a profession in its own right. Let us not portray cricket as just a bowler bowling to hit the wicket and a batsman trying to hit the ball as hard as possible. Cricket is subtle and surrounded by countless variations in tempo and style that make it a truly fascinating game. Its terminology is almost a foreign language and its different technical ploys can rival the moves in any game of chess.

Fortunately, it is played in the open air most of the time, which has obvious benefits and some less obvious, as wind and weather test the variety of skills in both teams.

The skills of batting are generally more obvious, if not more subtle, than other skills in the game—and this may be the reason for their greater appeal to many of those who watch. Having said this, it is the contest for supremacy between bat and ball that truly absorbs those who get to know the game in depth, with all its variances of skill and changing moods. So, by considering the requirements and skills of batting first, we can then take the role of the bowler to test our knowledge and give us some appreciation of the tasks involved in 'thinking' the batsman out, because most of the time that is what the bowler needs to do.

BATTING

Basics

No matter who you are, talented or otherwise, tall or short, strong or not so strong, of twinkling feet or built like a cart-horse, there are a few basics that need to be acquired. They are a good grip of the bat, a comfortable stance and a preparation for action, usually in the form of a back-lift.

Grip

Both hands should be close together, the top hand in particular gripping the handle firmly. The bottom hand can be more relaxed. No more than about an inch of handle should protrude beyond the top hand. The 'vees' formed by the thumb and forefinger are very important in that they should be 'in line'. This will enable both hands to work together freely. Batsmen of different inclinations will

Fig. 1 THE GRIP
Fingers and thumbs well round the handle, Vs in line; hands close together; back of top hand faces mid-off approximately.

Fig. 2 Wrong Grips.
(Top) Left hand too far in front. *(Bottom)* Left hand too far behind.

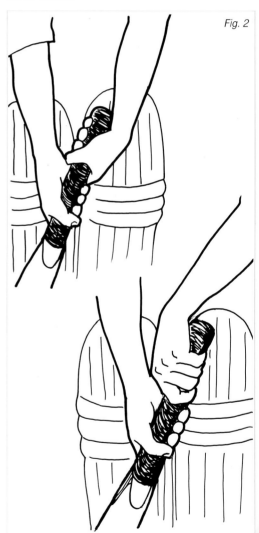

Fig. 2

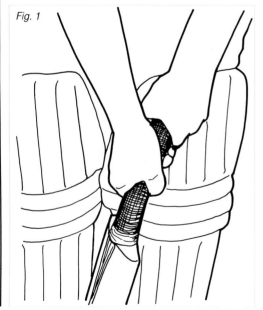

Fig. 1

Fig. 3

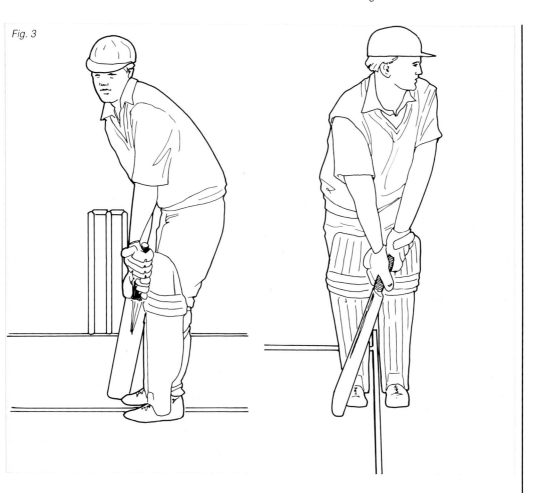

Fig. 3 STANCE
Eyes level; left shoulder points towards bowler; knees slightly flexed; weight evenly distributed, mainly on the balls of the feet.

position their hands differently on the bat handle. A defensively inclined batsman will position the 'vees' towards the splice of the bat. A purely attacking batsman with a fondness for the drive will tend to position the 'vees' towards the edge of the bat, although there is not quite the same control from this position. A good compromise is somewhere between the two.

Stance

Nature being what it is, no two batsmen can stand at the wicket in exactly the same position, but again there are sound basics from which the best results can be gained. The feet should be positioned on either side of the batting crease, about six inches apart, with the weight equally distributed on the balls of the feet. Too narrow a stance and the batsman will lose his balance, too wide a stance causes him to become 'fixed', restricting speed and range of foot movement. The back foot should be parallel to the crease. The front foot will find its own position. Knees should be slightly flexed for quick movement and the hips will be a little further open to the bowler than the shoulders. Shoulders will be in line, pointing straight down the pitch when the bowler is bowling right arm over the wicket. Adjustments can be made if the bowler changes his bowling position.

The most important single piece of advice I can give to any batsman, and probably worth mentioning now, is to always think (when practising at least) of the front shoulder making the first movement towards the line of the ball. This is of paramount importance when making any stroke as it will ensure that the head moves into the right position in relation to the feet and hips.

Whilst in the stance position, the head should be perfectly still with the eyes as level as possible, depending upon the flexibility of the neck. The side of the top hand will rest lightly against the inside of the thigh, the back of the top hand usually facing between mid-off and cover.

Avoid crouching, if anything 'stand tall' and position your head in line with the middle stump. This will give you an awareness of your position relative to the line of the ball. This alignment can be achieved when first going to the wicket by 'taking a guard' from the umpire or, in practice, from a bowler. Take guard simply by presenting a vertical bat at the batting crease from which you can mark the position of the middle stump on the crease, with the help of a person behind the middle stump at the bowler's end.

Of course, there are successful batsmen who do not conform exactly to these recommendations but not many who vary greatly from them. In recent years there has been a move to adopt a stance with the bat off the ground to allow the taller batsman to 'stand tall'. There is nothing wrong with this as it enables the batsman to avoid crouching. Other batsmen adopt an 'open stance', with the chest opening to face the bowler. This is not new, as pictures from the past show us. However, to get on the line of the ball, considerable shoulder turn is needed. For

(*Above*) GUARD—Thank you Umpire!

Fig. 4 BACK-LIFT
Both eyes on bowler's hand; head still; bat vertical with face 'open'; elbows clear of body with front arm 'extended' back.

(*Opposite*) GRAEME HICK'S classical back-lift is an example to all aspiring young batsmen.

some batsmen an open stance precipitates the essential shoulder movement into the line of the ball, but it is yet another movement and consequently adds to the problems of timing the stroke.

Back-lift

Such importance is attached to the back-lift these days that more and more batsmen are

Fig. 4

completing it whilst in the stance position and before any other movement into a stroke. Many of the older school of players and coaches are very critical of this new technique, but against fast bowling particularly it makes a lot of sense. One only has to think of American baseball where it has always been common practice for the bat to be taken back early to cope with the high speed throws of the pitcher. Conversely, the older school always refer to the great film of Gary Sobers during his great double century, for the Rest of the World XI against Australia in the Seventies. Dennis Lillee, one of the fastest and best bowlers ever, was bowling to Sobers, who had not moved a muscle from his traditional stance position when the ball left Lillee's hand! In this case, however, we are considering the ability of genius. Not everyone has the strength and reactions to lift the bat back and take it forward to the ball in the split second allowed by the truly fast bowler. We do not know the answer yet as to which technique is correct. Until we do, it must be a matter for individual experiment and choice. The main thing is, that whatever back-lift is used it should be a technically sound movement in itself, with the downswing that follows keeping the bat on the line of the ball.

Let the top hand control the back-lift. Allow the front arm to extend, flexing naturally as it pulls the shoulder under the chin, whether playing back or forward. Keep the head perfectly still and pick the bat up, if possible between wickets, allowing the face to open towards point. Some great batsmen have noticeably picked the bat up towards slips but have 'corrected' by 'looping' at the top of the back-lift to bring the bat down the line of the ball.

Playing the Ball

From the stance position, either traditional or modern, a batsman can hit the ball most effectively by moving the feet (through an initial movement of the front shoulder) either forward towards the anticipated pitch of the ball to make early contact or back away from the anticipated pitch of the ball to make later contact, depending upon where he thinks the ball is likely to pitch.

If the ball can be hit just after it bounces then it is easier to play forward to make a satisfactory hit. If the ball is likely to pitch a good distance away from the batsman it is easier to play back, allowing more time to make a stroke.

The 'pitch' of the ball may be defined as the point at which the bowled ball hits the ground. The 'length' of a ball (delivery) is defined as the point where the ball pitches in relation to the batsman when he is in his normal stance at the wicket.

Fig. 5 PLAYING THE BALL

Recognised Names for Different Lengths of Bowling

Good Length
This is the length bowlers try to pitch every ball. An appreciation of a good length can be acquired to some degree by the recognition of what is not a good length. The following descriptions of various lengths of delivery will clarify this point.

Long Hop
A delivery that pitches approximately half-way down the pitch, the long hop is generally considered to be the easiest ball to hit. In fact, it can normally be hit hard anywhere in front of the wicket on the leg-side. It is said that even a full toss is a better delivery than a long hop.

continued on page 75

Fig. 5

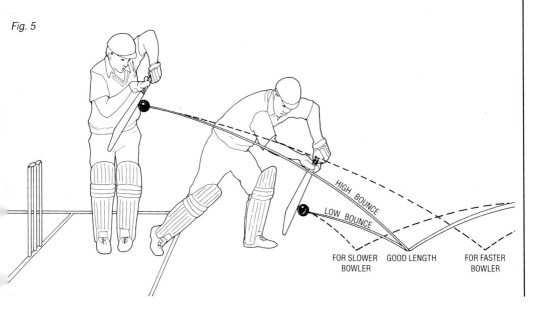

HIGH BOUNCE
LOW BOUNCE

FOR SLOWER BOWLER   GOOD LENGTH   FOR FASTER BOWLER

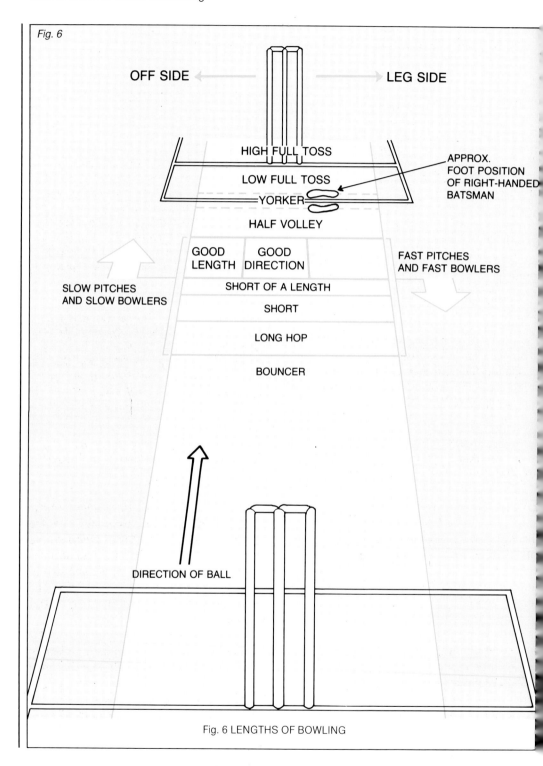

Fig. 6

OFF SIDE ← → LEG SIDE

HIGH FULL TOSS

LOW FULL TOSS

APPROX.
FOOT POSITION
OF RIGHT-HANDED
BATSMAN

YORKER

HALF VOLLEY

| GOOD | GOOD |
| LENGTH | DIRECTION |

SHORT OF A LENGTH

SHORT

LONG HOP

BOUNCER

SLOW PITCHES
AND SLOW BOWLERS

FAST PITCHES
AND FAST BOWLERS

DIRECTION OF BALL

Fig. 6 LENGTHS OF BOWLING

Recognised Names for Different Lengths of Bowling

Short Ball
This pitches nearer to the batsman than a long hop. Good batsmen look to score off the short delivery especially when it is pitched off the line of the stumps. Depending upon the direction of the ball the batsman can play any one of the attacking back strokes on a good surface. Even on a bad pitch the short ball can cost runs.

Short of a Length
Pitching just short of a good length is a defensive delivery on a good pitch, but it can be a useful wicket-taker on a difficult pitch (when the ball is lifting or keeping low).

Half Volley
Pitching beyond a good length, this is the delivery that every batsman should be looking to drive just as it hits the ground. When the ball is swinging it can be a wicket-taker unless the batsman gets to the pitch of the ball.

Yorker
Pitches approximately at the batsman's feet. It is a very effective wicket-taker if bowled with a little extra pace. In any case it is very difficult to score off.

Full Toss
Like the long hop, this delivery is looked upon by batsmen as a gift. The ball does not pitch at all and the height at which it reaches the batsman can determine the stroke. A high full toss will usually be pulled (or cut when wide of the off-stump) with a horizontal bat. A low full toss can be driven off the front, or back foot, depending upon the batsman's style of play.

Bouncer
This pitches in a similar area to the long hop, but is delivered at a fast pace. The ball pitches and lifts towards the batsman's chest and head. The best batsmen may be able to 'hook' the bouncer but many prefer to duck or sway out of line without playing a stroke.

Beamer
This is a head-high full toss, considered to be an unethical delivery if bowled by a fast bowler.

Bounce and Deviation

The bounce and lateral deviation of the ball on pitching are very important considerations for both batsman and bowler and add another complication to the subject of length and direction.

Whilst the length of a delivery gives an indication of the type of stroke that may be played, the anticipated bounce and deviation of the ball on pitching will also influence the batsman, possibly causing a change in technique within the circumstances of the game. For example, on surfaces from which the ball tends to bounce high, back strokes will predominate, batsmen only playing forward when they can get close to the pitch of the ball. When the ball tends to bounce low, the reciprocal is true, with the forward stroke coming into its own. When the ball deviates on pitching it is of course a welcome sign to the bowler, whether the deviation be accidental or by design. An accurate bowler can make life very uncomfortable for a batsman when there is any lateral deviation of the ball through either spin, swing or seam and only the technically well-equipped batsman will be able to cope. A sound defence will be all-important, letting the ball come to the bat rather than pushing through with the bottom hand. The ability to recognise the bad ball early and hit it hard and true is crucial.

Forward Strokes

There are those who believe that defensive strokes should be the last consideration of the batsman and it is true that the forward defensive prod, when overdone, is not the best sight in cricket. However, whilst this comment is valid, it is my belief that correct defensive technique is the cornerstone of batting and as such should be the first consideration for the learner. It is all right to think attack, but have the means at your disposal to combat the best of bowling. There is an old adage worth remembering: 'You cannot score runs in the pavilion.'

The forward attacking strokes and particularly the drive are perhaps the most interesting for the spectator and the most satisfying to the batsman. Defensively, the forward stroke, as already suggested, tends to be over-used and is, in fact, a product of the 'if in doubt, push out' philosophy. Forward play can be limiting as the range of strokes can only safely cover a much smaller area of the field than the back strokes. For this reason the good bowler will try to make the batsman play forward.

Fig. 7 FORWARD STROKES

Fig. 7

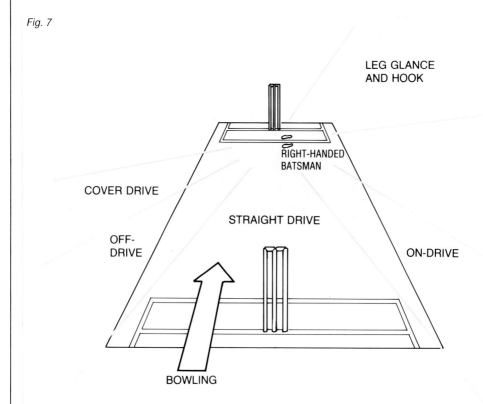

LEG GLANCE AND HOOK

RIGHT-HANDED BATSMAN

COVER DRIVE

STRAIGHT DRIVE

OFF-DRIVE

ON-DRIVE

BOWLING

Forward Defence

Played to a good length delivery pitched on the stumps or just outside the off-stump. Take care not to play the forward defensive too much when the ball tends to bounce high off the wicket (see Back Defence).

From a sound stance and controlled back-lift, the front shoulder will lead the head and hence the front foot towards the line of the ball. The weight will be transferred almost entirely on to the front foot with the front knee bent to close any gap between bat and pad. The front elbow is high on contact with the ball and a firm top-hand grip, with the wrist behind the bat handle, keeps the bat face vertical and checks its forward movement. A relaxed bottom-hand grip allows the bat handle to be angled forward with the top hand to keep the ball down on contact.

(*Above*) GRAHAM GOOCH, not normally associated with forward defence. Graham makes big scores because he can cope with the best deliveries.

Fig. 8 FORWARD DEFENCE
Head well forward in line with bat handle; top hand in control; front knee bent to close 'gate'. No follow-through.

Fig. 8

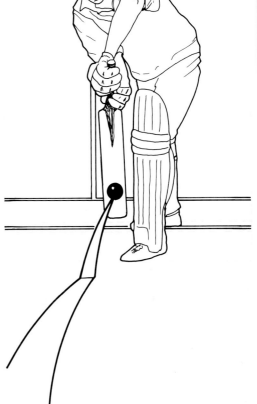

Forward Attack

The Drive

This is played to a low full toss or more usually a half volley, pitching anywhere between the line of mid-on to cover point. It is probably the most elegant of all the strokes and on a good wicket the most productive. The early basic movements of the forward defensive stroke are applied but obviously with different intent as the stroke progresses.

Cover/Off/Straight Drive

The front shoulder leads the head towards the line of the ball with the front foot just inside the anticipated pitch of the ball. From a high back-lift the full face of the bat comes down the line of the stroke. At the point of contact the bottom hand accelerates through the ball, pulling the rear shoulder under the chin and fully extending the bottom arm into a high, balanced and full follow-through.

The Check-Drive

In the check-drive the wrists will lock rather than break as in the full follow-through. This checked drive is frequently played against

Fig. 9 COVER DRIVE
From a high back-lift the front shoulder leads the front foot towards the line of the ball. With the weight fully on the front foot the hands follow through in the direction of the stroke.

Fig. 10 (*Inset*) Finish of CHECK DRIVE.

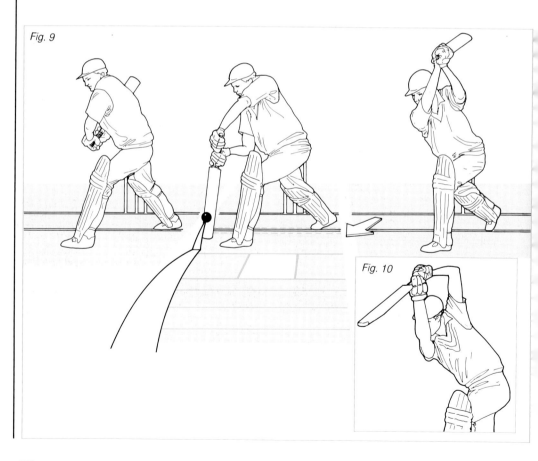

Fig. 9

Fig. 10

fast bowling when it is difficult to generate the full power needed for the full follow-through. It is also useful when teaching young children to drive on the off-side of the wicket, in that they often tend to swing across the line of the ball when trying to play the drive with a full follow-through. To play the check-drive the top hand (wrist) needs to be positioned firmly behind the bat handle.

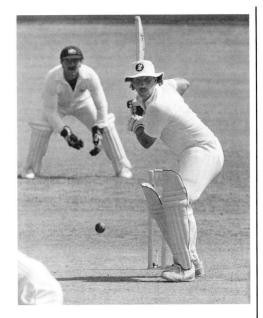

(*Right*) IAN BOTHAM—This magnificent position says more than a thousand words.

(*Below left*) DAVID GOWER cover-drives with effortless elegance.

(*Below right*) GRAEME HICK—The perfect example of the check-drive by one of the world's best young batsmen.

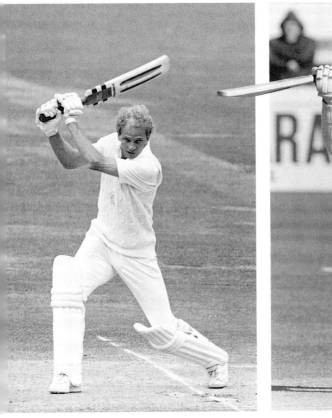

Fig. 11

Moving Out to Drive

To slow, flighted and sometimes medium pace bowling, when the wicket-keeper is standing back, the batsman may move down the wicket to drive. This needs very quick footwork and supreme confidence. Only the most accomplished of players are capable of consistently using this ploy. Do not carry through with the stroke if the correct driving position is not established, simply revert to a defensive stroke.

The On-Drive

As opposed to the off-drive and the cover-drive, the on-drive is probably the most difficult of all strokes to play. There is a tendency to hit with the bottom hand too soon, closing the bat face and taking it across the line of the ball. There is also a tendency to let the head fall over towards the off-side, causing the batsman to hit the ball in the air towards mid-wicket. A good tip is to drop the front shoulder and open the hip a little when moving into the stroke.

Forward Leg-Glance

Played to a full, good length ball going down the leg-side, this stroke can be an alternative to the on-drive and sweep, depending on field placing. It is a useful run-getter against slightly loose bowling. Play the stroke exactly as the forward defensive, turning the wrists on contact. Position the front pad to meet the ball if you miss.

Fig. 11 MOVING OUT TO DRIVE
High back-lift. Head and shoulder lead; back foot crosses behind front foot keeping body sideways. Play the normal drive as the weight transfers fully to the front foot.

Fig. 12 ON-DRIVE
The front shoulder dips as the front foot opens towards the pitch of the ball. The hips also open slightly as the hands lead a long flat swing of the bat—into a high follow-through.

Fig. 13 FORWARD LEG GLANCE
Commence this stroke as you would the on-drive but position your pad to meet the ball if it is missed by the bat. Be certain the ball would not have hit the wicket, turning the wrists on contact directing the ball wide of fielders.

Fig. 12

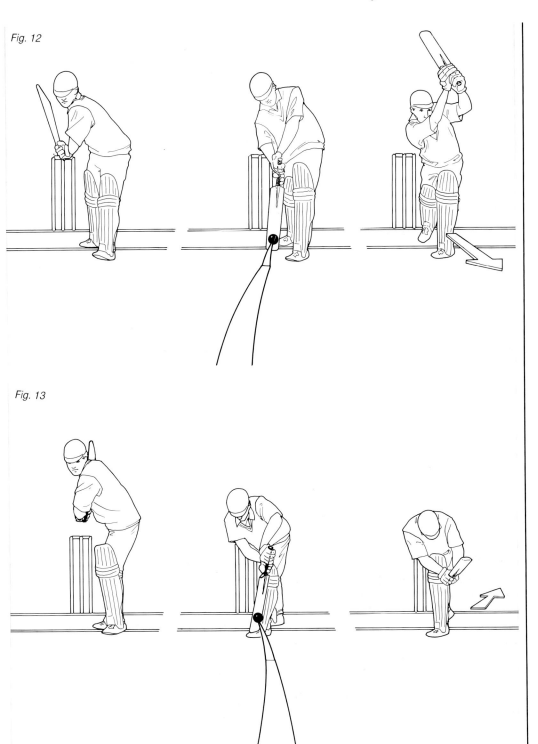

Fig. 13

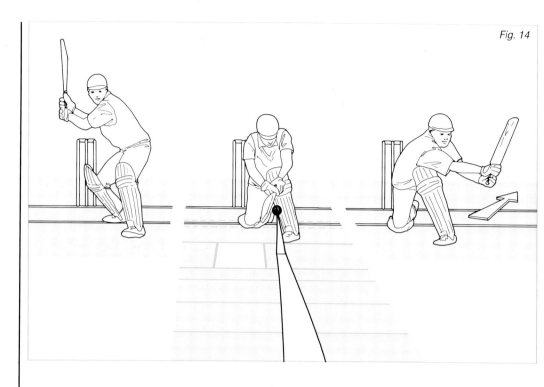

Fig. 14

The Lofted Drive

Played to a delivery just short of a half volley, or just beyond a good length, this is an occasion stroke. That is, it is played when the fielders are 'crowding the bat' and there is no fielder in the outfield. When runs are urgently needed the stroke may still be played, but make an effort to direct the ball away from the boundary rider, otherwise you will just 'give' your wicket away.

Sweep Stroke

Played to a good length ball pitched outside the leg-stump and turning in towards the wicket, the stroke can also be played as an alternative to the front foot leg-glance, i.e. to

Fig. 14 SWEEP
From a high back-lift the front shoulder leads the front leg directly on to the line of the ball. The ball is struck downwards at full arms' stretch.

a ball pitching on or outside the leg-stump and going down the leg-side. It is the only 'cross bat' forward stroke other than hitting the high full toss to leg. Commence the stroke as for the forward defensive with a high back-lift. Hit the ball down, making contact just after it pitches. The front leg bends fully, the rear leg trails. Make sure the ball hits the front pad if the bat fails to make contact. Learn to direct the ball wide of the leg-side fielders.

Back Strokes

Unless a batsman is a capable player of the back strokes he can never be classed as a truly top-class player. There are batsmen who survive and sometimes make big scores playing almost exclusively off the front foot; but those who master the back strokes have such an advantage in range of stroke-play, that their all-round value to the team, not to mention their entertainment value, is so much greater.

Back Defence

This is played to a good length or short of a length ball, likely to bounce high rather than low and pitched on the stumps or just outside the off-stump, the back defensive stroke is a much more difficult stroke to play than the forward defensive stroke.

From a sound stance and back-lift the front shoulder leads the back foot just inside the line of the ball, parallel with the crease. The head stays 'forward' to give the body a forward balance rather than leaning away. The weight of the body is carried almost entirely on the back foot which has moved back as far as possible commensurate with the speed of the ball through the air. The

Fig. 15 BACK STROKES

Fig. 15

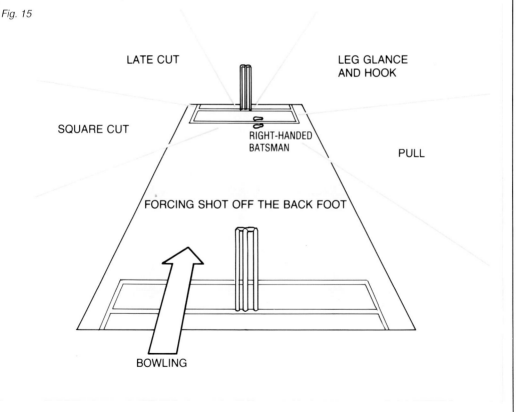

LATE CUT

LEG GLANCE
AND HOOK

SQUARE CUT

RIGHT-HANDED
BATSMAN

PULL

FORCING SHOT OFF THE BACK FOOT

BOWLING

front foot can be almost off the ground as it acts only as a balance. As in all vertical bat forward strokes the top hand is in firm control, with the bottom hand supplying only a thumb and forefinger grip. The front elbow is high and forward, the rear elbow (tucked into the side) helping to keep the bat vertical. The bat handle is angled forward by the top hand without any forward movement of the bat face.

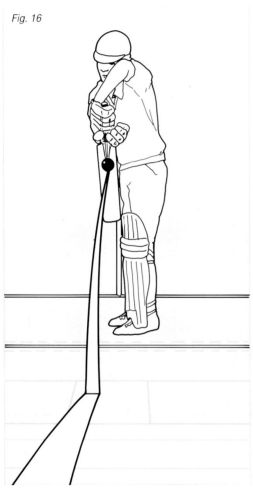

Fig. 16

Fig. 16 BACK DEFENCE
From the stance position the back foot has moved parallel with the crease, taking the head towards the line of the ball. Top hand controls the bat with the front elbow which is shoulder-high and the head slightly forward. No follow-through.

Attacking Back Strokes

Forcing Shot

This is played to a short of a length ball pitched just outside the stumps. Sometimes referred to as a back foot drive, this stroke is very much a modern stroke, developed through the surfeit of 'short of a length' defensive bowling prevalent in limited over games. It is played with a vertical bat, as an extension of the back defensive stroke but with different intention. From a higher back-lift the bat is accelerated through the ball, finishing with a full follow-through or a 'check' finish. As in the forward stroke the 'check' finish, giving more control, is applied by a high and forward front elbow with a locked front wrist behind the bat handle on and after contact.

Pull Stroke

This is played to a long hop (missing the wicket) or a short delivery pitched outside the leg-stump that bounces normally, but never more than chest height. Begin the stroke with the basic back-lift and movements for the back defensive stroke. Move quickly into position and take extra care to watch the ball on to the bat. As the back foot pivots, the body opens and the ball is hit at full arm stretch as the weight transfers to the other foot. When pulling the short delivery off such a pace that complete weight transfer

Fig. 17 FORCING SHOT
Follow the same initial movements of the back defensive stroke with different intention. The back foot should be parallel to the crease and just inside the line of the ball. Keep front elbow high on contact and the bat face on the line of the stroke. 'Check' finish.

Fig. 18 (*Inset*) Full follow-through.

Fig. 19 THE PULL STROKE
Begin this stroke with the same initial movements as the back defensive stroke. Let the back foot pivot as the body opens to hit the ball down at full arm stretch.

Fig. 17

Fig. 18

Fig. 19

is not possible, take care not to fall away from the ball too early. This can easily produce a half-hit stroke off the top edge of the bat. Direct the stroke in front of square-leg by getting the head behind the line of the ball, and hitting down.

The Hook Stroke

This is played to the 'bouncer' or high bouncing long hop over chest height, pitched on or outside the leg-stump. It is played with the same mechanics and with the same very quick footwork of the pull stroke. Position the head on the outside of the line of the ball with the object of 'directing' the ball rather than just hitting the ball down. (This is a stroke for experienced batsmen only.) Be prepared to duck under the ball or sway off the line if you are not quite committed or not in the correct position for the stroke. This stroke should be practised at length with a soft ball.

Square-Cut

This is played to a wide short delivery outside the off-stump that bounces at least bail height. From a sound stance and back-lift, the front shoulder and head turn towards the line of the ball. The weight moves completely on to the back foot which automatically moves across and points approximately in

(*Above*) GRAEME HICK plays the pull stroke for another boundary in his record innings of 405 not out.

Fig. 20 THE HOOK
Similar to the pull stroke but played to a very short ball bouncing at least to shoulder height. Move the head and back foot quickly outside the line of the ball.

Fig. 21 SQUARE-CUT
Note shoulder-turn into the line of the ball. From a high back-lift throw the hands and arms into the stroke making contact when the ball is approximately level with the body. The weight moves almost fully on to the back foot as the bat follows right through.

(*Opposite, Below right*) SUNIL GAVASKAR—A master batsman plays the square-cut.

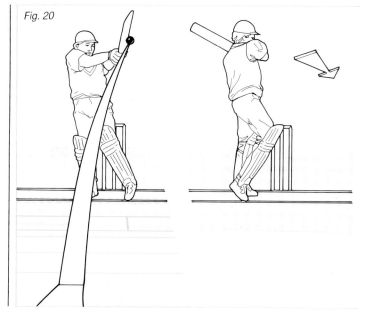

Fig. 20

the direction of the intended stroke. From a high back-lift, the ball is hit easily but hard at full arm stretch. The bottom hand controls the stroke and the wrists roll enough to direct the ball and keep it down. The back shoulder drives under the chin as contact is made with the ball, allowing a long follow-through of the arms.

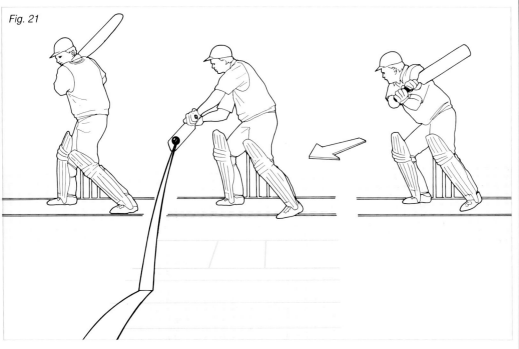

Fig. 21

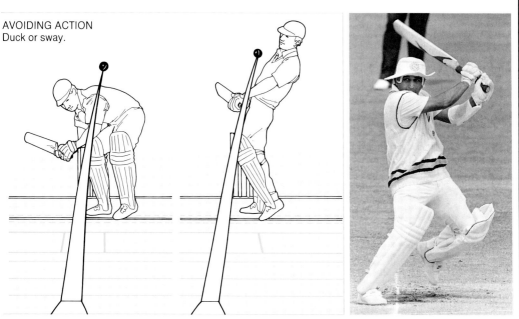

AVOIDING ACTION
Duck or sway.

The Late-Cut

This is played to a short of a length delivery only just wide of the off-stump. Similar to the square-cut, but hit closer to the body and not at full arm stretch. The stroke is played with the wrists and a late downward strike almost level with the stumps.

The Leg-Glance (Back Foot)

This is played to a short delivery either pitching leg-stump or just outside, but going down the leg-side. Do not play this stroke outside the body—it may result in a catch to the wicket-keeper. Neither should the stroke be played to a ball that would hit the wicket. Almost up to the point of contact play the stroke exactly as the back defensive stroke on the leg-stump. Keep the bat handle forward to play the ball down, bringing the bottom hand into the stroke as late as possible. Using the wrists, angle the bat and place the ball between the fielders.

Running Between Wickets

Along with fielding, good running between wickets is becoming an increasingly important factor in the winning or losing of cricket matches. Some of the exciting televised Cup Finals at Lord's, have shown just how important it is. In limited over matches and junior matches good and bad running between wickets is most apparent. In fact, it would be very interesting to discover how many run-outs there are in these matches as a percentage of the total wickets that have fallen to bowlers.

The important requirements for successful running between wickets are:

1) Work with three calls only: *Yes*, *No* and *Wait*.
2) If there is any doubt the call should be *Wait*.
3) Early calling is VITAL, and especially

Fig. 22

so if there is a second call needed after a *Wait* call.

4) Every run should be run as fast as possible, bearing in mind there is a likely 'about turn' at the other end.
5) The calling should be done by the striker, providing the ball is hit in front of the wicket or just behind square on both sides of the wicket. When the ball goes in other directions, the non-striker takes over the calling.
6) The non-striker should 'back up', that is, walk two or three paces down the wicket and be prepared to run after the bowler has released the ball.
7) Run the first run fast and slide the bat in behind the crease at full arm stretch. Turn and be ready to run the next run.
8) The first caller should call for the next run more as an enquiry, requesting an answer from his partner who very often will be running towards the 'danger end

Fig. 23

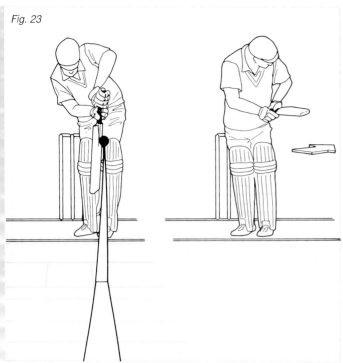

Fig. 22 LATE-CUT
Similar to the square-cut, this stroke is played with the wrists, hitting the ball down, wide of the slips.

Fig. 23 LEG-GLANCE (Back foot)
Do not play this stroke outside the body—an easy catch to the wicket-keeper could result. Play as the back defensive stroke, using the wrist at the last moment to flick the ball wide of the fielders.

(*Below*) Good BACKING UP wins matches.

(the wicket nearest the fielder who is throwing the ball back).

9) Always slide the edge of the bat into the crease at full arm's length when completing a run. If possible, turn towards where the ball is expected to be. Unless the bat or some part of the batsman's person is grounded behind the crease when the wicket is broken, he can be given run-out. When running two or more runs it can be an advantage on turning to change the hand holding the bat and make it easier to see the ball.

10) It is dangerous to run for a mis-field unless it is a very obvious run to both batsmen.

11) Runs can be scored off a wide or a no-ball, but equally batsmen can be run-out off either.

12) Batsmen should know which is a fielder's throwing arm—it could be both!

13) Running between wickets should be practised.

BOWLING

Certain aspects of bowling have already been covered in the Batting section, in particular length, bounce and deviation of the ball. These subjects are also important in developing the techniques of bowling and the more the bowler knows of batting techniques, the better equipped he will be for his bowling task. There are, of course, other require-

MALCOLM MARSHALL—The best do not always conform, but apart from the open action he does.

ments of the good bowler and the main one is a knowledge of and an ability to bowl a good direction. In fact, good direction is just as, if not more important than, good length.

Direction

Bowling a good length outside the off-stump can very often keep runs down or even result

Fig. 24 The importance of direction

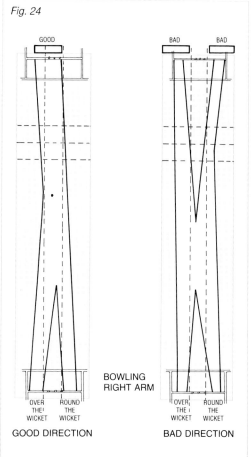

Fig. 24

GOOD DIRECTION

BAD DIRECTION

BOWLING RIGHT ARM

in a dismissal through a batsman's frustration. Bowling a good length outside the leg-stump, however, can give runs away, as either the sweep or leg-glance can take toll of this direction of bowling without undue risk. Good length without good direction is bad bowling and unlikely to take wickets consistently. Good direction generally describes deliveries that if missed by the batsman will hit the stumps or just miss the off-stump.

The key to good direction is the position from which the ball is delivered. This in turn depends upon the expected movement of the ball, either in the air (swing) or off the wicket (spin/seam). A delivery position from which the ball swings or spins too much to find the edge of the bat, when pitched on the line of the stumps, may need to be adjusted by a bowler, providing the ball is not likely to hit the stumps, that is.

How successfully this adjustment can be made without losing length or direction, or degree of movement is a measure of the bowler's ability. A good guide to initial direction is that the bowler should aim to set the line of the ball as near as possible between wicket and wicket, with any margin of error being towards the off- rather than the leg-side.

The Basic Action

In looking at the various batting strokes and how they are performed against different deliveries we are immediately reminded of what is practically important in good bowling. Without question, a sound, repeating basic bowling action is required by any bowler as a prerequisite of a good length and direction and before the more subtle skills of bowling can be acquired.

This basic bowling action can be considered and analysed as a number of separate components, each of which is vital to the complete action. The main four components are the grip of the ball, the run-up, the delivery and the follow-through.

The Grip

Depending upon the type of delivery intended, the grip will vary, but as always the variations will be based on sound principles.

The ball should be held in the fingers and not in the palm. The first two fingers should be placed on either side of the seam, comfortably and just wide enough to obtain maximum control of the ball on release. The inside of the thumb should rest just alongside the seam immediately opposite the first two fingers. The third finger simply acts as support to the ball.

Fig. 25 THE BASIC GRIP

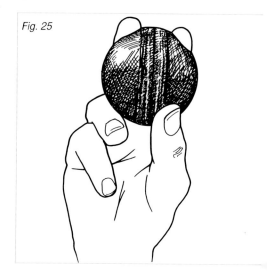

Fig. 25

The Run-Up

The object of the run-up is to enable the bowler to move into the delivery stride perfectly balanced and with the momentum necessary for the delivery intended.

Start slowly, with your intentions very much in mind. Gradually lengthen your stride and increase speed without losing rhythm. The penultimate stride in the run-up should be the longest and the fastest. Consciously gather yourself as you 'bound' into the delivery stride.

Fig. 26

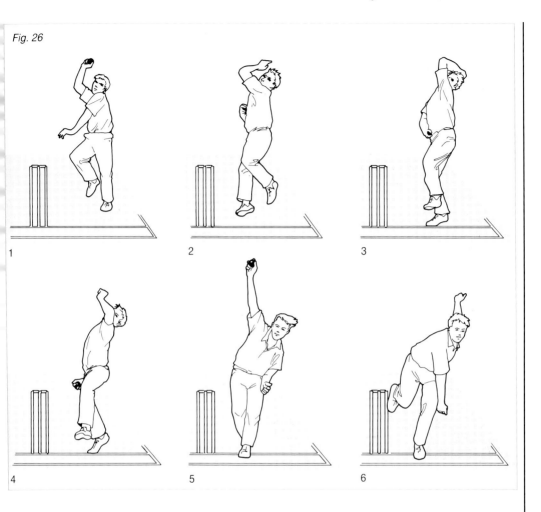

The bound should be, if anything, a continuation of the forward momentum, high enough to turn the shoulders sideways but not so high that it will cause too much loss of forward impetus. Look to land at the beginning of the delivery stride, with the back foot parallel to the bowling crease. This will help towards a strong body action through the delivery stride, especially if you throw the front arm up and back to create a lean away from the batsman, with the back arched for maximum height of the bowling arm on delivery. The length of the run-up will vary with the type of bowler. Obviously, the faster the bowler, the longer the run-up required to

Fig. 26 BASIC BOWLING ACTION
The actions of great bowlers vary but the majority conform to certain fundamentals—a correct grip, a smooth, economical run-up, a well balanced delivery and a full follow-through.

1/2 'The bound'. High enough to allow a full turn of the shoulder, without reducing momentum.
3 'The coil'. In this basic action, as against the 'open' action, the front foot lands parallel to the crease. The eyes look over the front shoulder.
4 The 'spring' begins to uncoil through the delivery stride.
5 The delivery stride is completed with a high action, the front arm having generated maximum momentum in the delivery.
6 A full follow-through completes a good action, the head looking over the front shoulder at the batsman.

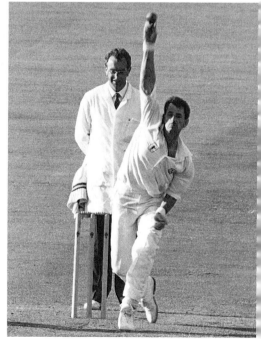

(*Top, far left*) THE BOUND—IMRAN KHAN, a magnificent athlete at his best.

(*Top, left*) THE COIL—DENNIS LILLEE, Australia's best.

(*Opposite, below*) THE DELIVERY STRIDE—RICHARD HADLEE, unquestionably New Zealand's best.

(*Below*) FOLLOW-THROUGH—RICHARD HADLEE, the perfect model for any young bowler.

help generate speed through the bowling action. Too long a run-up, apart from being tiring, can be responsible for a loss of momentum through the delivery stride. Too short a run-up can result in the bowler straining to achieve the required momentum. Most bowlers do not put enough practice into establishing their correct and most effective run-up.

The Delivery

The beginning of the delivery stride leads the body into the 'coil' position (a 'key' set-up for any bowler).

Let the high front arm bend to pull the body through the delivery stride, staying sideways as long as possible. The front leg flexes as it lands, to absorb the shock, and tends to straighten as it takes the weight of the body and begins to pivot. The bowling arm comes over to release the ball at maximum height and the shoulders swing square to the batsman.

At the moment of release the fingers will be behind the ball, with the wrist stiff for accuracy and swing. (Only to obtain maximum pace will the wrist be flexed back.) The faster the bowler, the longer the delivery stride, but there is an optimum. Too long a delivery stride restricts momentum, too short a stride restricts body action.

The Follow-Through

A full, vigorous follow-through is an essential for all bowlers, whatever type—fast or slow. All the bowler's movements through-

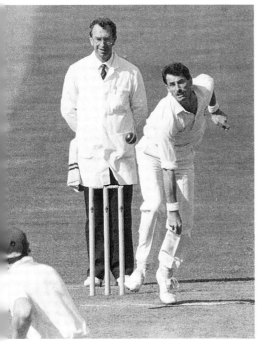

out the bowling action are directed towards the off-stump.

The front arm in the delivery stride is again very important in the follow-through, as it extends down and back, pulling the other side of the body into the follow-through and allowing the bowling arm to come right across the body after the ball has been released. The head looks over the bowling shoulder as it thrusts towards the batsman. Deceleration continues as the bowler runs straight towards the batsman, bearing in mind that he is not allowed to run on the pitch more than four feet past the bowling crease and within one foot of the middle stump.

Types of Bowling

Whether right- or left-handed, bowlers can be categorised, with different skills being applied in each category.

Fast Bowling With pure speed and accuracy being the primary consideration.

Swing Bowling With the ball swinging (or swerving) in the air in one direction or another as it approaches the batsman.

Seam Bowling When the bowler has the ability to constantly land the ball on the vertical seam, causing lateral deviation as it pitches in the right conditions, i.e. well-grassed wickets.

Medium Pace Cutters Applying spin to the ball by cutting the fingers down one side or the other as the ball is released. In certain conditions (soft or dusty wickets) lateral deviation off the pitch can be obtained.

Pace bowlers, whether fast or medium, whilst specialising in one category or the other, can generally add to their capability by acquiring the skills to bowl cutters.

Spin Bowling
Finger Spin (Off-Spin and Slow Left Arm Spin) As against simply cutting down the side of the ball, a greater degree of spin can be applied, usually by the first finger working within a specific grip to maximise the speed of the ball's sideways rotation as it is propelled forwards towards the batsman. The slower the ball, of course, the greater the deviation on pitching.

Wrist Spin Maximum spin can be imparted to a cricket ball by using mainly the third finger and a 'turning over' of the wrist, to give an additional 'flip' to the ball as it is released.

Bowling Techniques

Fast Bowling

Pure fast bowling is one of cricket's greatest pleasures to watch. The fast bowler should concentrate on supreme fitness and a good basic action. Speed is nearly everything, but subtle variation in pace is still important, as is accuracy. Other skills can come after rather than before the ability to bowl extra fast.

Swing Bowling

Due to the fact that the cricket ball is manufactured with a seam (stitched leather) protruding around the circumference, it is possible to cause the ball to swing or swerve in the air on delivery. This is achieved by an accurate release of the ball with the seam vertical but inclined in one direction or another. Atmospheric forces acting against the inclined seam cause lateral movement of the ball in its forward flight. The ball will swing more or less depending upon its condition. A new ball with a protruding seam and a smooth all-round surface will swing easier and more, for example, than a ball with a rough surface and only a slightly protruding seam. A heavy atmosphere also contributes towards greater swing as the side forces on the ball increase. Swing bowlers usually preserve the swing characteristics of the ball by keeping one side of the ball polished, creating a difference of pressure on either side. For maximum swing the polished side of the ball is tilted towards the batsman.

The Out-Swinger

This swings in the air away from the right-handed batsman towards the slips.

Grip and Action—The grip varies from the basic grip in that on delivery the vertical seam points towards the slips. The side of the thumb is on the seam in this instance.

The out-swing action requires a very definite sideways position through the delivery stride. After releasing the ball the arm will swing across the body past the hip. The higher the

Fig. 27 An explanation of SWING BOWLING.

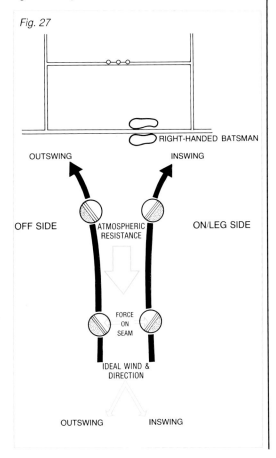

Fig. 28

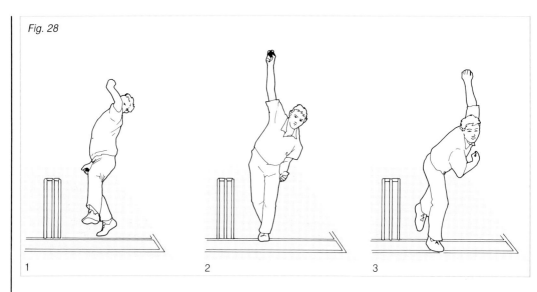

1   2   3

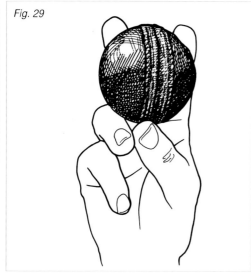

Fig. 29

Fig. 28 OUTSWING
1   A good sideways position looking behind the front
    arm; right foot parallel to crease.
2   High delivery. Fingers behind the ball which is
    delivered with a firm wrist.
3   A full follow-through with the bowling arm
    stretching past left thigh.

Fig. 29 OUTSWING GRIP

Grip and Action—The ball of the thumb will
be flat against the seam, and on release the
vertical seam will be pointing towards fine
leg.

The in-swing action requires the ball to be
'pushed' towards the off-stump from a more
open-chested delivery position. It is likely
that in the delivery stride the back foot will
be pointing in the direction of the batsman,
rather than parallel to the crease, as in the
case of the out-swinger.

Seam Bowling

For the seam bowler to be effective, the seam
must project well clear of the surface of the
ball. The skill of the seam bowler lies in his

arm action, the later the ball will tend to
swing in its flight. A low, slinging arm action
will tend to make the ball swing early in its
flight.

The In-Swinger

This swings in the air into the right-handed
batsman and towards fine leg.

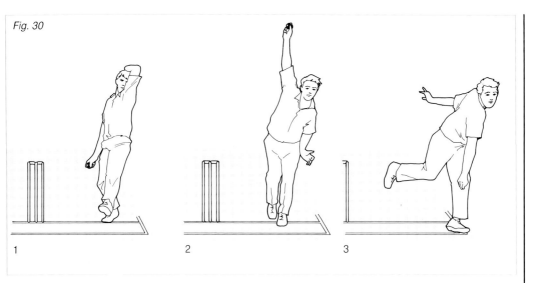

Fig. 30

1   2   3

Fig. 30 INSWING
1   Rear landing foot tends to be pointing down the pitch. Eyes look inside raised front arm.
2   High delivery with fingers and firm wrist 'pushing' the ball towards the batsman.
3   The bowling arm comes through towards the wicket-side of the delivery in a lesser follow-through than the outswinger.

Fig. 31 INSWING GRIP

Fig. 31

ability to constantly pitch the ball on the vertical seam, creating a lateral deviation in one direction or another.

Grip and Action—The grip for seam bowling is exactly as the basic grip. The wrist position is very important at the point of release, as it may have to be inclined very slightly one way or another to obtain the desired seaming effect. Seam bowling is limited in application. To be really effective, a 'green' pitch is required, that is, a well-grassed, slightly damp pitch, which acts as a cushion to the seam. The natural finger action on the ball is a slight dragging back of the two top fingers at the instant of release. This stabilises the ball. The good seam bowler relies heavily on variation in pace and extreme accuracy.

Cutters

The Off-Cutter

The great advantage of the off-cutter as a foil to the out-swinger is that once the batsman knows that a bowler can bowl it, he is more likely to play at the slightly wider out-swinger.

Fig. 32

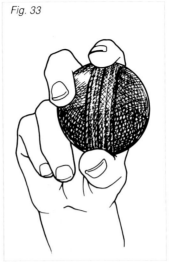
Fig. 33

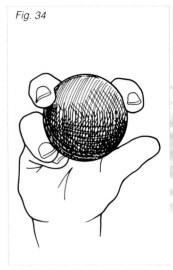
Fig. 34

Grip and Action—The grip is similar to that for the out-swinger, but with the first finger wedged alongside the seam, which points in the same direction as for the out-swinger. Some bowlers use a straightforward off-spin grip. As the ball is delivered, the first two fingers cut across the ball, the first finger pulling the seam down in a clockwise direction.

The Leg-Cutter

As the off-cutter is a foil to the out-swinger, so the leg-cutter is to the in-swinger, as it is usually bowled with an in-swing action. It is, however, one of the most difficult deliveries to bowl as is evident from the very few bowlers who attempt it. Sydney Barnes of the Golden Age was the first to consistently bowl the leg-cutter and it gave him great success. More recently, Alec Bedser used it effectively on wet wickets in the late Forties and early Fifties.

Grip and Action—The leg-cutter can be bowled using either of two grips. One, a version of the normal in-swing grip but with

Fig. 32 LEG-CUTTER GRIP

Fig. 33 OFF-CUTTER GRIP

Fig. 34 SPIN GRIP

the middle finger wedged against the seam, and the other, with the first three fingers equally spaced across the seam and the thumb in support—a leg-spin type of grip.

In the first instance, the normal in-swing action is used with the middle finger cutting down the inside of the ball on delivery and applying leg-spin. As the seam is not rotating to constantly make contact with the wicket there is a 'hit and miss' element in this delivery which can be disconcerting for the batsman. The second method gives more consistency in the right conditions (wet or dusty wickets) as it is bowled virtually like a fast leg-break.

Spin Bowling

Watching a game of cricket without seeing a spin bowler perform can be likened to listening to an orchestra without hearing the piano.

Finger Spin/The Off-Spinner

This is the delivery that pitches and turns from the off to the leg, when bowled to a right-handed batsman.

Grip and Action—The first finger is the main spinning finger, hence the term finger spin. The top joint of this finger crosses the seam. The second or middle finger takes up a similar position, again the top joint lying across the seam if possible. The two fingers are spread as wide as possible, to give the maximum spinning leverage. The third finger rests lightly along the seam, acting as a support. The thumb takes no part in the spinning of the ball. The ball must be held in the fingers.

The body action is basic in that it is sideways, with the bowling arm taking a full swing into a high delivery.

The ball is delivered against a braced left leg, the delivery stride being slightly across the crease and short enough for the bowler to 'stand tall'. The spinning action simulates the opening of a door, dragging the seam in a clockwise direction.

A full follow-through is as essential to the spin bowler as it is to the fast bowler, the bowling arm whipping across the body past the left hip.

Finger Spin/Slow, Left Arm Bowler

Known in the game as an SLA, the slow, left arm bowler is simply a mirror of the off-spinner in that the principles of spin, basic action, flight etc. are exactly the same. However, simply because the bowler is left-handed a completely different set of problems are presented to the batsman. For example, the normal finger spin delivery delivered by a left-handed bowler will spin away from the right-handed batsman towards the slips.

Finger Spin Variations

The great off-spinners, in particular Jim Laker, Freddie Titmus, Ray Illingworth and John Emburey, have all had the ability to bowl what appears to the batsman (and sometimes the wicket-keeper) to be a heavily spun off-spinner, but in fact the ball does not spin at all, if anything it just drifts away from

JOHN EMBUREY—A man I must have in my side; off-spin bowler and much more.

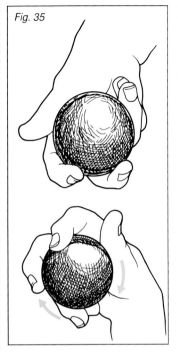

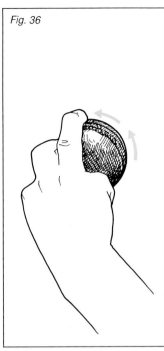

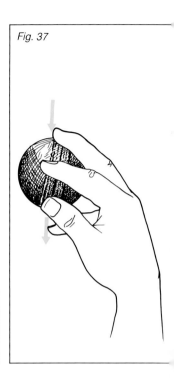

the right-handed batsman. None of these bowlers would have reached such heights without having learned this variation which deceives even the very best batsmen.

I have spoken to Jim Laker, Ray Illingworth and John Emburey, and they have demonstrated to me how they grip the ball for this variation—all have a different style. I can only say that somehow they seem to undercut the ball at the moment of release, still giving the batsman the impression of spin whilst in effect slightly changing the angle of the seam. Of course, the off-spin bowler can bowl a blatant floater using the first finger to guide what is virtually an out-swinger, but it is usually quite obvious to the batsman. An off-spinner without the ability to vary the amount of spin and produce variations will never be a master of the art.

The same can be said of the slow, left arm bowler, who will pose different problems for the batsman, one of which will be the

Fig. 35 LEG-SPIN GRIP AND WRIST ACTION

Fig. 36 GOOGLY WRIST ACTION

Fig. 37 TOP-SPIN WRIST ACTION

'quicker arm' ball swinging into the right handed batsman in the hope that he will be on the back foot and a possible LBW victim. This delivery is simply the bowler's floater or under-spinner, as previously described.

Wrist Spin

The term wrist spin defines that type of spin bowling in which an uncocking or flipping of the wrist on delivery generates the extra spin that can be applied in this form of bowling.

The Leg-Spinner

The leg-break is a delivery that spins from leg to off when bowled to a right-handed bats man by a right arm bowler.

Grip and Action—The ball is cupped firmly in the first three fingers and base of the thumb The seam lies across the joint of the first two fingers. The third finger is bent and lies alongside the seam. A good basic action is suitable for the leg-break with the wrist and third finger playing the major roles as the ball is released. Just prior to release the wrist is cocked inwards (towards the front of the wrist). As the ball is released the wrist flips the fingers forward and twists in an anti-clockwise direction. The third finger moves across the seam and drags it in the same direction, assisted by the thumb and first two fingers.

The Googly

The leg-spinner's 'secret weapon', the googly, is an off-break bowled with a leg-break type of action. No single delivery can give more pleasure to a bowler than that which deceives the batsman into thinking it is a leg-break when it is, in fact, a googly. The best googly bowlers practise for hours to develop an action that is as near that of a leg-break as possible when viewed from the batting crease.

Grip and Action—The orthodox grip is the same as for the leg-break. In an attempt to further deceive the batsman, leg-spin bowlers adopt different actions for the googly, the idea being that the batsman may think the less obvious googly action is a leg-break and play for it accordingly.

There are two basic wrist actions for delivering the googly. Either the ball must travel over the fingers and the back of the hand, or the ball must be released directly over the side of the hand. This second delivery is achieved by leading the delivery with a bent wrist to allow the ball to flip over and impart off-spin with the third finger at the very last instant.

The Left Arm Wrist-Spinner

The left arm wrist-spinner is a very rare animal indeed. I can only think of three, all Australians, who bowled it regularly in first-class cricket. They were Fleetwood-Smith who played in the Thirties and George Tribe who played in the Forties before coming to England to play in Northern League cricket. Tribe later played for Northamptonshire and completed 'the double' (100 wickets and 1,000 runs in an English first-class season) in seven consecutive years, in the Fifties. Also, Jack Walsh who did not play for Australia but bowled with distinction for Leicestershire in the Forties and early Fifties. Being so unusual was to some degree the secret of their outstanding success. All the art and guile of the normal leg-spin bowler was suddenly presented 'in reverse' to the unsuspecting batsman. What a pity we do not still see them today.

Wrist Spin Variations

A useful variation on the leg-break and the googly, is the top-spinner. The grip and wrist action for the top-spinner are exactly the same as for the leg-spinner, except that instead of spinning the ball almost at right angles to the line of flight it is over spun towards the batsman, giving the impression of gathering pace from the pitch as it bounces.

The flipper is a 'mystery ball', perfected initially by Clarrie Grimmett, the famous Australian leg-spin bowler of the 1930s, and later bowled with success by a number of great Australian wrist spin bowlers whom I have named earlier. It is the most difficult delivery of all to perfect and I mention it here only to whet the appetite of the reader. After a very close study, both live and on film, of Abdul Qadir, the Pakistan wrist spin bowler, (one of the few capable of bowling the 'flipper'), it seems that as the normal leg-break is

about to be bowled, at the last second the ball is flipped with a clockwise twist rather than an anti-clockwise spin, under rather than over the fingers. One has the impression that at the last moment the ball is 'pushed' towards the batsman with the third and fourth fingers. Very little, if any spin is imparted to the ball.

Flight and Variation of Pace

Pace, length, direction, bounce, lateral deviation, variation in pace, off-spin, leg-spin, top-spin, out-swing, in-swing, off-cutter, leg-cutter, seamer are all terms that apply not only to bowling in general but more specifi-

ABDUL QADIR—The world's best wrist-spinner by far, bowls (a) the Leg Break and (b) the Googly. Easy to pick from a photograph; in action, a different 'kettle of fish'.

cally to the ball itself once it has left the bowler's hand.

Not yet discussed is the term 'flight' which is of the utmost importance in bowling. It may be said that flight and variation of pace are one and the same thing, but whilst they have similarities they do not mean the same. A flighted delivery leaves the bowler's hand in an upward rather than a downward arc, so that the batsman has two planes of movement to consider as the ball approaches. He has to decide where the ball may pitch and

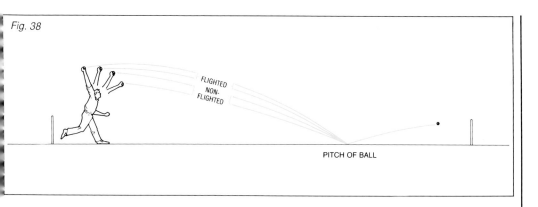

Fig. 38

FLIGHTED
NON-
FLIGHTED

PITCH OF BALL

Fig. 38 FLIGHT OF THE BALL

what the anticipated length may be. On good batting surfaces flight, when allied to subtle change of pace, good length and direction and varying degrees of spin or swing, can be a 'winner' in every sense.

The possibilities, if properly applied, are many and the bowler who has developed such skills is special indeed. Bishan Bedi, the great Indian left arm spin bowler, was a fine example of what flight can mean, both in terms of successful results and delight for the spectator.

Summary of Bowling Techniques

Looking back at the various technical explanations of the different types of bowling, I am conscious that a few extra words in the form of a summary may be helpful to those who may not be conversant with the intricacies of bowling.

It is important to understand that the leg-side (or on-side) of the wicket is that side on which the batsman's legs are positioned when in the normal stance at the wicket. Again, in the normal stance the batsman's back foot would be pointing to the off-side.

The name of a type of bowler is usually determined with a right-handed batsman as the norm, for example:

1) An off-spin (break) bowler (finger spin) spins the ball so that on pitching it deviates from off to leg.
2) A leg-spin (break) bowler (wrist spin) spins the ball so that on pitching it deviates from leg to off.
3) A slow, left arm bowler (finger spin) spins the ball so that on pitching it deviates from leg to off.

4) A googly is bowled by a wrist spin bowler. When bowled by a right arm bowler it is an off-break (to a right-handed batsman) bowled with a leg-break type of action. When bowled by a left arm bowler it is a leg-break (to a right-handed batsman).
5) A 'Chinaman' is a left arm wrist spinner's off-break (to a right-handed batsman) bowled with a leg-break type of action.
6) Cutters, both off and leg, can be considered as medium-paced finger spinners.
7) An out-swing bowler swings the ball in the air towards the off-side (the slips).
8) An in-swing bowler swings the ball from the off- to the leg-side (fine leg).
9) Right and left arm pace bowlers swing the ball out or in, using reciprocal grips and actions as in the case of the off-spin and slow left arm bowlers.

Bowling is indeed a complex matter and I suggest that this text be related to a good practical demonstration which as always will convey more than a thousand words.

105

FIELDING AND WICKET-KEEPING

At all levels of the game in recent years, fielding has experienced the greatest changes. No longer is it the poor relation of other skills. Fielding has become a spectator sport in itself, for each position has its requirements both physically and mentally.

Cricket is a game of ebb and flow. As a match progresses and constantly changes, depending upon the many circumstances of play, so do the roles played by the fielders in support of their bowlers. One minute they are attacking, the next defending. Within the requirements of the good bowler or captain should be the knowledge to sometimes do both at the same time. When batsmen of different abilities are at the wicket, that compromise is often required to combat their strengths and probe their weaknesses.

Fielding may be divided into four different areas:
1) The outfield
2) The infield
3) The close catchers
4) Wicket-keeping.

The Outfield

At one time this was the home of the least athletic members of the side or a resting place for fast bowlers, but the outfielder of today is expected to have speed of foot, a powerful and accurate throw and safe hands to catch the longest and highest of hits. Once purely a defensive fielder, today the outfielder faces every run as a challenge, and an entertaining one at that.

The Infield

Cover point, mid-wicket and those who lie in wait at similar distances from the wicket are the speed merchants and very often required to be a team's best fielders. Mobility for the one-handed pick-up at speed, combined with accurate and *early* throwing ability are essential. Good fielders in these positions can virtually dominate, even oppress, the batsman at the wicket.

Close Catchers

One aspect of cricket has remained the same throughout the ages and that is close catching. 'Catches win matches' is as true as ever. I am inclined to think, however, that to field in 'suicide' positions, albeit wearing helmets, tends to reduce the effectiveness of bowlers, who must surely be under pressure to bowl 'safe' rather than 'sound' in those circumstances.

Wicket-Keeping

Of all the skills of cricket, wicket-keeping seems to have lost most in recent years, although in the last year or so, with a host of very promising young wicket-keepers in the first-class game, there is a refreshing tendency to return to the 'art' of wicket-keeping, rather than the wicket-keeper being simply a straight first slip with gloves on, trained mainly as an acrobat. I am of course completely biased in thinking that if the wicket-keeper stood up to the wicket for medium-paced bowling the game could be enlivened and another dimension added for the interest of spectators. I also think we would see good batsmen getting just as many runs, with mediocre batsmen being restricted.

Wicket-keeping can be compared to batting. There are attacking wicket-keepers and defensive wicket-keepers—artistes and tradesmen. I should love to have seen Herbert Strudwick and J.J. Blackham who both stood up to the wicket to the fastest of bowlers.

Great wicket-keepers are born and not made. There are those who do the job by simply putting on a pair of gloves and catching what they can. But the wicket-keeper should be far more than a catcher. Along with the captain, he should be a motivator, quietly or otherwise. He should be the player who sets the standards for the rest of the fielders in the manner in which he goes about his job—in appearance, in style, with an enthusiasm that can only be infectious and add to his team's enjoyment. At the same time the wicket-keeper needs to be a serious student of the game as it is his job to have a good knowledge of all the types of bowling he is likely to keep wicket to. It is also a bonus in his support of the captain, or as a captain, for him to be able to accurately assess the strengths and weaknesses of the batsmen at the wicket.

JACK RICHARDS gathers the ball as DAVID BOON makes his ground.

Fielding Techniques

Whilst the requirements of fielders in a match vary with the positions they occupy, the skills and techniques of fielding in the various areas of the field tend to overlap. For example, all fielders have at some time to stop the ball and throw it to the wicket-keeper. It can either be intercepted and stopped, or chased and stopped. Throwing and catching techniques depend upon the fielder's distance from the wicket.

Stopping the Ball

Interception—defensive

The term 'long barrier' speaks for itself and is in fact just that. By placing the right foot (if you are right-handed) at right angles to the path of the ball and dropping on to the left knee, a 'long barrier' is created. It is the safest method of stopping the ball and whilst it may be termed defensive, the fielder can quite quickly move into a good sideways throwing position, especially in the outfield when a long throw is required.

Interception—attacking

There are a number of methods of attacking interceptions and which one is used is dependent upon the fielder's distance from the wicket. Outfielders and deep infielders will usually be quickly on to the line of the ball, picking it up in two hands in front of the right foot (for a right-handed throw) as the body bends and turns sideways into the throwing position. A quicker pick-up and throw can be achieved from close range by running face-on to the line of the ball then making the pick-up and underarm throw with one hand. This method is sometimes

used from a longer distance, making an over-arm and very early throw whilst off-balance. Not everyone can attempt this type of throw as it needs athleticism of the highest order and much practice.

Retrieving

Good retrieving and throwing save countless runs in the field. Almost invariably the ball is picked up against the right foot. If the ball is not travelling too fast, a very early pivot and turn is possible. From short distances the fielder can jump and twist in the air as he throws, 'throwing on the turn', as it is called. Again speed and mobility are essential.

Throwing

Good throwing is necessary for any fielding side. Underarm throws are very effective from close in, but the most spectacular are the long flat and powerful throws from the outfield, achieved with a flat or over-arm action.

An early release of the ball is the secret of achieving run-outs. The batsman can very often be surprised by the early release when he is least expecting it. One of the finest sights in cricket is the close run-out achieved by a top-class fielder—and what an inspiration it can be to the team. Clive Lloyd, the great West Indian cricketer, in his younger days one of the greatest fielders ever, once told me that he achieved many run-outs by deceiving the batsman early in his innings. He would run in and field the ball normally for a few overs and then when the opportunity came he would step up one or two gears, very often catching the batsman 'on the hop'.

DAVID GOWER—(*left*) The long barrier, (*centre*) Two-handed interception for safety, (*right*) One-handed interception for speed. (*Below*) The throw.

Catching

As in many other aspects of cricket, catching is very much a matter of confidence, achieved by hard practice, fitness and concentration on every ball.

Close Catching

It is essential to concentrate hard, as close catching chances are usually few and far between. The slightest lapse in concentration when a catch comes completely loses the opportunity and more often than not it is the best batsmen who give early chances to close catchers. Obviously, a missed catch early in the innings can be disastrous. Close catchers should avoid becoming 'set', as taut muscles can stiffen and be responsible for a slow reaction time. Do not stand too close in to the batsman—it looks brave but more catches are missed by being too close than by being too far back. Of course, one has to be realistic and if the wicket is such that the ball is not carrying easily to the wicket-keeper, it is a guide for the close catchers to be that much nearer the bat. Avoid too wide a stance, it makes low catching that much harder. Too narrow a stance does not allow 'spring' for the wider catches. Watch a top-class goalkeeper prepare to save a penalty,

109

you will note that his feet are no more than shoulder-width apart.

Infield Catching

Infield catches can be the most varied (mishit drives, skyers over the shoulder) and they nearly always look easier than they actually are. Cover point and mid-wicket fielders, particularly, should practise taking the variety of catches they are likely to have against the most difficult background for sighting the ball. In a match, the infielder, more than any other fielder, has the problem of taking the skimming, shoulder-high catch against a background of spectators.

The Outfielder

The outfielder these days is as much a 'glamour' fielder as he was an 'also ran' in the past. In today's cricket there can be no hiding place and the 'boundary rider' is

(*Above*) DAVID GOWER—Close catching, for the camera.

(*Opposite, above*) GREG CHAPPELL—Supreme slip fielder, catching for keeps!

(*Opposite, below left*) DAVID GOWER—Infield (skim) catch, baseball style.

(*Below right*) HIGH CATCH, BASEBALL STYLE— MIKE GATTING takes a catch when it counts; World Cup 1987, Bombay.

required to be fleet of foot, with a powerful and accurate throw. The nail-biting catches are always his, and he is expected never to miss one. A good tip for the outfielder is to sight the ball before moving in one direction or another. Once you have sighted the ball, never let your eyes off it but get on to the line of flight as soon as possible.

Both outfielders and infielders should practise 'baseball' type catching (hands inverted with fingers pointing upwards). This method is a very effective alternative to the traditional method for catches coming above chest-height.

Wicket-Keeping Techniques

It has been said by the uninformed that simply catching the ball consistently is everything in wicket-keeping. Obviously, the fewer balls the 'keeper drops, the better he is at the job, but there is much more to it than that.

Stance

Generally, a squatting position is adopted, standing up or back from the wicket. A minority of wicket-keepers favour a crouching position when standing back akin to that of a slip fielder. This position enables the less mobile wicket-keeper to cover a wider catching range than may be possible from the squatting position.

The stance is very important, being the platform for any movement to 'take' the ball,

As good as there is!—The stance of a world record holder, BOB TAYLOR (1,563 victims).

whether standing up or back. In both instances it is wise not to move into the stance position too early as it is easy to become too 'set', allowing muscles to tighten and so slow down reactions by that vital fraction of a second. The stance position should always provide a good view of the bowler's delivery stride and above all a sight of the ball leaving the bowler's hand. It is vital not to move to the left or right (leg-side or off) too early, before having seen the line and trajectory of the ball.

Taking the Ball

Firstly, good concentration should enable you to ignore any movement of the batsman, although with experience you can anticipate the leg-glance. Assume that *every ball is yours*.

Prepare to take the ball with the arms relaxed and as straight as possible, especially down the leg-side. This will allow the hands to give that much easier when taking the ball. Try to keep the head steady and catch the ball naturally, mainly in the right on the off-side of a right-handed batsman and vice versa on the other side of the wicket, with the palms facing the ball. There is a theory that wicket-keepers should try to catch the ball in the hand nearest the wicket so that deflections on the off-side will go into the wicket-keeper's other hand, but I disagree with this totally.

Do not get up too early. Let the ball come to you. Do not snatch.

Standing up to the Wicket

Make your stance within easy reach of the wicket, about half a pace back from the stumps, but make sure that you can see the

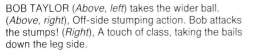

BOB TAYLOR (*Above, left*) takes the wider ball.
(*Above, right*), Off-side stumping action. Bob attacks
the stumps! (*Right*), A touch of class, taking the bails
down the leg side.

direction of the ball as it leaves the bowler's hand. Get behind the line of the ball but be prepared to sway off-line to take the lifting ball. Be ready to attack the stumps for a stumping or run-out chance by transferring your balance towards the wicket as you take the ball. That is, look to get your weight on to the foot nearest the stumps. Take the ball as close to the bat as possible when a batsman plays back or cuts. You may catch a really thick edge.

Try (and practise) for a fast hand action—one- and two-handed, to remove the bails. Run-outs and stumpings are very often split second affairs. Practise, also, taking every conceivable length and bounce of ball, for stumpings and run-outs.

Standing Back

Establish your position as soon as possible

BOB TAYLOR standing back—Concentration is everything.

with regard to the pace of the wicket and the general bounce of the ball. Look to take the ball just below waist-height as it begins to drop in its trajectory. You may find it necessary to move nearer the stumps once the new ball loses its shine and hardness.

You can anticipate leg-side catches, but not off-side catches. Avoid getting 'wrong-footed' by moving too early down the leg-side.

In general, help to keep the tempo of the game going. Let the captain know (if requested) when you feel a bowler is losing his 'nip'. Be sure to return the ball to the bowler at an easily catchable height, via fielders if necessary.

CAPTAINCY AND TEAM TACTICS

Captaincy in cricket is perhaps more important than in any other sport, if for no other reason than the variety of responsibility really does mean the cricket captain has to be 'all things to all men'.

The most important requirement of a captain is to have the respect of the team. This must be earned and maintained, not necessarily by leading from the front or by being 'the best' at everything, but by treating every single member of the team in a considerate manner, and that includes those who are not playing in the match. A team will only respect their captain if they realise that he has a good knowledge of the game, is firm in his decisions and without favourites. In nearly every case, and particularly in the higher levels of the game, the captain should be worth his place as a player, although there can be exceptions. For example, Mike Brearley of Middlesex was an outstanding, in fact, a great Captain of England without being quite good enough to get in the side as a batsman. Results proved conclusively that he was more than worth his place, purely for his tactical skills and ability to manage the players.

I have spoken at length to many of those who played under Mike and they are unanimous in their view that when he was captain, no matter what the situation, they felt that England would somehow win. He had the unique ability to make every member of his side believe in himself and consequently play to the best of his ability. But not every captain can be so talented.

Good captains are usually good planners, and planning starts well before the start of the match itself. A knowledge of the opposition, the conditions of play and an influence on the selection of a side suitable for the job in hand are all important. Ninety-nine per cent of players thrive on sensible encouragement. Few react positively to unpleasant comment or action by the captain, and this includes being 'dressed down' in front of the rest of the team. Good captains should be good coaches. This is very important when young players come into a team, as invariably they will look to their captain for technical guidance.

Before Taking the Field

In any match there are practical preliminaries that the captain needs to check or have checked before declaring his team and tossing up. Firstly, he needs to know that all

MIKE BREARLEY—The Captains' Captain.

115

the players selected are present and fit to play. Final fitness tests for any doubtful starters will need to be conducted. An inspection of the wicket and the ground in general is then in order. Possibly with the assistance of a senior player of some experience, he will make an assessment of how the wicket might play. He will balance his conclusions against the composition of the squad and decide on the final eleven and whether to bat or field should he win the toss. Within the hour before the match is due to start, later rather than earlier, a good captain will ensure that all the team, including the twelfth man, have 'warmed up' and are ready for all-out action from the first ball. Nothing is more galling to a team than to see their so-called fast bowler loosen up *after* the match has commenced, having in his first over bowled a slow long hop for the batsman to hit for four. Dropping a 'sitter' in the first over is just as galling, and can happen if the fielder concerned has not had a few catches in practice beforehand. In the team talk prior to taking the field, the captain will have reminded the team of any special tactics that may be tried against individual batsmen.

The Toss

It is a cricket tradition for captains to toss a coin before the match, after teams have been declared, to decide which captain shall have the choice of batting or fielding first.

The winning of the toss can be important because, depending upon different circumstances, it may be better for a team to bat or field first.

A captain may elect for his team to bat if,

a) the wicket is firm and dry at the start of the match and is likely to progressively take spin as the surface wears.

b) rain is possible during the match. A wet wicket will often make batting much more difficult, favouring spin, cut, or seam bowling.

Note: The ball will travel so much quicker on a dry rather than a wet outfield. Another consideration is the wet ball which is always more difficult to grip.

A captain may elect for his team to field if,

a) limited time/overs are played. In short matches the team batting second are generally able to control their batting tactics more effectively, in that they will know the position of the game throughout their innings. This is not the case when batting first.

b) at the start of a match a wicket contains moisture or is wet. It may be in the time before the wicket becomes fully dry again, that the pace bowlers can take advantage of the conditions.

c) there is a very grassy wicket at the start, holding a little moisture and again favouring pace and particularly seam bowling for a period. Such grassy wickets, providing they are firm, tend to get better as the match progresses.

d) there is a good pace bowler in his team—a pace bowler is most effective when the ball is new. In some club or school games only one new ball is used in a match and in this case some captains feel that it is worth taking advantage of this by fielding first.

In normal circumstances it may be said that when a wicket is dry and firm to start, then the longer the match and the more likely it is to benefit the side batting first. Having said all this, only in retrospect can a captain be proved right or wrong—and even then his team has to win for him to be proved right!

In the Field

The first ball is perhaps the most important in the match. If it is good, bringing the batsman forward into a stroke and maybe beating him, the fielding team is off to a good start. If the ball is short and wide, and sails harmlessly through to the wicket-keeper, the batsman has seen the pace of the wicket and feels that much better.

After an over or two the captain and the bowlers will have assessed the conditions more accurately and will have adjusted the field placings accordingly. Unless a bowler is extremely accurate or the batsman particularly defensive it is generally wise not to be over-optimistic at the start of an innings. There is nothing like establishing a position of strength from which to attack. Unless the fielding side take early wickets, over-emphasis on attack can give the initiative to the batting side from which a winning position can be too easily attained early in the match. Be realistic, do not deceive yourself over the quality of your bowlers. If wickets fall however, then is the time to apply pressure on the batsmen, particularly the batsman who has just come to the wicket.

Very often the better of the two batsmen at the wicket tries to commandeer the strike. The captain and the team as a whole should be aware of any such situation and try to frustrate the player concerned, if possible. It can help to upset the batsman's concentration.

Captains should make certain that fielders do not field too close. Catches are missed by fielders being too close and more runs are given away by fielders moving in too far, too fast, too early. Runs are more easily prevented by lying back and then running in fast for a clean pick-up and early throw on the run, than by being too close and failing to cut off the hard hit ball. Fielders should be positioned to cope with the different styles of batsmen. For example, a tall batsman will tend to hit the ball straighter than a shorter batsman, who will be more likely to cut and pull the ball squarer with the wicket. Again, the ball will tend to go fine on quicker wickets and squarer on slower wickets. The captain has much to think about and needs the full co-operation of all the team. The captain can get very useful information from the wicket-keeper as to how much the ball is moving either through the air or off the wicket. The wicket-keeper will also know that much earlier than the other fielders when a bowler is tired or has lost his 'nip'.

One of the biggest mistakes made by inexperienced captains is to over-bowl leading bowlers in their first spell. Many is the time that in trying to capitalise on early wickets a captain persists with the successful bowlers, only to see them flag and then not have enough 'steam' later to make a comeback. This can easily result in the 'tail wagging' as they say, with runs coming from the unexpected quarter. The best captains will try to balance their attack by resting a main strike bowler before completing a full spell of overs. This ensures that he can be fit to come back into the attack fresh, with maximum potential to dismiss the remaining batsmen. Having said this, there are times when it is worth taking a risk by bowling the main bowlers 'out' in an effort to dismiss the opposition in the shortest possible time for the lowest possible score. It depends very much on how conditions favour the bowlers and whether or not the wicket is likely to improve. These tactics can 'backfire' but this is when chance can take a hand to swing the game one way or the other.

When a young bowler is playing, and especially if he is a spin bowler, it is essential to select the best time to introduce him into the attack. Usually it can be after the batsmen at the wicket have been tied down for a spell. There is a chance they may relax and take unwarranted risks against the new bowler. Again, it is wise not to set a predominantly attacking field for a young inexperienced bowler; it can only create extra pressure.

A sign of inexperience in captaincy is very often shown to the batting side by ineffective field placing. On more than one occasion I have seen matches lost by lack of attention by the captain in setting the field for different batsmen at the wicket or different bowlers, and also by his letting the best and most reliable catchers and throwers wander out of position.

When Batting

On the face of it the captain's most important role is when the team is in the field. But when batting the dressing-room atmosphere is also very important, especially when the game is balanced and a wicket one way or another can mean so much. It is in the dressing-room that the captain can really come into his own in the way he supports the team and the individual batsmen. In many teams the 'star' batsman's success or otherwise can influence the team's morale to a surprising degree. Yet very few matches are won by individual batsmen. In fact, it is usually an inspired effort from the last few batsmen when the 'chips are down' that wins important matches. Good captains realise that a team effort by the batting side is just as important as a team effort in the field. The best teams encourage each other all the time, the captain sees to that.

At the start of an innings, it is important that the early batsmen are fully aware of the tactics to be employed and whose job it is to do what. This does not mean that tactics should not change as the game progresses and different situations arise. Frequently one batsman can act as sheet anchor whilst others play strokes to keep up the required scoring rate.

I notice that these days in the England side, if there is an opportunity allowing right- and left-handed batsmen to be together at the wicket, then it is taken at the fall of a wicket. The combination of right- and left-handed batsmen being at the wicket should not be underestimated by the captain: there is no doubt that it makes accurate bowling that much more difficult. It is the captain's job to make sure that the batting tempo is right for the position of the game. This part of his job is no more evident than towards the end of a close match when it is easy for panic to set in.

Other Requirements

Of all the requirements of a captain, none is as important as his attitude and capability as a fielder. Many are the fine teams whose captain is neither an early batsman nor a leading bowler, but very definitely he is an outstanding fielder and a trier in every respect. There is no reason why the wicket-keeper should not be a captain, providing he can retain his concentration for both jobs and has the respect of the team. He certainly has the advantage of being closest to the action in the field.

So what else should an erstwhile skipper be, apart from 'all things to all men'? Above all, he must have a sense of humour, because win or lose, the game should be about enjoyment for all involved, and that does not mean just the players. There are those behind the scenes who need to be appreciated and it is the captain's job to see that his team do just that. The umpires, the scorers, the ladies who make the teas. Where would we be without them? Neither should we forget the groundsmen, who are seldom recognised for their contribution. What a job all these people and many more do for cricket. Captain, it is your job to see that nobody, but nobody is missed, not even the committee!

FAMOUS PLAYERS
Denis Lillee appeals successfully for a catch by wicket-keeper Rodney Marsh. Centenary Test,
Australia v. England in Melbourne, 1977.

(*Opposite, top left*) Imran Khan, Pakistan. (*Top right*) Ian Botham, England. (*Below*) Sunil Gavaskar, India.

(*Above*) Sir Garfield Sobers, West Indies.

(Far Left) Richard Hadlee, New Zealand.

(Left) Greg Chappell, Australia.

(Above) Gordon Greenidge, West Indies.

(Right) Viv Richards, West Indies.

FAMOUS GROUNDS
(*Opposite, above*) World Cup final, Calcutta, 1987. (*Below*) The new Mound Stand at Lord's 1987.

(*Above*) The Old Pavilion at sunset, Sydney, 1983.

(*Overleaf*) Test match at Port-of-Spain, Trinidad, 1986.

Field Placing

As is stated more than once in this section of the book, thoughtful field placing is one of the most vital factors in the winning or losing of a cricket match. It is a captain's duty to have made a study of it, particularly with regard to his own bowlers. It is also important that each bowler has made a point of knowing exactly where his fielders should be in every different circumstance. Obviously, 'every different circumstance' covers a very wide range of possibilities and because of this, some sort of compromise between captain and bowler is the best way of achieving the desired result. Good captains usually appreciate that the experienced bowler will have a definite idea of where he wants his field. Sensible diplomacy is the best method of achieving the necessary compromise but if this cannot be achieved the captain of the team must always be 'in charge'.

The most important aspect of field placing is to consider how the range of fielding positions can cope with the variables listed below:

1) The type and ability of the bowler.
2) The style and ability of the batsman.
3) The condition of the wicket.
4) The type of match—limited overs, one-day, two-day etc.
5) The state of the game.
6) The state of the outfield.
7) The size of the ground.
8) The atmosphere.
9) The condition of the ball.

However, I am loth to specify a set field for different bowlers, as these days the subject gives a much wider scope for captains and bowlers to use their own initiative. The diagram on page 120 illustrates and lists the number of identifiable fielding positions. Some combination of nine placings from a possible thirty-seven is the object.

Possible attacking situations
1) First few overs of the innings.
2) Bad wicket, 'green wicket', spinner's wicket.
3) Wickets falling regularly.
4) Defensive batsmen at the wicket.
5) Before an interval.
6) New ball available.
7) Wickets to be taken at all costs, i.e. big score in hand.
8) One end open, i.e. tail-end batsman at the wicket.

Possible defensive situations
1) Limited number of overs to bowl.
2) Very good batsman's wicket.
3) Good stand under way between two good batsmen.
4) One end closed—good batsman and tail-ender together. Defend the better batsman, attack the tail-ender.

The points made are of course generalisations and invariably some balance between attack and defence is the most effective policy.

Other important factors in field placing are:

1) Do not try to set a field for bad (inaccurate) bowling—change the bowler first.
2) Know how different bowlers generally obtain wickets, and do not depart too radically from a successful formula.
3) Stick with sound principles. If the wicket has bounce, keep as many close catchers as possible, particularly slips.
4) If the wicket is slow and of low bounce the infielders can pick up catches from mis-hit drives. Make sure you close gaps and encourage the batsmen to hit 'over the top'.
5) Recognise the importance of the condition of the outfield, slow or fast.

Fig. 39

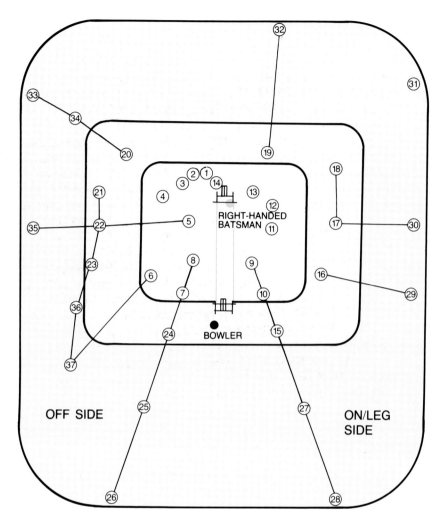

FIELDING POSITIONS

CLOSE FIELD	**INFIELD**	**OUTFIELD**
1 FIRST SLIP	15 MID-ON	25 DEEP MID-OFF
2 SECOND SLIP	16 MID-WICKET	26 LONG-OFF
3 THIRD SLIP	17 SQUARE-LEG	27 DEEP MID-ON
4 GULLY	18 BACKWARD	28 LONG-ON
5 SILLY POINT	SQUARE-LEG	29 DEEP MID-WICKET
6 SHORT EXTRA	19 SHORT FINE-LEG	30 DEEP SQUARE-LEG
7 SHORT MID-OFF	20 SHORT THIRD-MAN	31 LONG-LEG
8 SILLY MID-OFF	21 BACKWARD POINT	32 DEEP FINE-LEG
9 SILLY MID-ON	22 POINT	33 DEEP THIRD-MAN
10 SHORT MID-ON	23 COVER POINT	34 THIRD-MAN
11 FORWARD SHORT-LEG	24 MID-OFF	35 DEEP POINT
12 BACKWARD SHORT-LEG		36 EXTRA-COVER
13 LEG-SLIP		37 DEEP EXTRA
14 WICKET-KEEPER		

6) Watch out for the outfielders who wander out of position. It is easier to take a catch in the outfield coming towards the ball, than to turn to make the catch.

7) Encourage the batsman to play strokes across the line of the ball. For example, if an off-spin bowler is turning the ball a lot to a right-handed batsman, the cover point position can be left open, encouraging a stroke directly against the spin. Use this principle, especially when attacking, for all types of bowling.

8) Remember that when a batsman plays strokes directly against the spin or swing, the ball can easily 'pick up' off the wicket, giving a low catch on the drive.

When looking to set a field for a particular bowler, I strongly recommend consultation with a good coach or an experienced bowler of the type concerned. So, rather than making scores of improbable diagrams, I have included illustrations for a few standard 'fields' as a basis for discussion and possible adjustment. In each case assume a right-handed batsman is at the wicket.

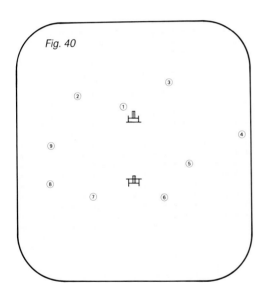

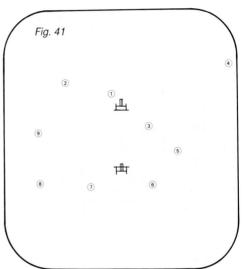

Figs. 40–45 STANDARD FIELDS

Fig. 40 Leg spin/Googly

1 FIRST SLIP
2 SHORT THIRD-MAN
3 SHORT FINE-LEG
4 DEEP SQUARE-LEG
5 MID-WICKET
6 MID-ON
7 MID-OFF
8 EXTRA COVER
9 COVER POINT

Fig. 41 Slow left arm

1 FIRST SLIP
2 SHORT THIRD-MAN
3 FORWARD SHORT-LEG
4 DEEP BACKWARD SQUARE-LEG
5 MID-WICKET
6 MID-ON
7 MID-OFF
8 EXTRA COVER
9 COVER POINT

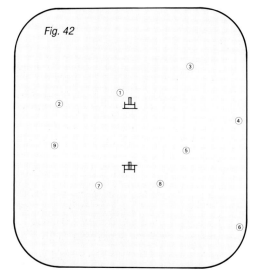

Fig. 42 Off-spin

1 FIRST SLIP	6 LONG-ON
2 BACKWARD POINT	7 MID-OFF
3 SHORT FINE-LEG	8 MID-ON
4 DEEP SQUARE-LEG	9 COVER POINT
5 MID WICKET	

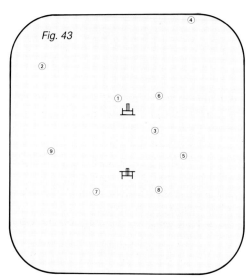

Fig. 43 Inswing

1 FIRST SLIP	6 BACKWARD SHORT-LEG
2 THIRD MAN	LEG
3 FORWARD SHORT-LEG	7 MID-OFF
4 DEEP FINE-LEG	8 MID-ON
5 MID WICKET	9 COVER POINT

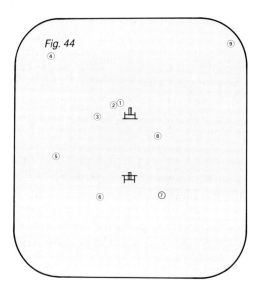

Fig. 44 Outswing

1 FIRST SLIP	6 MID-OFF
2 SECOND SLIP	7 MID-ON
3 GULLY	8 MID-WICKET
4 THIRD MAN	9 LONG-LEG
5 COVER POINT	

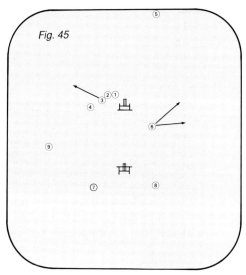

Fig. 45 Fast bowler

1 FIRST SLIP	6 FORWARD SHORT-LEG
2 SECOND SLIP	LEG
3 THIRD SLIP	7 MID-OFF
4 GULLY	8 MID-ON
5 DEEP FINE-LEG	9 COVER POINT

ATTITUDES

In the main, the skills and techniques described in this book are those used most effectively over the years by a majority of the best players—a distillation of success, if you like. There are, of course, very successful exceptions to the orthodox methods described. In fact, it is very difficult to define orthodox. What is unorthodox in one generation becomes orthodox in the next. Bob Willis took over 300 Test wickets with what was generally considered to be a poor action. Malcolm Marshall of the West Indies, one of the finest fast bowlers ever, is hardly a carbon copy of the classical New Zealander Richard Hadlee, but he is equally effective. Unorthodox batsmen have scored centuries for centuries and fortunately they continue to confound the critics of today. In appearance at the wicket at least, Graham Gooch and Chris Broad are prime examples. And what of Ian Botham? So unorthodox to the casual observer, so orthodox to the analyst. Botham can be the most 'correct' hitter of a ball there has ever been in cricket.

So far I have only mentioned the physical skills. Without application and strength of mind, physical attributes, whether based on power or technique, cannot take a player to the top. Developing the right *attitude* is the key to success, either through the intelligent use of what one was born with, or by acquiring an effective substitute (if that is possible): the natural player as opposed to the manufactured player—Gower or Boycott, Compton or Hutton.

Fortunately, no individual can be programmed to react like a computer. If Viv Richards receives a half volley just outside the off-stump he may hit it for four through the covers or he may achieve the same result by hitting the ball through mid-wicket. This provides the spectator with the fascination of watching the virtuosity and unpredictability of outstanding talent. No one would want to see every half volley pitched outside the off-stump, hit for four through the covers, as though by machine.

Ability can be acquired in different ways—it can be obtained through instruction and by experience. Gifted players will very likely develop their talents by experience and minimum instruction, whereas others, not so gifted, will need a more even combination of the two. Then it will be a matter of attitude as to which player achieves success.

One of the most important aspects of attitude in cricket, as in other walks of life, is to recognise one's limitations. How often do we see a batsman play really well whilst scoring twenty or thirty and then get out with a stroke that he does not normally play very well? Similarly, there are bowlers who by limiting their range of deliveries in a match will make a good contribution to the team effort, until maybe in frustration they will 'try something' beyond their ability and let the batting side regain the initiative.

Another area of cricket where attitudes can be of immense importance is in practice and fitness training. If, as in the previous instance, a batsman loses his wicket by consistently playing strokes beyond his ability, what is wrong with putting in a few hours of practice on that particular stroke? A few minutes will not suffice. Hours are needed to correct what might only be a minor fault. Fast bowling and fitness go together as much as any pairing in cricket and it is usually by not achieving a reasonable level of fitness, that most fast bowlers fall by the wayside. There is a new slogan in use: *Your attitude is showing*, and so it does. If you are a cricketer reading these words, let your attitude be worth seeing.

METHODS OF PLAY AND COMMON FAULTS

Within the boundaries of an individual's skills and attitude must be the method by which he gets the most out of these. Under pressure, faults can easily develop and these need to be recognised early if they are to be eradicated or minimised. The following checklists will highlight some of the problems that occur all too easily in matches, when outside influences can affect a player's technique.

BATTING CHECKLIST

1 Concentration is the first priority in batting. Attitude on the day and previous practice are all-important.

2 Watch the ball closely—right through the bowler's run-up and particularly as it leaves the bowler's hand.

3 Programme yourself for each bowler and each delivery. Think positively. Think back or forward, depending upon all the circumstances, that is, the expected pace of the ball, the state of the wicket and particularly the state of the game. For example, playing on a fast wicket against a very fast bowler, you will be programmed back but ready to come forward if necessary.

4 Learn to pace yourself within the requirements of the state of the game. It is not a bad idea to think of advancing your score in sixes or tens or even twenties, taking stock after achieving each target. In other words build your innings, and not necessarily slowly!

5 Conversely, it is no use playing entirely within an individual scoring plan if the state of the game demands an unorthodox approach. For example, if a very high scoring rate is required in comparatively few overs, un-orthodox methods will need to be applied. You should have thought about this previously, even reproduced your intentions in practice beforehand. In your mind's eye you should have visualised yourself hitting the ball harder and further than you have ever done before. If you have, you will be half ready to do just that.

6 Most anxious batsmen move too early—steel yourself to wait just that fraction of a second.

7 Be realistic—recognise that it will be more effective to play strokes to hit the ball squarer on slow wickets and straighter on hard wickets.

8 Remind yourself of the value of quick footwork, especially when batting against slow bowlers.

9 I know some batsmen who can really hit the ball hard and yet do not score as quickly as one would expect. The reason for this is that they do not vary the weight of their strokes. Learn to hit the ball 'soft' on occasions, to bring the field in.

10 Sort out your fielders and know their capabilities. Many are the runs missed through lack of this knowledge.

Common Batting Faults

The basic fault in batting technique is in not leading all strokes with the front shoulder and head. In forward strokes this means the head falls over towards the off-side which can cause the bottom hand to come into the stroke too early, pulling the bat across the line of the ball. In back strokes it results in the back foot opening up too early when it should be near enough parallel to the crease in all but the pull and hook strokes. This again causes the bat to come across the line of the ball, with all its inherent problems.

Having said this, batsmen should be aware that in the horizontal bat strokes, such as the pull and the square-cut, the bat comes naturally across the line of the ball and should do, providing it is as near horizontal as possible.

Another major batting fault, sometimes affecting the best of players in defence, is not

BOWLING CHECKLIST

A good action is all-important to a bowler, but I know a lot of bowlers with good actions who are not successful. There are other factors to take into account:

1 *Planning* is the key to bowling success.

2 Study batsmen closely. Know that tall batsmen are likely to be forward players. Look to get them on the back foot early in their innings. Smaller batsmen tend to pull and cut off the back foot. Make sure you keep the ball well up to them.

3 Improve accuracy by consciously gathering yourself as you come into the delivery stride—this is very important.

4 Spin and swing need to be controlled. How many times have you seen a bowler beat the bat with too much swing or spin? Learn to control the amount by experimenting with the position of the seam on delivery and by varying your delivery position.

5 Every bowler should be able to bowl over *and* round the wicket.

6 Set targets for accurate bowling, i.e., no more than one delivery in four overs pitched on the leg-side of middle stump, a difficult target.

7 No matter what your pace, bowling is to do with guile. Subtle variation in pace, angle of attack, even length, all contribute to putting doubt into the batsman's mind.

8 Do not worry if you do not possess the classic side-on action. How many wickets you obtain and at what cost are what really count. Striking rate is also very important, that is, overs/wickets. I should like to see bowling statistics incorporate this ratio. For example, it is no use taking wickets at a low cost if you do not take them often enough. A bowler's runs/over-rate are also important these days—rather too important. Set your targets in all these areas, but identify which is truly most important for your team.

9 Field placing is vital to bowling success. Make a study of it and recognise that different batsmen require different field settings. Know **exactly where your fielders should be to within a foot!**

10 Remember two things. You cannot take wickets if you are not bowling and the more overs/hours you bowl the more wickets you will take.

keeping the bat handle forward in advance of the bat face. In other words, instead of allowing the ball to come to the bat, the batsman pushes at the ball with too much bottom hand. Any deviation of the ball can find the edge of the bat and travel upwards from the edge, rather than down as it would if the bat was vertical and angled forward from the handle.

Correct technique is, of course, concerned mainly with reducing the chances of dismissal and this applies particularly to batsmen who want to improve performance in terms of figures. Those with great flair may be able to flout sound technique, but only up to a point. In fact, improving technique can help the most gifted batsmen to hit the ball even better. For example, hitting power can be increased by developing maximum extension of the front arm (left for right-handed batsmen) on the back-lift and the rear arm on the follow-through. Watch a top golfer in action for a good illustration of this. The aim is to achieve maximum speed of the bat at the point of impact.

Common Bowling Faults

a) Incorrect grip for intended delivery.
b) Not enough thought and work put into establishing a proper run-up—exemplified by bowling no-balls without check in practice.
c) No lean away from batsman, or arching of the back moving into the delivery stride.
d) Too high a jump into delivery stride, losing momentum at an important point in the action.
e) Too long or too short a delivery stride for the type of bowler.
f) Poor use of non-bowling arm, resulting in an inadequate follow-through.

FIELDING CHECKLIST

1 Ground fielding—avoid looking up at the batsman before you have picked the ball, in a run-out situation particularly.

2 Be careful not to move in too much from your original fielding position in either the outfield or the infield, especially on a fast wicket and outfield. Remember it is easier to run forward than back.

3 Controlled fielding is the best fielding.

4 Be aware of the bad sighting backgrounds in the field—forewarned is forearmed.

WICKET-KEEPING CHECKLIST

1 Do not stand back in 'no man's land'.

2 He who hesitates. . . .

3 Check your gloves before every match—these are a wicket-keeper's lifeline.

4 Always practise one-handed catching especially in your weaker hand—everyone has one.

5 Be an attacking wicket-keeper.

6 Byes are usually the result of bad bowling, so remember you cannot always be responsible for byes. Be your own judge.

7 Do not use your pads to stop the ball.

8 Apart from the leg-glance, do not anticipate. That is, do not move too early before you have some idea of the line of the ball, especially when standing up to the wicket.

CHAPTER THREE

The Training of Cricketers

Earlier in this book I quoted W.G. Grace from his famous book, *Cricket*, published in 1891. Part of the quote reads, 'but, to acquire all-round proficiency I am strongly convinced that constant practice and sound coaching have all to do with it.' So, it seems that coaching was not an unknown subject in the nineteenth century, but it can hardly be said that it was as popular as it is today. Of course, as the game spread, so did coaching, but it was mainly individual coaching at the county grounds, by the professionals, for members and their sons.

At about the same time as the County Championship became well established, retired professionals became full-time coaches at the public schools. There is no doubt that this development not only greatly enhanced cricket in the first half of the twentieth century, but also very conclusively established the value of good coaching. It is worth noting the high percentage of county and Test players that came from a public school background and, for that matter, still do, although not in so high a ratio these days, as coaching is more widely available and quality cricket is played on a larger scale. Nowadays, in fact, there is a National Coaching Scheme, initiated by MCC in the early Fifties but subsequently taken over and further developed by the NCA through the Cricket Council. The development of the National Coaching Scheme has changed the face of coaching considerably, particularly in the numbers of enthusiastic club coaches, many of whom are working school teachers who know more about cricket coaching than ever before. A figure of more than five thousand people currently involved can be no exaggeration when it is known that over ten thousand coaches have qualified at various levels over the last few years.

Nevertheless, this does not tell the full story by any means, for in 1952, sixteen years before the formation of the Cricket Council, the MCC Youth Cricket Association had been formed and an MCC Coaching Scheme launched nationally. Three marvellous men of cricket were responsible—Gubby (now Sir George) Allen, Harry Altham and Harry Crabtree. Gubby Allen instigated the initiative in the MCC Cricket Committee of 1948 when he posed the question in his own forthright manner, 'What are we doing about coaching in the state schools?' Harry Altham created the scheme during his brilliant Chairmanship of the MCC Youth Cricket Association, and Harry Crabtree, Essex cricketer and educationalist, developed the project practically. It was Harry Crabtree who devised group coaching as a means of coaching a number of youngsters together. It was the cornerstone of the MCC scheme and in my opinion the greatest single influence on the progress of practical coaching in cricket history. Of course, the one-to-one, player–coach situation is the best, but accepting this, the idea of serving a ball on to a selected length and direction to suit a particular stroke can be used very effectively. This is the principle of group coaching (see page 131).

The foregoing paragraphs give some indication of the meaning of cricket coaching in the United Kingdom. Being realistic, this is only a sign of the times, as the desire for success in sport has multiplied countless times. Whether we like it or not sport is big business and not only at the highest levels. Participation in sport is a national objective and as such its promotion becomes important and consequently so does success at all levels of participation. When success in sport is important, so is coaching or training, to give it a wider interpretation. Certainly it is in most sports, and there is no reason why it should be any different in cricket.

(*Opposite*) NCA NATIONAL COACH, LES LENHAM, gives a young batsman the feel of where his head *should* be.

Sir George Allen

Gubby Allen, as he has been known in cricket for more than fifty years, has almost certainly been the most significant single influence on the English game in the mid-twentieth century. In the Thirties he was a good enough fast bowler to play in the controversial 1932/3 series in Australia alongside Larwood and Voce, although he did not agree to bowl 'bodyline' when asked to do so by Jardine, a comment on his position in the game even then.

The list of his achievements in cricket that follows does not by any means tell the whole story. For example, his greatest pride is in the influence he has been able to exert on the development of coaching in the last forty years. As I have already written, it was through his early initiative together with that of his great friend Harry Altham that a National Coaching Scheme was developed.

His strong personality has dominated cricket for nearly fifty years. Autocratic, shrewd, straightforward and a man of great principle, he does not suffer fools in any shape or form. I have been privileged to work with this great man of cricket on a number of projects and I learned much from the experience. He has a charming sense of humour just under the surface and a simple warmth not associated with his public image. His feeling for cricket and MCC is unsurpassed.

Gubby Allen played for Middlesex as an amateur from 1921–50. He played for England in England in 1930, 1931, 1933, 1934 and 1936 (Captain). In Australia he played in 1932/3 and in 1936/7 (Captain). In New Zealand he played in 1932/3 and in the West Indies in 1947/8 (Captain). He was President of MCC in 1963/4 and Treasurer from 1964–76, also Vice Chairman of the Cricket Council from 1974–6 and Chairman of Test Selectors from 1955–61.

As a player he came into the category of a

SIR GEORGE ALLEN.

genuine all-rounder but he was first a fast bowler with 778 first-class wickets under his belt at 21.22 each. Eighty-one of these wickets were taken in twenty-five Test matches. Sir George has virtually lived at Lord's for many years, his house backing on to the Harris Memorial Garden. Like W.G. Grace, I cannot but feel that he will always have a presence there.

The Coach

Before commenting on the requirements of the cricket coach, it may be a good idea to identify who the cricket coach is.

At the higher levels, coaching can be or even should be a profession, but there is nothing wrong with any father or mother coaching their children at the earliest age. In fact, it is essential if a young cricketer is to absorb the correct basic skills for him to start at an early age. Learning about cricket is no different from being introduced to reading and writing in the home environment. Hence my hope that this book will find its way on to the family bookshelf.

Coaching involves a whole spectrum of people, I am glad to say, and whilst this is not a coaching book, I hope there is enough information about the skills of cricket and coaching in it, to persuade anyone with an interest to try their hand at a pastime that will give them and those they encourage years of pleasure.

Remember that the traditional cricket net is far from being an essential for coaching. Neither is a hard ball. In fact, when encouraging the very young a soft ball should be used. Bat shapes are also just as useful as the real thing when playing fun cricket in the garden, on the beach or wherever, although experience as both father and grandfather tells me that even three year olds prefer something realistic. Cricket need not be an expensive game to learn or play. Read something about the basic skills and link what you learn to some of the suggestions made in this chapter. Remember that whilst other qualities and qualifications are necessary and can be aspired to, over ninety per cent of people

GROUP COACHING—Enjoyable action.

thrive on encouragement.

Also an asset, is an appreciation of what to do or not to do in fitness training, especially when dealing with mature young cricketers. I have seen one or two quite unnecessary injuries to players who have been under the wing of someone without the knowledge and experience of proper fitness training—but this is the responsibility of the serious coach. Also a responsibility of the serious coach is the need to investigate the potential of psychology in cricket coaching. It is used very successfully by coaches in other sports at national and international level. So why should cricket be any different?

Group Coaching and Skills Practice

Batting

The principles of group coaching are ideal for developing batting skills. The idea is simply to give the batsman an opportunity of playing/practising a specific stroke repeatedly. This is accomplished by setting out a prepared surface to accommodate all the

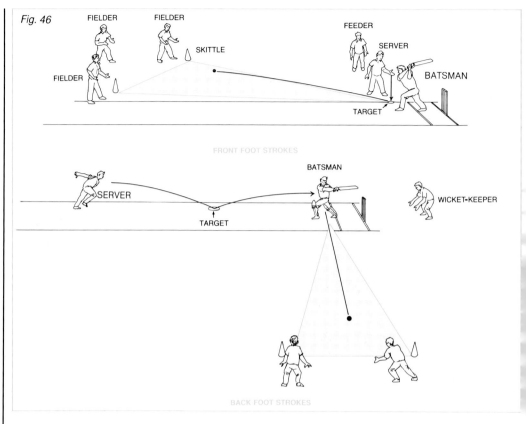

requirements. Lay out the area for the group concerned.

The drawing shows an ideal number of five/six for batting, although two can manage the routine, especially in an enclosed area.

It is important for the bowler/thrower to practise accuracy for the batsman to obtain maximum benefit. Obviously different strokes can be practised in minimum time

Fig. 46 BATTING PRACTICE

Fig. 47 BOWLING PRACTICE

and everyone in the group will get an opportunity. In the more sophisticated group coaching sessions these days, a bowling machine can be used very effectively.

Bowling

Bowling practice can be most effective in pairs, simply bowling to each other over an agreed distance, with targets that can be varied in size and position (both in length and direction) to suit each bowler.

Fielding

As in bowling, fielding practice can be accomplished in pairs or small groups. This can include all types of fielding and catching.

Wicket-keeping

Of all the skills of cricket, wicket-keeping is probably practised the least. Perhaps this is because, being only one of eleven in the team, the 'keeper's influence seems minimal. However, with a little co-operation from team-mates, wicket-keeping practice can be very effective. Three/four players are needed—the wicket-keeper, a bowler or bowlers and a batsman. The role of the batsman is vital, in that he is required to convincingly play at the ball but deliberately miss on a high percentage of occasions.

Goal Setting

One of the most effective coaching techniques that can produce the most spectacular improvement in players at any level is the setting of achievable goals.

Goal-setting applies equally to short, medium and long term aims, although it has been found to be most effective in the short term. Achieving goals gives great self confidence to players and, on the principle that success breeds success, goals should be set to give no less than a seventy per cent chance of success. It is also important, when setting goals, to ensure that the goal is acceptable to, and entirely under the control of, the player.

Your level of involvement will of course influence your attitude towards coaching and subjects such as goal setting, but bearing in mind earlier comments on the value of ensuring sound introductory experience to children, there is nothing lost by parents having some knowledge of these techniques, which are so important to the professional coach.

When conducting skills practice using

Alec and Micky Stewart represent all that is best in professional cricket. The Oval, 1992.

group coaching methods, or otherwise, goals can be set through competition. In batting, for example, by scoring points for hitting the ball through defined targets, or, in bowling, a competition for hitting a target marked on a wicket can easily be set up. Obviously the same can be done for fielding and wicket-keeping. Without creating this sort of press-ure, coaching and practice become very boring for players. Easy practice is not practice!

COACHING TIPS

1 Ask questions—demonstrate answers.
2 Action speaks louder than words.
3 Keep an open mind—even if you are or were a good player.
4 Fail to prepare, prepare to fail—a maxim for players and coaches.
5 Record as much as you can and check before coming to any conclusions.
6 Practise what you preach—make sure your standards are high, before setting them for others.
7 Remember, anyone can encourage a win-ning team.
8 Good coaching is hard work—work harder.

Cricket Practice

What is that oft quoted remark attributed to many great performers in various sports when luck is mentioned as being the reason for their success? Some refer to their bank account, but the comment I like is the one from Gary Player, the great golfer: 'The more I practise, the luckier I get.'

Cricketers have varied greatly in their attitude to practice. Traditionally, it has been treated not as a means of improving skills and technique, but more as a light physical work-out. This attitude has been promoted, particularly when exceptional

talent has crossed the stage and the natural flair of the great player has clouded the logic that might well have been heeded by many of the less gifted. Sadly, one or two of these 'great' players in promoting their own image have done nothing for those that need to work for success. This is not quite the case with some, however, and the record-breaking Geoffrey Boycott is an outstanding example of what can be achieved by using practice, almost to the point of obsession, to eradicate technical faults. In fact, Boycott's achieve-ments have had some influence on today's younger players and with new technical innovations and a stronger acceptance of coaching, practice is becoming more and more effective.

There are a few factors that confirm these comments:

1 Group coaching principles allow pro-longed repetitive practice of individual skills.

2 Even more concentrated practice of individual batting skills can be accomplished using a bowling machine, which can be set to deliver balls at a set speed, length and direc-tion to suit the batsman's requirements.

3 The use of video equipment is a great incentive to practice. Recordings from televised matches also help when assessing a player's technique under pressure as against his technique in the more relaxed atmo-sphere of a practice session.

One of the most illuminating aspects of practice that I have seen in recent years occurred when watching Ian Botham practis-ing batting at the Lord's nets just before a Test match in the early Eighties. Ian seemed to be trying to drive every ball he received as far as he could, almost as a golfer would on a driving range. My first reaction, bred on my experiences in a different and older school, was to think, 'Hello, this lad's showing off! We all know what a big hitter he is.' How stupid of me, how blinkered a view! Ian is so right—how very sensible it is to practise hitting sixes, when sixes are your stock in trade and what the crowd pay to see. How right it must be for young players to experiment in practice, endeavouring always to maximise their potential and extend their horizons.

There are important, even vital, criteria for worthwhile practice. These are, firstly the quality of the playing surface—wicket, pitch, call it what you like—must be good. Secondly, the ball should be of the right quality and in good condition. Thirdly, the background should be considered. It is not possible to practise effectively if the batsman cannot see the ball properly. These points may also come under the heading of safety, and of course, *safety* for all concerned should be the first of all priorities.

Net Practice

'He's down at the nets, or up at the club—or pub,' we say, and have done for generations.

THE NETS at LORD'S.

In fact both pursuits are usually fun, almost complementary to each other.

Net practice is very often viewed as a physical work-out, rather than a time to polish up skills and seriously try to correct faults. Whatever, the following comments are meant for the players who see net practice as a means of improving their skills.

I have already mentioned safety in cricket and the necessity for good conditions, particularly wickets. Net practice can also be much more enjoyable if it is properly organised, preferably by a coach or the captain of the team. It is important to make sure that everyone attending 'the nets' gets a fair 'crack of the whip'. For example, there should be space behind the stumps so that the wicket-keeper can practise. If there is more than one net, the better players should be grouped together, as should different age groups. Casual net practice is probably a cricketer's most likely source of injury. There can be much 'messing about', and many players fail to appreciate the value of a proper warm-up session before practice. Regarding the netting itself, it is worthwhile checking its condition. If the nets are double and treble, the length of the netting should

Middle Practice

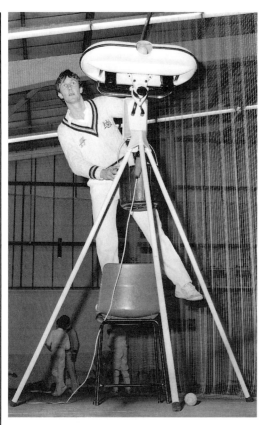

THE BOWLING MACHINE—Use it with care.

Middle practice, or match practice, is not generally accepted as particularly useful and I am at a loss to understand why. Perhaps it is the inconvenience of preparing suitable conditions, or alternatively, and more likely, is the fact that it does not occupy enough players in the time available. However, middle practice should not be undervalued, as it is probably the best way of putting players under pressure other than in a match itself. Maximum activity can be had, if played as a variation of pairs, eight-a-side or six-a-side cricket, when two or more matches can be played at the same time if facilities are available. Match practice can be more useful in setting goals for players, with the benefits that this undoubtedly brings.

It is particularly important to stage eleven-a-side match practice also, reproducing the conditions that might apply in a real match. Both sides of a situation need to be considered. Practise as a team the task of obtaining various target scores against the clock, if possible on different types of wicket and circumstances. The fielding side in this type of practice will benefit just as much as they develop tactics to stop the opposition reaching their target. This type of middle practice is also marvellous for helping to develop the skills of captaincy. Some sort of incentive can be introduced which adds spice to the affair. I well remember a practice match we arranged at Northampton one year when we played against Derbyshire for a firkin of ale. I can tell you there was a lot of pressure on all of us to win.

Conversely, it is worth practising a defensive situation, when the team batting are simply trying to save the match and the fielding side want two or three wickets to win with only a few overs left. This is a situation that occurs frequently in cricket and usually the team that wins is the one that applies the best tactics and keeps its nerve.

protect players in adjacent nets. The width of a net is important also. Anything less than twelve feet is really not good enough.

Whilst net practice can be criticised, and I have pointed out the valid reasons for criticism, over the years well organised net practice in good conditions has proved to be a significant contributor to the progress of young players. The very high proportion of public school cricketers who have reached the highest levels in cricket is a testimony to the value of good net practice, especially when organised as a school policy. In recent years, group coaching principles have been applied very successfully in nets, very often using a bowling machine to give a repeated delivery for practising a particular stroke.

Other Aspects of Training for Cricketers

Within the overall training of cricketers there are of course many other considerations. Properly organised fitness training programmes for groups and individuals are becoming appreciated more and more by players, and it is showing in their performances. One only has to see a first-class team in the field these days. The West Indies teams of the Eighties are an outstanding example, as their trainer is an integral part of the team.

Fitness Requirements for Cricket

Whether you are a specialist batsman, bowler or wicket-keeper, general fitness training will follow a similar pattern. Any variation will come from the emphasis placed on the physical requirements of each particular skill and the individual involved.

A training programme for any cricketer will look for improvement in strength, stamina, mobility, agility, speed of running, speed of reaction, speed of movement, recovery rate and concentration. However, it is logical that in the performing of the various skills, some aspects of fitness will take precedence over others. A well-designed programme will recognise the need for this.

Bearing in mind the multitude of variations possible, I will limit my advice here to brief notes on warming-up procedures. These are, or should be, an ingredient in any practice or match.

Warming Up

As I have already indicated, in the past (and even now in some sections of cricket), properly scheduled fitness training was almost

FITNESS can be shared—IAN BOTHAM and VIV RICHARDS; Worcestershire v. Somerset, 1986.

BOWLING is HARD WORK—So is getting fit for it!

frowned upon. In fact, to use a word of today it was not 'macho' to be associated with anything so 'non-cricket'. A couple of knee-bends, arm stretches and maybe a toss of the head were the nearest thing to a genuine warm-up. One has the feeling that partaking in specific fitness training in the Golden Age, or even later, would in some eyes have been tantamount to cheating!

However, for those who wish to reap the benefit, a warm-up session should last approximately ten minutes, never more than fifteen minutes. Light jogging and/or the gentle but correct performing of skills related to your role in the game is sufficient and should be enough to produce a light sweat. Mobility exercises should also be under-taken, stretching muscles and 'pressing' joints gently and well within their limits.

Psychology and Training

Physical fitness training obviously makes sense, but sport, and cricket in particular, is not only a physical activity but also very much a game in which the mind is important. If this is true, and few cricketers will deny it, mental training can also be a subject worth exploring.

Sports psychology is a comparatively new subject in itself, in cricket it is practically unknown. Yet, I am convinced, with very limited experience and knowledge of the subject, that much can be gained by a crick-eter or a coach in at least opening their minds to the possibilities that may be presented. Of course, we all practice psychology to some degree and we know it works, so it is quite logical to look into what has been achieved in other sports through a qualified approach.

A few practical areas may be mentioned that are already successful. *The mental rehearsal* is very much akin to the physical warm-up in that it is aimed at preparing a player for the match ahead by visualising one or more aspects of the performance. *Con-centration* needs to be practised if one is going to improve it—there are methods. The same applies to *relaxation* and the development of *self confidence*—so important for the successful player.

As in physical fitness training, mental training is a subject for specialist advice and, more than in physical training even, a little knowledge can be dangerous. Nevertheless, if interested cricketers read these comments, I can only earnestly recommend them to seriously investigate the possibilities. They should contact the National Coaching Foundation or, as a starter, read the books produced on the subject.

Cricket Games

In the last ten or more years there is no doubt that there has been a revolution in cricket.

Whilst the first-class game has made enormous strides in spectator interest, playing cricket over anything from one to five days and providing regular entertainment to cater for every taste, the recreational game has not been far behind. Like the first-class game, the recreational game has realised that if it is going to appeal to the junior sportsman of today, certainly in the learning years, it needs to be something other than the traditional game. For many youngsters wanting, in fact needing, activity and involvement, the eleven-a-side game is played over too long a period, with minimum rather than maximum participation for the majority of players. So it was with cricket in junior schools not that long ago, but young cricketers learning the game today get as much, if not more, varied physical activity than they do in many other sports. Cricket is now played by juniors (and seniors for that matter) in such a way that everyone has a fair 'crack of the whip'.

This new method of playing cricket involves batting in pairs and giving players the opportunity to bat for a prescribed number of balls, regardless of whether or not they lose their wickets. In fact, when a wicket is lost, the batsman or a team has runs deducted from a starting total rather than departing from the wicket. The awful first ball 'duck', is no longer seen as a 'character builder' for eight year olds being introduced to the game. Everyone, or at least the great majority, bowls, and reduced numbers in the field make sure that everyone is 'on their toes' and physically involved.

In the following pages I comment on and give the rules for just a few cricket games enjoyed in clubs and schools, some of which are specifically designed to be played indoors.

Pairs Cricket

A game between pairs of players that can easily occupy up to eight pairs (sixteen individuals). The game can be played with a soft ball indoors, or outdoors with a hard ball and protective equipment.

Fig. 48 WORK CARDS

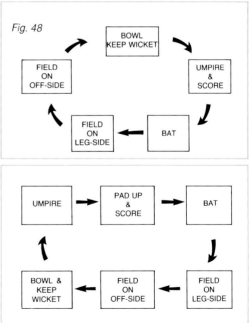

Rules

Each pair bats for an agreed number of overs regardless of whether or not they are dismissed.

Each pair starts with an agreed score (say 100) and deducts an agreed number of runs each time they are dismissed. Juniors may deduct 6 or 8 runs depending upon age and ability. Normal scoring of runs applies but special scoring systems can be devised as required. After a pair have batted for the agreed number of overs the players rotate and another pair bats. It is a good idea to make up a card to suit the number playing (see Fig. 48). For example, in a five pair game, pair one can bat, pair two bowl and keep wicket, pair three score and umpire, pair four field on leg-side and pair five on off-side. More fielders can be added if necessary, or a pair can be padding up if hard balls are used.

Eight-a-Side Cricket

KWIK cricket, Team cricket and Softball are all popular versions of eight-a-side cricket;

SOFTBALL in action.

KWIK cricket perhaps being the most well known. This type of cricket has developed from the pairs game and become the most popular of outdoor/indoor games for young cricketers. Thousands of teams are playing regularly in competitions or simply for fun, throughout the cricketing world.

Eight-a-side cricket can be played equally effectively with a soft or a hard ball, depending upon environment, equipment available and so on.

Rules

1 Each team shall comprise eight players.

2 The length of the pitch shall be eighteen yards (sixteen yards for under eleven cricket), as normal for hard balls.

3 Cricket stumps should be used when possible. If not available, any suitable alternative may be used at the discretion of the organiser.

4 Each game shall consist of one innings per team, each innings to be of twelve (six-ball) overs duration (sixteen or twenty overs when time permits).

5 The batting side shall be divided into pairs,

each pair batting for three overs (four or five overs in sixteen- or twenty-over games).

6 No player on the fielding side may bowl more than a quarter of the total overs (i.e. four in a sixteen-over game). The wicket-keeper may not bowl.

7 Each team shall commence batting with a team score of 200 runs.

8 Each time a wicket falls, runs must be deducted from the team score (six for under eleven, eight for under thirteen, ten for under fifteen and so on).

9 When a batsman is dismissed, he should immediately change ends with the non-striker (on all but the last ball of the over or after a run-out).

10 It is recommended that no fielder shall be allowed to field within eleven yards of the batsman's middle stump, except behind the wicket on the off-side (eight yards when playing with a soft ball). (Call *no ball* for contraventions of this rule.)

11 The Laws of Cricket shall apply outside local rules defined by the organiser.

Variations of eight-a-side cricket to suit the needs of the particular situation are obviously possible and desirable. These variations can be developed by enterprising organisers. For example, when eight-a-side cricket is played indoors with a soft ball, six-a-side scoring can be used.

Six-a-Side Cricket

This very popular game, first played in 1972, was the brainchild of Mike Vockins, Secretary of Worcestershire CCC.

Equipment

The Reader indoor cricket ball, obtainable from leading sports retailers, has been specially developed for this mainly indoor game and is strongly recommended, although tennis balls or similar may be used for junior games. Normal cricket balls can be used when playing outside. Portable stumps or suitable replicas are necessary and a good playing surface is essential. Artificial (non-turf) surfaces can be laid if available and suitable.

When hard cricket balls are used, all normal protective equipment should also be adopted.

KWIK CONTINUOUS CRICKET at Headingley, 1988.

SIX-A-SIDE CRICKET INDOORS.

Facilities

Sports halls or gymnasiums measuring a minimum of 100 x 60 x 20 ft are recommended for adult games although the size can be varied to suit local conditions. When played by youngsters with tennis balls the area can be appropriately less.

Rules

1 Teams consist of six players each.

2 Each innings shall consist of a maximum of twelve six-ball overs.

3 No bowler should bowl more than three overs. In the event of a bowler becoming incapacitated, the over shall be completed by a bowler who has not bowled three overs even if he bowled the preceding over.

4 Two batsmen shall be at the wicket at all times during an innings. In the event of a team losing five wickets within the permitted twelve overs, the last man can continue batting, with the fifth man out remaining at the wicket as a runner.

5 When a batsman reaches a personal total of 25 he retires but may return to the crease in the event of his side being dismissed within the twelve overs. Retired batsmen must return in the order of their retirement and take the place of the retiring or dismissed batsman. Retired batsmen cannot return to the wicket until such time as the fifth wicket has fallen.

6 Negative or short-pitched bowling should be no-balled.

7 The laws relating to wides should be strictly interpreted by the umpire.

Results

The team scoring the most runs in its innings is the winner. If the scores of both teams are equal, then the team losing the least wickets is the winner. If the teams are still equal, then each member of both teams should bowl one ball (overarm) and the team hitting the stumps the greatest number of times is the winner.

Scoring

1 A ball struck to hit the boundary wall

behind the bowler without touching the floor or any other wall or ceiling counts as six runs. It, however, the ball touches the floor but does not touch any of the other walls or the ceiling and hits the boundary wall, then it counts as four runs.

2 A ball struck to hit the ceiling or one or more of the side or back walls counts as one run, even if the ball subsequently hits the boundary wall. Two additional runs are scored if the batsmen complete a run. (If the ball is struck to hit the ceiling or side or back wall and the batsman is then run out, one run is scored.)

3 Two runs are scored if the striker plays the ball and it does not hit a wall direct and the batsmen complete a run.

4 A bye counts as one run if the ball hits a wall; a leg-bye counts as one run if the ball hits a wall. In each case if the batsmen complete a run, two additional runs are scored.

5 Two byes or two leg-byes are scored if the batsmen complete a run without the ball hitting a wall.

6 No-ball:
  a) If the batsmen do not run when a no-ball is called, a penalty of one run is credited under extras. This applies even though the ball hits the ceiling, a side or a back wall.
  b) If the batsman does not strike the ball and completes a run, two runs are credited under extras. This applies whether or not the ball hits the ceiling, a side or a back wall.
  c) If a striker hits a no-ball the number of runs resulting, as specified in rules 1, 2 and 3 above, are added to his score but not the penalty in addition.

7 Wide:
  a) If a wide ball is called, a penalty of one run is credited under extras even

though the ball hits the ceiling, a side or a back wall.
  b) Two runs are credited under extras for every run completed by the batsmen but not the penalty in addition. This applies whether or not the ball hits the ceiling, a side or a back wall.

8 An overthrow hitting any wall counts as one run to the batsman. The batsmen should not change ends.

9 No runs are scored if a batsman is caught out off the walls or ceiling.

Methods of Dismissal

Apart from the normal methods of dismissal contained in the Laws of Cricket, the following variations apply:

1 The batsman can be caught out by a fieldsman after the ball has hit the ceiling, the netting or any wall except directly from the boundary wall, provided the ball has not touched the floor.

2 The last not-out batsman will be given out if the non-striker running with him is run out.

3 The batsman or the non-striker will be given not-out if the ball rebounds from a wall or ceiling and hits a wicket without being touched by a fieldsman.

Continuous Cricket

This is mainly a fun game, very often used to finish off a junior practice session indoors. Any number can play in two equal teams. Two skittles or similar, or chair to represent wickets, two bat-shapes and a tennis ball, or similar, are all the equipment needed.

Rules

1 The number of complete innings per team should be decided before starting the game.

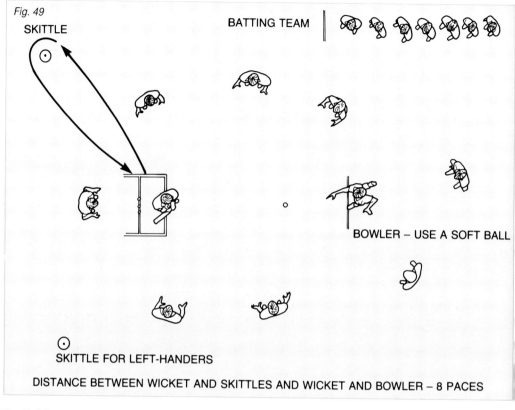

Fig. 49

SKITTLE

BATTING TEAM

BOWLER – USE A SOFT BALL

SKITTLE FOR LEFT-HANDERS

DISTANCE BETWEEN WICKET AND SKITTLES AND WICKET AND BOWLER – 8 PACES

Fig. 49 CONTINUOUS CRICKET

2 The bowler may bowl regardless of whether the batsman is at the wicket and the ball must be delivered underhand, bouncing only once before the wicket.

3 The batsman must run if he hits the ball.

4 To score a run, he must run round the skittle and be in position to receive the next delivery.

5 The batsman can be bowled out or caught only, and the umpire must call *Out* immediately the batsman is dismissed.

6 The next batsman remains seated on the batting chair until the previous man is given out.

7 No-ball is given if the ball bounces more than once before reaching the wickets or if the bowler delivers the ball in front of the bowling mark.

8 Fielders must not be allowed within eight paces of the batsman.

CHAPTER FOUR

The Structure of Cricket

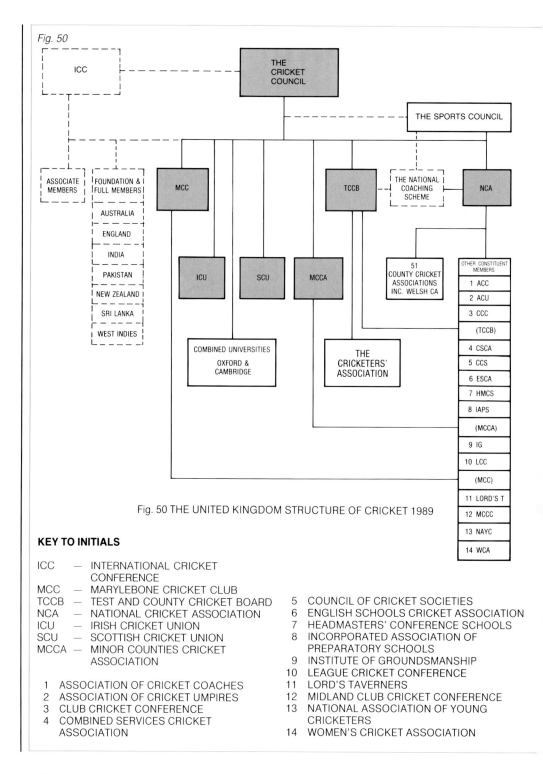

Fig. 50

Fig. 50 THE UNITED KINGDOM STRUCTURE OF CRICKET 1989

KEY TO INITIALS

ICC — INTERNATIONAL CRICKET CONFERENCE
MCC — MARYLEBONE CRICKET CLUB
TCCB — TEST AND COUNTY CRICKET BOARD
NCA — NATIONAL CRICKET ASSOCIATION
ICU — IRISH CRICKET UNION
SCU — SCOTTISH CRICKET UNION
MCCA — MINOR COUNTIES CRICKET ASSOCIATION

1 ASSOCIATION OF CRICKET COACHES
2 ASSOCIATION OF CRICKET UMPIRES
3 CLUB CRICKET CONFERENCE
4 COMBINED SERVICES CRICKET ASSOCIATION
5 COUNCIL OF CRICKET SOCIETIES
6 ENGLISH SCHOOLS CRICKET ASSOCIATION
7 HEADMASTERS' CONFERENCE SCHOOLS
8 INCORPORATED ASSOCIATION OF PREPARATORY SCHOOLS
9 INSTITUTE OF GROUNDSMANSHIP
10 LEAGUE CRICKET CONFERENCE
11 LORD'S TAVERNERS
12 MIDLAND CLUB CRICKET CONFERENCE
13 NATIONAL ASSOCIATION OF YOUNG CRICKETERS
14 WOMEN'S CRICKET ASSOCIATION

No matter what your sport, if it has any substance it is likely to have something of a history and be represented throughout the country by a variety of organisations dedicated to preserving the values the sport has nurtured in its leaders. So it is with cricket, but as the game goes from strength to strength, so do the different organisations and their roles become less defined. For all sorts of reasons, the true names and purposes of the many different organisations are often converted into unrelated initials and misleading titles, that perplex those who follow cricket, giving them little idea of who actually does what. For example, what is the difference between MCC and MCCA? Is ACC something electrical and wasn't ICC quoted in the *Financial Times* this morning, or was it ICI? My colleagues reckon it would be a worthy few pages if I could at least try to bring some semblance of order and recognition to 'what means what' in cricket and where in the jigsaw lie the various pieces.

I can think of no more useful start than to construct a diagram to simplify the task.

The Cricket Council

The Cricket Council is the governing body for cricket in the British Isles (The United Kingdom of Great Britain and Northern Ireland, the Channel Islands, the Isle of Man and the Republic of Ireland). Its constituent members are TCCB, NCA and MCC. In addition, the MCCA, the ICU and the SCU are entitled to appoint one representative at meetings of the Council, although these representatives are not entitled to vote.

In the British Isles the Council fulfils the following roles:

a) acts as the spokesman for the whole of cricket.

b) promotes the well-being and development of cricket.

c) is responsible for the conduct and organisation of cricket.

Background to the Formation of the Cricket Council

Prior to 1968 MCC had generally and traditionally been 'in charge' of cricket in the United Kingdom. Over the years the influence of this private club was immense. There is no question that throughout the world and particularly in this country the volume of cricket played, its world status and simply the amount of work contributed to 'setting up' the game, was a marvellous testimony to MCC. Cricket needs be thankful that MCC was there to hold the reins for so long. Even in 1952 MCC members contributed £15,000 to the MCC Youth Cricket Association, the forerunner of NCA.

County cricket in this period was represented by the Advisory County Cricket Committee and the counties ran Test cricket through a Board of Control. Both bodies were in close liaison with MCC. Three main influences radically changed the set-up as it stood. In 1964 the Government set up the Sports Council to progress the development of all sport in the United Kingdom. The fact that this new body was able to grant well over £1,000,000 in the first few years to fifty-seven different sports indicated the importance of its role in the future of cricket. The second influence came through the then Minister of Sport, Mr Denis Howell, who informed the cricket authorities that government aid could not be granted to a private club but could, within the brief of the Sports Council, be given to a national governing body for cricket, if there was one. The third influence was the parlous financial state of cricket, with the first-class counties struggling for survival and consequently having little if any money to invest in the grass roots of the game. Thus, the creation of the Cricket Council became an obvious solution.

The International Cricket Conference

The ICC is the forum from which member cricket playing countries throughout the world administrate and make rules for the playing of cricket to defined standards. The Conference is responsible for the status of Test matches played between foundation and member countries. This includes the appointment of umpires and the making of qualifying rules for players in Test matches and one-day internationals. ICC also classifies first-class matches.

A match lasting three days or more between two sides of eleven players is the basic qualification for a first-class match. It is the responsibility of foundation and full members of ICC to decide the status of the match in their individual countries.

The inaugural meeting of the Imperial Cricket Conference (it became the International Cricket Conference as recently as 15 July 1965) was held at Lord's on the 15 June 1909, and it was attended by representatives of the MCC, the Australian Board of Control and the South African Cricket Association.

FREDDIE BROWN CBE, man of cricket—Former Captain of England, Chairman of the Cricket Council, President of MCC, President of NCA and much more.

The Indian Board of Control, New Zealand Cricket Council and the West Indies Board of Control were first represented at a meeting held on 31 May 1926. The Board of Control for Cricket in Pakistan was first represented at a meeting held on 21 July 1953. South Africa ceased to be a Member of the Conference on leaving the British Commonwealth in May 1961.

On 15 July 1965, when the name was changed to International Cricket Conference, a new set of rules was adopted. The Board of Control for Cricket in Ceylon (now Sri Lanka), Fiji Cricket Association and United States Cricket Association were elected associate members on the same day.

The Bermuda Cricket Board of Control, Danish Cricket Association, East African Cricket Conference and Royal Netherlands Cricket Association were elected associate members on 14 July 1966. The Malaysian Cricket Association was elected an associate member on 12 July 1967. The Canadian Cricket Association was elected an associate member on 10 July 1968. The Gibraltar and Hong Kong Cricket Associations were elected associate members on 10 June 1969. The Papua New Guinea Cricket Board of Control was elected an associate member on 24 July 1973. The Argentine, Israel and Singapore Cricket Associations were elected associate members on 23 July 1974. The West African Cricket Conference was elected an associate member on 20 July 1976. The Bangladesh Cricket Control Board was elected an associate member on 27 July 1977. The Board of Control for Cricket in Sri Lanka was elected a full member on 21 July 1981. The Kenya Cricket Association and the Zimbabwe Cricket Union were elected associate members on 21 July 1981.

The Sports Council

Amongst the many titles listed in this 'Structure of Cricket', none will be recognised less than the Sports Council and yet few will have made such a contribution to cricket's future in recent years.

The task of providing facilities and developing sporting activities is one of the most challenging facing any country. It was against this background that, in 1972, the Sports Council was established by Royal Charter to develop sport in this country. The Sports Council is an independent body which has overall responsibility for British sports matters. There are separate councils for Scotland, Wales and Northern Ireland and all four work together closely to ensure a consistent approach to common problems.

The Sports Council consists of a Chairman, a Vice Chairman and twenty-two members who are appointed by the Secretary of State for the Environment. The full council meets four times a year and considers general sports matters, in addition to reports and recommendations from its four main committees—Policy and Resources, National Resources, Regional Resources and Publicity, Information and Research.

Apart from the service offered by the Sports Development Unit, there are other specialist units at the headquarters—Technical, Research, Information and Press and Publications, offering advice to anyone concerned with sport and recreation.

In fulfilment of the objectives of its charter, the Sports Council receives an annual grant from central government which it uses to develop sport. The Sports Council seeks to:

a) promote general understanding of the social importance and value of physical recreation.

b) increase provision of new sports facilities and stimulate fuller use of existing facilities.

c) encourage wider participation in sport and physical recreation as a means of enjoying leisure.

d) raise standards of performance.

Capital grants are made towards the provision of facilities which cater primarily for local community use, as well as national and regional projects. The Council supports special projects such as prototype schemes, conversions of existing buildings and projects in areas of special need, particularly those which are low cost and provide for youth participation. Capital grants and loans are also available to voluntary clubs for the development of facilities. Recurrent grants are made to the governing bodies of sport and physical recreation to improve administration, develop participation and improve standards of performance through coaching, preparation training and international events.

Sports Council staff in nine regional offices have the responsibility of implementing the policies of the Sports Council in developing sport according to regional needs, interests and conditions.

In recent years the Sports Council has been responsible for millions of pounds coming into cricket, nationally and through individual grants to regions and clubs.

The Test and County Cricket Board

The TCCB are responsible mainly for:

a) the organisation, administration and promotion of the first-class County Championship and any other competition concerning the first-class counties.

b) the organisation, administration and promotion of Test and other International matches in the United Kingdom, and official tours to and from the British Isles. The eighteen counties (and the year of their formation) that comprise TCCB are:

Derbyshire	1871	Essex	1895
Glamorgan	1921	Gloucestershire	1870
Hampshire	1875	Kent	1864
Lancashire	1865	Leicestershire	1895
Middlesex	1864	Northamptonshire	1905
Nottinghamshire	1864	Somerset	1891
Surrey	1864	Sussex	1864
Warwickshire	1895	Worcestershire	1899
Yorkshire	1864	Durham	1992

Denis Silk: Cambridge University and Somerset CCC, President of MCC (1993–94) and Chairman of TCCB (1995–   ). A true man of cricket in every sense.

The TCCB administration headquarters along with those of MCC and NCA are based at Lord's Cricket Ground.

The county programme takes in:

The County Championship—generally accepted as being started in 1873 with nine counties (Derbyshire, Gloucestershire, Kent, Lancashire, Middlesex, Nottinghamshire, Surrey, Sussex and Yorkshire). Played over three days until recently when four-day matches were introduced on a limited basis. The points scoring system alone has changed over twenty times, nevertheless, the County Championship is the most coveted team trophy in cricket as it remains the test of a team's performance in all aspects of the game throughout the summer.

The NatWest Trophy—formerly the Gillette Cup, a sixty overs-a-side knock-out competition that has produced the most thrilling one-day matches since its inception in 1963.

The Benson and Hedges Cup—inaugurated in 1972, is both a league and a knock-out competition, with matches being played over fifty-five overs each side, taking place mainly in the early part of the county programme. In recent years the competition has become very popular for, like the NatWest Trophy, it produces exciting cricket in a one-day competition.

The AXA Equity League—a forty overs competition, has brought cricket into millions of homes since its inception in 1969.

Every Sunday afternoon one of the county games is televised and whilst this has had its critics, there is no doubt it has added to the summer scene, particularly in the standard of fielding it produces.

Every summer, under the direction of TCCB, one or more of the six other major cricketing countries tour the United Kingdom. Usually at least five Test matches are played in addition to at least three one-day international matches. During the English close season TCCB arrange a programme of tours abroad through ICC when England play a similar programme to that undertaken in the summer. Every four years a World Cup Tournament based on one-day limited over matches is staged. All members and associate members of ICC participate in the World Cup. Cricket is a very busy game all over the world at all levels these days.

J.D. (DON) ROBSON became Chairman of the National Cricket Association in 1977. Very much a man of the North-east, over the years he has had an immense influence on the development of the recreational game.

The National Cricket Association

The NCA is responsible for the organisation, administration and promotion of the recreational game, including the National Coaching Scheme.

The objects of the association are:

a) to encourage the playing of cricket in accordance with the Laws of Cricket and in the best traditions of sportsmanship.

b) to represent and further the interests of the constituent members and to be a channel of communication between such members and the Cricket Council.

c) to administer a coaching scheme on a national basis.

d) to recommend to the Cricket Council application for government grants in respect of:
   i) the administration of the association
   ii) the financing of representative amateur teams at home and abroad
   iii) the provision of coaching
   iv) any other projects for the betterment of cricket.

Constituent members of NCA are fifty-one County Cricket Associations:

Bedfordshire ACC	Durham CA
Berkshire CA	Essex CA
Buckinghamshire CA	Gloucestershire CA
Cambridgeshire CA	Guernsey CA
Cheshire CA	Hampshire CA
Cornwall CA	Herefordshire CA
Cumbria CA	Hertfordshire CA
Derbyshire CA	Hunts &
Devon CA	Peterborough
Dorset CA	Isle of Man CC

151

Isle of Wight CC
Jersey CA
Kent ACC
Lancashire CA
Leicestershire CA
Lincolnshire and
  South Humberside
  CA
Middlesex CU
Norfolk CA
Northamptonshire CA
Northumberland CA
Nottinghamshire CA

Oxfordshire CCA
Rutland CA
Shropshire CA
Somerset CA
Staffs CA
Suffolk CA
Surrey CA
Sussex CA
Warwickshire CA
Welsh CA
Wiltshire CA
Worcestershire CA
Yorkshire CA

Scottish Districts (four):
Border Cricket
  League
East of Scotland CA

Northern District CA
Western CA

Irish Districts (four):
Leinster CU
Munster CU

Northern CU
North West CU

Seventeen other constituent members are: Association of Cricket Coaches, Association of Cricket Umpires, Club Cricket Conference, Combined Services Cricket Association, Council of Cricket Societies, English Schools' Cricket Association, Headmaster's Conference Schools, Incorporated Association of Preparatory Schools, Institute of Groundsmanship, League Cricket Conference, Lord's Taverners, Marylebone Cricket Club, Midlands Club Cricket Conference, Minor Counties' Cricket Association, National Association of Young Cricketers, Test & County Cricket Board, Women's Cricket Association.

The affairs of the association are governed by a council known as the NCA Executive. All constituent members are represented on the council. The day to day management of NCA is undertaken by full-time executives and staff working on behalf of a management committee supported by four sub-committees:

Coaching
Cricket
Finance and General Purposes
Junior and Youth

Through the County Cricket Associations between six and seven thousand cricket clubs are members of NCA. Each club pays an affiliation fee dependent upon the number of teams that play regularly for the club. The other constituent members represent a considerable number of different active cricket interests. For example, ACC has over two thousand registered coaches, ACU has several thousand umpires, and an army of young cricketers play in schools of all denominations represented by ESCA,

(*Opposite*) CRICKET'S BACK ROOM BOYS! NCA National Coaches with the author and (far right) Secretary of NCA, BRIAN ASPITAL. Left to right: LES LENHAM, DAVID WILSON, BOB COTTAM (now with Warwickshire CCC), GRAHAM SAVILLE, BOB CARTER, DOUG FERGUSON.

(*Below*) NCA/NAT WEST UNDER-13 EIGHT-A-SIDE FINALS AT SHERBORNE. This marvellous national competition attracts 900 teams from clubs throughout the country.

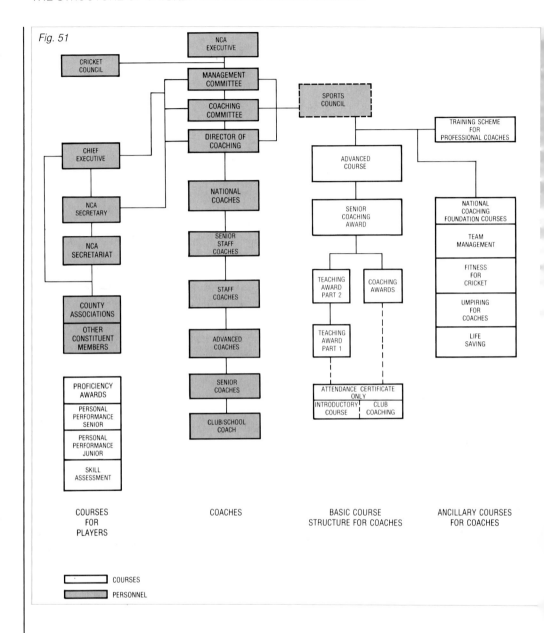

Fig. 51

COURSES FOR PLAYERS	COACHES	BASIC COURSE STRUCTURE FOR COACHES	ANCILLARY COURSES FOR COACHES

COURSES

PERSONNEL

HMCS and IAPS. The NAYC organises representative cricket and major youth festivals at the under-nineteen level for over twenty counties. At international level under-nineteen teams are selected through the combined influence of all constituent members, plus TCCB and MCC, and play regularly at home and abroad. In all, NCA run seven major national competitions, most of which are sponsored.

The National Coaching Scheme employs Director of Coaching at NCA's Lord's head

Fig. 51 THE STRUCTURE OF THE NATIONAL COACHING SCHEME 1989

quarters and National Coaches located in various regions of the country, with the widest brief in the development of cricket and NCA in particular.

The structure of the coaching scheme, as can be seen from the diagram, involves many people and organisations. It is generally based on a series of coaching award courses for coaches, each of which gives a different level of qualification, from the very basic to the very advanced. All courses are supervised and monitored through NCA appointed staff. The corner stone of the scheme is a panel of over one hundred NCA Staff coaches working with National Coaches and individual county cricket associations to ensure the efficient tutoring and examination of over one thousand candidates every year.

Conferences, master classes and special courses for young players are run by NCA every year. It is interesting to note that many county and Test players of the Eighties first made their mark playing in NCA, NAYC and ESCA festivals and competitions from the age of twelve. Coaching of young players at all levels of ability is undertaken through the combined efforts of NCA and ESCA. Since 1992 as many as forty Test Cricketers and two hundred County Cricketers have played for this England U19 team.

Michael Atherton (left) and John Crawley (right) have both come through the various levels of youth cricket training in school and NCA and both have captained England U19 teams with distinction.

MINOR COUNTY PLAYERS

BEDFORDSHIRE	M. I. McLaren	1972
CHESHIRE	S. A. Milner	1972
SHROPSHIRE	B. R. B. Jones	1980
STAFFORDSHIRE	K. Moore	1974

Marylebone Cricket Club

MCC is a private cricket club, founded in 1787, whose home is the Lord's Cricket Ground situated in London, NW8. More about MCC can be found earlier in this book (see pages five to seven).

MCC is responsible for all aspects of the Laws of Cricket and also for the organisation, administration and promotion of senior tours to associate member countries of ICC. By allowing the use of Lord's Cricket Ground for Test matches the MCC is playing a further considerable role in cricket.

Having been such an influence on the development of cricket throughout the world, MCC are generally thought to have a far greater role in the game than in fact they have, although it was only in 1968 with the formation of the Cricket Council that their historic role was diluted.

The Minor Counties Cricket Association

The MCCA was formed at a meeting in Birmingham in March 1895.

Counties that do not come into the category of 'first-class' (see the definition of first-class cricket on page 148) are eligible to become members. The minor counties currently registered are noted along with the year of their formation as follows:

Bedfordshire (1899), Berkshire (1858), Buckinghamshire (1891), Cambridge-shire (1844), Cheshire (1894), Cornwall (1895), Cumberland (1853), Devon (1901), Dorset (1896), Durham (1895), Hertfordshire (1895), Lincolnshire (1870), Norfolk (1827), Northumberland (1896), Oxfordshire (1779), Shropshire (1850), Staffordshire (1871), Suffolk (1864), Wiltshire (1881).

The Minor Counties Competition (Championship) requires each participating county to arrange two, two-day innings, home and away matches with a least four other counties. This format has changed little over the last fifty years. Over the years many first-class county second elevens have participated and in fact they have frequently won the championship, although this is not possible these days as there is a second eleven championsip in existence for the first-class counties which prohibits their involvement in the MCCA competition.

Minor counties cricket has gained an enviable reputation for the manner and the spirit in which matches are played. To some degree the cricket has been a nursery for many fine players who have progressed into the first-class game. Conversely, many household names have returned to play in minor counties cricket after a career in the first-class game.

In recent years and currently, a high position in the Minor Counties Championship has guaranteed places in the lucrative limited over competitions played in the first-class programme. This has ensured a very competitive atmosphere in matches as there is quite a lot at stake financially.

A representative minor counties team has always played a match against the major touring team of the day, invariably acquitting themselves well. Of the many well-known minor counties' players and characters from the past are A.P.F. Chapman, H.E. Dollery, Bill Edrich and Jack Ikin. Popular and successful captains from Cheshire have been David Bailey and Freddie Millett, but one man who has been outstanding, not only in minor county history but in the history of world cricket, is the immortal S.F. Barnes. Sydney Barnes played for Staffordshire between 1904 and 1934 and took 1,441 wickets at an average of 8.15 runs per wicket. He also scored several hundreds for the county.

The Association of Cricket Coaches

The first general meeting of ACC was held in Nottingham on 8 March 1975. The renowned Essex cricketer and coach Harry Crabtree was elected President. Peter Sutcliffe was Chairman and Mike Speak was Secretary. Other stalwarts of the time were Mike Fearnley, Ted Jackson and Colin

A meeting of the NCA Executive at Lilleshall in the early 1980s. Every major cricket organisation in the UK has attended these meetings twice annually for the last twenty-five years.

Gilkes, to name but a few. The association was formed to give those coaches who qualified within the National Coaching Scheme a continued link with NCA coaching developments and interests throughout the country. At the time NCA had little, if any, communication with newly qualified individual coaches.

The success of the association which now has over 2,000 members more than justifies its formation. In another sense it also confirms the success of the National Coaching Scheme through which over 1,000 coaches qualify annually at different levels.

Nowadays ACC members form the coaching arms of many county cricket associations. ACC runs an annual conference and publishes a comprehensive house journal. Like the members of the many organisations mentioned in this chapter, ACC members make an immense contribution to the development of cricket as they influence the young players in clubs and schools throughout the United Kingdom.

David Gower and Ian Botham in their heyday in the 1980s.

The Association of Cricket Umpires

Of all the different organisations that exist in cricket, none can be of greater importance than the ACU.

However and wherever cricket is played, whether it be in a junior school knock-about or a Lord's Test match, without umpires we would have no real game. Furthermore, without reasonably proficient umpires the game would suffer. The umpire can make or break a game of cricket just as much as can the referee in football.

The ACU was founded in 1953 through the initiative of Tom Smith, and for a further twenty-five years Tom was its General Secretary. He did a wonderful job for umpiring and cricket. His book, *Cricket Umpiring and Scoring*, is essential reading in cricket circles. Now with a worldwide membership of several thousand, the association obviously has a very important role to play. Its main objective is to ensure that umpiring is of the highest possible standard in every sense. Training courses leading to examinations allow umpires to have a qualification and thereby a recognition of their knowledge and ability. In recent years, scoring has become part of the ACU responsibility in that training and qualifications for scorers are part of the ACU structure.

The Club Cricket Conference

The CCC was founded in 1915 to work in the interest of club cricket and club cricketers. Its members are 2,300 amateur clubs, comprising about 250,000 cricketers in the counties of Bedfordshire, Berkshire, Buckinghamshire, Cambridge, Devon, Dorset, Essex, Hampshire, Hertfordshire, Kent, Middlesex, Norfolk, Northamptonshire, Oxford, Suffolk, Surrey, Sussex and Wiltshire.

The affairs of the CCC are administered by a council of cricketers, past and present, nominated by member clubs. The council, assisted by a full-time Secretary, represents a vast amount of experience in the game at all levels.

The CCC has many past achievements, not least its active co-operation in the formation of the National Playing Fields Association (NPFA). It has campaigned vigorously and successfully in the interests of clubs and their members, often resulting in legislation at government or local government level, particularly in matters relative to ground preservation and rating assessment. The CCC works closely with the NCA.

Combined Services Cricket Association

With due respect to the RAF, it needs little imagination to visualise the important role the Army and Navy have played in cricket history. The transported and the transporter, if you like, took the game to many other lands hundreds of years ago. It is recorded through the pen of a young naval padre that as early as 1676 in Aleppo the game of 'krickett' was played.

The Services had a connection with the very important occasion in 1744 when the first code of Laws for Cricket was drawn up at the famous Artillery Ground by members of the very influential London Club. The Honourable Artillery Company had owned the ground since 1638, so it is not unreasonable to think that soldiers played there from the very earliest days.

However, in spite of the longevity of Services cricket, the first official inter-Services match between the Army and the Navy was not played until 1908 at Lord's. Not long after that the RAF and the Army did battle at The Oval in 1919. Since the earliest days Services cricket has always enjoyed a great reputation, not only for the calibre and

159

character of its players but for the marvellous atmosphere that pervades its many matches. I well remember my National Service days and the happy and long-lasting associations with men from every rank and walk of life.

I believe that as many as twenty-six National Service cricketers subsequently played Test cricket and I am sure their experience in Services cricket did them no harm at all. How well I remember the astute captaincy of Alan Shirreff and the huge hitting of Bob Wilson. Also J.H.G. Deighton who was an outstanding bowler, played thirteen seasons of Services cricket and was good enough to play in any county side.

Today Services cricket is very much alive, and every July the Combined Services team play at Lord's with just the same spirit as ever, representing all that is best in the game.

The Council of Cricket Societies

Of all the environments in which cricket blooms, none can be warmer than that of a cricket society. One of my personal joys over the years has been in visiting many active societies located throughout the country. The CCS represents its member societies and more importantly a host of cricketing people whose genuine welcome and feeling for cricket is unsurpassed anywhere. There are now approximately thirty societies with a membership getting on for 10,000. They usually meet once a month over the autumn and winter, when speakers from all corners of cricket provide entertainment and serious cricket discussion. Sometimes it is a film evening, occasionally a quiz, it can be a special dinner; but whatever, it is always a cricket occasion and a living testimony to the feeling there is for cricket in this country. Whether your welcome comes from the splendid environs of St James, where *the* Cricket Society (formed in 1945) meet or the lively halls of Wombwell (1951), you will

know they are all the same, as hands are shaken all round and the questions start. Happy memories bring to mind Jack Sokell, Eric Rice, Geoffrey Copinger and a host of others who preserve the life of cricket on the darkest of winter evenings in every corner of the land.

The English Schools Cricket Association

The ESCA was formed in 1948 and represents all types of schools from both the independent and state sectors of education. Every English county is now a member of ESCA and they all run competitions in age groups ranging from under-eleven to under-nineteen. In recent years over 700 matches per year have been played at county and international level under the banner of ESCA.

Individual schools play in major national competitions, financially supported in many instances by the Lord's Taverners. In recent years as many as 2,000 primary schools play in an eight-a-side competition, culminating in finals at Edgbaston, the home of Warwickshire County Cricket Club. Now linked with this is the nationwide junior programme, KWIK CRICKET, initiated by TCCB and developed through ESCA, NCA and thousands of cricketing people dedicated to the 'grass roots' game.

International matches are played regularly against Ireland, Scotland, Wales and touring teams from other cricketing countries. Coaching plays an important part in the ESCA programme and in the various age groups NCA National and Staff Coaches are engaged in the training of the most talented players.

As can be imagined, in a caring organisation such as ESCA many stalwarts have contributed to its very healthy current position. In the early days the legendary Harry

Altham inspired those around him to give ESCA every support. Today's President, Hubert Doggart, is a man of similar ilk, helping to keep the high standards for which ESCA is known. Cyril Cooper MBE, General Secretary for years, has devoted a lifetime to schools cricket, and such men as W.T. (Robbie) Robbins, Ken Ingman, and Dick Procktor along with many others form the tip of an iceberg of men who have contributed more than will ever be known. Indeed, the strength of schools and junior club cricket today can only give parents or the population as a whole, the realisation that as long as the game and the young people that play it are in such good hands they will not come to much harm.

The ESCA Handbook published annually tells its own story of schools cricket and is well worth reading.

The Headmasters' Conference Schools

The HMC is the representative body of about 240 of the most prestigious independent secondary schools, including all those public schools which have historically played such an important role in developing the game. Inter-school fixtures go back to the late eighteenth century and Eton *v.* Harrow is the oldest fixture at Lord's, dating back to 1805. All HMC schools have extensive fixture lists with more than 40,000 boys playing cricket regularly on some of the loveliest and best maintained grounds in the country.

There is a tradition of representative cricket dating back to the first Public Schools' XI selected in 1903, with matches against MCC and the Combined Services. Now this representative cricket is linked with that provided by ESCA so that all schoolboys from whatever sector of education have an equal chance of being selected for national schools' sides. The huge majority of HMC schools are affiliated to county schools' associations, often making their facilities available for coaching and matches. ESCA is recognised as the national schools' body, but the strength of the cricketing infrastructure within HMC schools and their commitment to the nurturing of cricketers of all abilities gives them a very important role in the game.

The Incorporated Association of Preparatory Schools

This association of independent junior schools was founded at the turn of the century to ensure that the very best scholastic and sporting standards were maintained by its members. The playing and proper coaching of cricket was a priority in their policies, to such an extent that the results of cricket matches very often took precedence over everything else in the school curriculum. Consequently, a long tradition of cricket exists in IAPS, with some 110,000 boys now regularly playing competitive cricket each season. Neither will the impetus change, as today more emphasis than ever is placed on proper coaching and the observance of cricket's ethics and traditions. The talents of junior cricketers on the playing fields of Britain are a source of great pride to those who foster these budding international stars. Such men as Tony Pullinger and Mike Glover from the Dragon School and many others like them will continue to ensure that cricket is a game worth playing as a cornerstone of the sporting heritage that makes such an important contribution to the social fabric of the country.

Institute of Groundsmanship

In the early evening of 10 January 1934, eleven keen groundsmen, anxious to preserve and develop their role, met in The

London Stone, a public house on Common Street in the City of London. After some discussion, and no doubt refreshed by a glass or two of ale, they decided to contribute £1 each to found an organisation now well known as the Institute of Groundsmanship. The first President was William Bowles, the Head Groundsman of Eton for almost fifty years.

Today the Institute plays a more than important part in the progress of sport in this country. In particular, groundsmanship of the highest quality is vital to the future of cricket. As such the importance of this progressive organisation cannot be over estimated.

Ireland, Scotland and Wales

Whilst all three countries come under the auspices of the Cricket Council, each has developed its role in cricket in different ways. Although other sports, such as soccer in Scotland and rugby union in Wales and Ireland, are predominant, cricket has its considerable place and holds it very proudly as an important part of each country's sporting heritage.

Ireland

Cricket was first played in Ireland in the early part of the ninteenth century and whilst clubs were formed in North and South, it was not until 1923 that cricket in Ireland came under the single banner of the Irish Cricket Union. There are now many clubs in Ireland, with strong junior sections ensuring the development and progress of the game. Traditionally Irish cricket has been closely linked with MCC and the well-known Irish hospitality has been appreciated by many representative teams. The ICU are nowadays prospering new links with NCA particularly through coaching and by entering teams in interna-

tional competitions. In fact, in 1987 Ireland were the host country for the International Youth Tournament involving six different countries.

Scotland

The Scottish Cricket Union came into being in 1909 but Scottish representative cricket has been played since 1865. In fact, in 1882 the Scottish claimed an historic victory against the touring Australian XI. Over the years there has been great rivalry and generally a very even contest between Scotland and Ireland. Like Ireland, Scotland has very close links with MCC and always provides good opposition to any representative touring team. It is perhaps fair to say that the development of Scottish cricket owes much to the accent placed on cricket in the well-known boarding schools such as Fettes, Melville, Loretto, and others, although the Scottish clubs themselves have always set high standards. Some of the world's great players have been engaged as club professionals. Of the Scotsmen who have played cricket at the highest level, M.H. Denness is perhaps the most famous—he captained England on nineteen occasions.

These days Scottish cricket is closely linked with NCA, and club teams representing Scotland have had much success in the national competitions. One of the six NCA regional National Coaches is based in Scotland and much progress is being made, particularly in the introduction of cricket into junior schools. On the senior front, Scotland continues to play against first-class opposition in limited over games, individual players often having conspicuous success.

Wales

Whilst cricket in Scotland and Ireland follows not a dissimilar pattern, Welsh cricket is quite different in that Glamorgan represents

Wales in the first-class game and is one of the counties that form the TCCB. Glamorgan County Cricket Club was formed in 1888 at Cardiff and attained first-class status in 1921. Always a team worth watching, especially in the field, Glamorgan won their first championship under the inspired leadership of Wilf Wooller, arguably the greatest of all Welsh sportsmen. He played rugby with distinction for Wales and since his very first game for Glamorgan has been in the heart of Welsh cricket—a man of integrity, intelligence and fierce Welsh pride. The County Championship was again won in 1969 under the captaincy of Tony Lewis, another Welshman of outstanding personality and quiet charm, nowadays a well-known broadcaster, author and journalist. Tony's contribution to cricket has yet to be measured, but when it is, there will be few in the game's history to surpass it.

Occasional imports have graced Glamorgan teams, Majid Khan of Pakistan being the most respected and probably the best batsman, but it was the home-grown players such as Emrys Davies, Haydn Davies and Don Shepherd who gave them the solid platform on which Glamorgan's reputation was built. Many fine players have represented Glamorgan, some of them learning the game in the competitive atmosphere of Welsh league cricket.

Due to the geographic structure of Wales, as in many other places, there appeared a north/south divide, certainly in cricket terms. This is not unusual in any country as transportation in cricket until recent times restricted co-operation of any form, simply on economic grounds. Nevertheless, as in Ireland and Scotland, club and league cricket maintained a position in both the North and the South, through such clubs as Bangor and Swansea, until in 1969 the Welsh Cricket Association was formed. Linked to NCA and with a similar structure, the WCA is going from strength to strength. The development of young cricketers in Wales has been supported by the appointment of Tom Cartwright, one of cricket's finest coaches, as the Welsh National Coach. The future of cricket in Wales is secure.

The League Cricket Conference

League cricket has been played for over a hundred years but not until 1962 did the different leagues readily come together. Probably this late formation of a body with such influence in cricket was simply a result of the success and independence of each individual League. The LCC is as northern orientated as its related organisation the CCC is southern orientated. Together they form a mass of cricket experience, knowledge and opinion that has been a great support to the promotion and development of the NCA.

Up to sixty different leagues contribute to the LCC, representing an enormous number of cricket clubs and players. Every cricket organisation has its personalities and the LCC is no different from the others, with Doug Schofield and Bob Cherry being just two of that special group of cricketing people that make this game what it is.

Lord's Taverners

The Lord's Taverners, 'born' about 1950, was the idea of Martin Boddy, one-time opera singer turned actor. Martin came to the conclusion that the group of cricket lovers, many of them fellow actors, with whom he would often share a beer whilst watching the cricket at Lord's, should get together and perhaps contribute to those less fortunate. Martin Boddy had two special friends, Michael Shepley and Spike Hughes, fellow actors and cricket enthusiasts. The three launched the Taverners with the hope of raising a few pounds for the National Playing Fields Association so that young cricketers might learn to enjoy the game in better conditions than they might otherwise have done. The legendary doyen of English cricket, Sir Pelham Warner, became the first Taverner and HRH Prince Philip warmed to the idea of becoming Patron and 'Twelfth Man'. From those early days the Lord's Taverners through their hundreds of distinguished members from all walks of life has raised millions of pounds as a sporting charity.

Their objectives are:

a) to provide a sporting challenge for youngsters and, in particular, through the playing of team games such as cricket.

b) to provide through the NPFA adventure playgrounds for underprivileged children and 'help keep them off the streets'.

c) to provide minibuses for handicapped children to enable them to get into the fresh air and away from the confines of hospitals and homes. The buses are named 'New Horizons'.

Between 1982 and 1986 the Lord's Taverners donated the magnificent sum of £747,691 to 'grass roots' cricket, and their marvellous efforts continue.

Midlands Club Cricket Conference

Founded in 1947, the MCCC has had enormous influence on the development of cricket over an area which, some might say, extends beyond the Midlands, such is the strength of this organisation.

Today, with six hundred plus member clubs, it continues to foster all that is best in the game. A very comprehensive Annual Handbook well identifies its role, and a list of past Presidents, not least of which is the legendary former Secretary of Warwickshire, Leslie Deakins, gives some idea of the quality of its management.

The National Association of Young Cricketers

The NAYC was formed in 1963 by members of the National Club Cricket Association, who were concerned by the lack of interest in youth cricket from authorities other than schools. Within one year, twenty-two counties were members of NAYC and from those early days literally thousands of fine young cricketers have been encouraged to reach the very highest levels of performance. The Oxford and Cambridge Festival and the annual NAYC v. MCC match at Lord's are the highlights of an inter-county programme that sees all the best in the development of young cricketers. Many stalwarts have played their part in guiding players into cricket from every part of the country and none more so than Jack Overy OBE from Kent who first became Chairman of the Association in 1967. Today NAYC is closely associated with NCA and continues its busy programme through many counties. The Hilda Overy Trophy has been keenly competed for since 1969 and is today ample evidence of another success story in cricket.

The Cricketers' Association

The thought of a cricketers' association within the first-class game, representing the interests of contracted players, could have been nothing but a figment of the imagination to those who knew cricket before the 1960s. Until then the professional cricketer had little say in the conduct of the game and even less in the collective welfare of professional players. Perhaps the economics of county cricket before the Second World War and the rigid views that prevailed made it impossible for a common voice to be heard. In most circumstances I imagine there was no need for a representative view and if there had been it was unlikely that it would have been given a hearing. The balance between good amateur players and successful professionals was such that both were happy in their positions. Looking on from afar there seems to have been a respect from both sides, born of tradition and controlled by those who held the purse strings of the county cricket clubs.

However, the wider freedom in society after the two wars progressively gave birth to a different attitude. The decline in cricket's fortunes in the early Sixties further opened the door to the entrepreneurs of business and thus to the increase in financial backing that resulted in giving the players (by this time the number of true amateurs was minimal) a desire for an influential voice in their own destiny.

It was destiny that brought Fred Rumsey of Derbyshire, Somerset and England into the right place at the right time. He was certainly the right man as he inspired the beginnings of the association in such a way that it was accepted by the hierarchy almost immediately. The election of John Arlott as President proved to be another blessing and with the further thoughtful, but firm, guidance of Warwickshire's Jack Bannister as Secretary the mix was as perfect as it could be. From then on the Test and County Cricket Board and the Cricketers' Association affairs were conducted as a partnership. County captains David Brown of Warwickshire and Geoff Cook of Northants became respected Chairmen and, all in all, the examples set over a period of twenty years could well be a model for government in any sphere. Difficult times there have undoubtedly been, but all have been negotiated with dignity.

The Universities

Any dialogue on the structure of cricket could never be complete without some discourse on the role played by the Universities and particularly by the two great cricketing universities, Oxford and Cambridge.

The first Varsity Cricket Match took place between Oxford and Cambridge in 1827. It is the oldest first-class fixture and has taken place regularly since then with the exception of the war years. The match was and is played at Lord's. Many volumes would be necessary to bring together all the illustrious names and deeds of the cricketers who have represented the dark and light blues of Oxford and Cambridge. The list of rival captains alone identifies men who have captained England and the county clubs, in some cases almost exclusively for well over a hundred years. Cricket administrators who have dominated the first-class game and MCC throughout cricket history are similarly made up of Oxford and Cambridge cricketers, highlighting the importance of these great institutions. That cricket has evolved into the game it is today, with its high standards being recognised throughout the world, is to their eternal credit.

Perhaps the one man who should be congratulated above all others is the man who began it all, Charles Wordsworth. He not only originated and organised the University Cricket Match but also the Boat Race. In 1829 he performed in both within two days. Unfortunately, in organising the Boat Race to take place before the cricket match he was not able to do himself justice as a batsman at Lord's. His hands were still very sore from rowing! I have no doubt however that a man of such initiative and versatility did not allow such a possibility to occur again.

Obviously, with the traditions of Oxford and Cambridge being so firmly established, it was unlikely that the other 'red brick' universities would develop a similar role in cricket.

However, in recent years there have been signs that changes are in the offing, with Loughborough and Durham leading the way. In fact, there is now a Combined Universities team that plays against the first-class counties in national limited over competitions. A sign of the times no doubt, but never should the contribution that Oxford and Cambridge have made to cricket be forgotten.

The Women's Cricket Association

The WCA came into being in 1926 when a group of hockey and lacrosse players in Colwall, Worcestershire, decided to form a body to promote women's cricket. Colwall remains the venue for the annual women's cricket week.

In 1929 the 5oz ball was adopted as standard use for women, against the 5½oz ball used by men; and in 1931 the Australian Women's Cricket Council was formed. The first Test between England and Australia was in Brisbane in 1934, the two sides meeting again in 1937 in England. The 1987 tour of England by Australia marked the fiftieth Jubilee of Test cricket between the two countries.

The first recorded women's cricket match in England was in 1745 on Gosden Common, Bramley, Surrey, and a highly successful commemorative match was played at the same venue in June 1986, to mark the WCA's diamond jubilee.

These days a full calendar of events is run for juniors (under-nineteen) and young England (under-twenty-five) as well as for seniors. There are regular indoor and outdoor six-a-side competitions and a recently introduced eight-a-side indoor tournament.

The headquarters of the WCA is located at Edgbaston, home of Warwickshire County Cricket Club.

The England team at Lord's following their famous victory over New Zealand in the final of the 1993 World Cup.

CHAPTER FIVE

Cricket Equipment and Grounds

EQUIPMENT

There is a popular misconception that cricket equipment is expensive and this precludes the playing of the game to some extent. It is true that, as in all sports, individuals like to have their own special or favourite equipment and sometimes, as in the case of a hand-finished bat for example, the price of such individuality can be relatively high. However, many clubs and schools provide cheaper, hard-wearing equipment that is quite adequate. In fact, the cost of equipment varies considerably and every need can be catered for with the less expensive kit without detracting in any way from the enjoyment of the game.

Of course, within cricket's traditions the English leather ball with its hand-stitched seam is preserved with great care for the first-class game and Test matches, but there is absolutely no reason to consider traditions to that degree when money is tight and the players are simply looking for an enjoyable game. I am sure many readers will, like me, have learned to play the game with an old tennis ball or a 'corkie' and a bat shape cut out of an old wooden box.

As in most things, you pay for what you get in material terms, but in sporting enjoyment this is not necessarily the case. However, as a young player improves it is quite understandable that he will look, or perhaps hope for a bat autographed by a favourite Test cricketer.

Of all the items of cricket equipment, a cricketer's bat is the most personal and enduring. In the museum at Lord's bats used by the legendary batsmen in cricket history are preserved. They are well worth seeing, especially when you consider how they came to be there. Imagine Bradman's 334 at Leeds in the Thirties. But how on earth did W.G. Grace manage to score a double century with a bat looking like it does in the dullness of a glass showcase? In fact, there is not that much difference between the bats of today and those of two hundred and more years ago. They are still made from English willow, they are still produced with a feeling for their use. I have met most of the bat manufacturers and many of the craftsmen they still employ. Of all the tools of a trade, bats are still very special.

So, how do you select one? If you are a young player you should take the advice of an experienced coach or player. Take your time in making a choice and look for the following qualities. Firstly, the bat has to be the right weight. A good test is for the batsman to complete a full back-lift, using the top hand only on the bat handle. Once a bat of the right weight and handle has been selected (short or long handle, depending upon the height and stance of the individual batsman), balance is the key factor. A well balanced bat with the weight located at the 'sweet spot' in the middle of the bat, will pick up easily and immediately feel comfortable to the batsman. When a batsman comes across a bat that is well balanced and has a comfortable feel about it then that is the bat to have—and such treasures are not always the brand new, expensive items that one would expect. Australian Jock Livingston, a fine cricketer and a good friend who has spent many years in the sports trade, tells me that bats with few vertical grains are generally softer with more spring in the face than the close-grained bats which tend to be harder-wearing.

If you are buying a bat or bats for the club, do not turn your nose up at the vellum covered varieties. They can be very good value for money in the rough and tumble of life in the dressing-room—and they withstand the rigours of rain and rough treatment much better than their more sophisticated relatives.

Once a bat is selected it should be 'broken in' by progressively bouncing a good leather ball on the face. Before 'breaking in', a good quality bat oil (linseed) should be applied to both the front and the back of the bat to act as a weather seal, avoiding the splice. Most manufacturers give instructions on bat care and maintenance. Remember to clean all the dirt off your bat after every innings—it can be a pleasurable occupation if the bat has done you proud and scored a lot of runs. Make sure the rubber grip is in good condition—nothing is more annoying than to find yourself at the wicket with a bat that you cannot grip properly.

I recommend the purchase of good quality pads—they last much longer and are far better value for money. If you are a wicketkeeper, the 'Rod Marsh' style pads without the knee-flaps are good (but not for batting). If you are on a tight budget a pair of the lightest batting pads are adequate for wicketkeeping. Remember to cut the leg straps to the right length, when first purchased they are often too long and untidy. Buckskin is more expensive than canvas but longer wearing. Keeping pads clean and very white helps to preserve them.

Wicket-keeping gloves mean as much if not more to the 'keeper than a personal bat does to its owner. Properly selected and prepared gloves are a wicket-keeper's lifeline. The difference between the personal gloves of a top-class wicket-keeper and those 'boards' that may be a part of the club 'kit' are such that even if the world's best wicket-keeper uses the uncared for 'boards', as I call them, I guarantee that he would not last long in the team. If you are the wicket-keeper who has to use the communal gloves, obtain permission to look after them personally.

New gloves should be 'broken in' by striking the face with the bottom of an old bat. This will soften them and form a good 'cup' in each palm, ready for a lot of ball-catching in both gloves. An application of leather dressing on the gloves will generally soften the backs so that they can be easily removed to throw the ball 'by hand' in run-out situations. Chamois or good quality cotton inner gloves are essential to prevent finger injuries, and for comfort I favour a not too tight elastic band round the wrist. Some wicket-keepers bind their fingers or the inners themselves with adhesive tape but this is not essential unless you are regularly keeping wicket for long periods.

Batting gloves, whilst not quite as individual as wicket-keeping gloves, are nevertheless important. If a batsman is to control the bat effectively throughout an innings, soft, well-fitting gloves are essential. Batting gloves, again like wicket-keeping gloves, should give the user 'feel'. At the same time it is essential that proper quality protection is built into the design of the gloves. Finger injuries, often serious, are simply a direct result of wearing poor quality batting gloves with inadequate padding.

If you are to enjoy your cricket it is important to be well shod. Modern cricket boots are marvellous in every respect. They are light and extremely comfortable without costing the earth. Spikes are an essential for bowlers in all weathers. In dry weather and for use indoors, rubber-studded footwear for batting, fielding or wicket-keeping is satisfactory. Keeping footwear clean and very white is as important, or should be, as cleaning your teeth. In fact, in all aspects of dress, clean and well cared-for gear reflects the character and usually the quality of the player—and his team. Good woollen socks are important for foot health and a woollen vest on cold days will save hours of discomfort later, especially when bowlers have perspired and tend to stiffen up in cold weather. Neither is it much use having a sweater if it is not a warm one.

Caps do not seem to be as much a part of the cricket scene as they were, but some players find them useful to keep hair from flying about and distracting attention from the action part of the game.

Helmets, at least for both batsmen, are an essential. I am not certain whether they should be offered to fielders—I know they are at the moment but I think there should be a minimum distance allowed between fielder and batsman. Helmets for fielders can, in my opinion, have an adverse effect on the game, by giving the fielder the confidence to field too close to the bat. This not only inhibits the batsman but in some instances also the bowler who tends to bowl 'away' from the close-in fielder to avoid contributing to possible injury.

Of all the items of cricketing equipment, however, it is quite obvious that bats and balls hold the most special place in history. Through these traditional 'tools of the trade', and those that use them, the game of today has been moulded. In 1979, Hugh Barty-King was responsible for writing a most entertaining book with the equally delightful title of *Quilt Winders and Pod Shavers*. Published by Macdonald and Janes Ltd., it is more than a history of bat- and ball-making. It presents another fascinating picture of life in the early, golden days of cricket.

Cricket Bat Manufacture

The bat had evolved in shape from a simple club-like stick to the recognisable ancestor of the modern implement by the mid-eighteenth century. In those days it was fashioned from solid wood, and the jar that resulted from hitting a ball hard was a palm-tingling experience. Then, in the 1850s, a Lord's cricket professional, Thomas Nixon, made a bat with a resilient, shock-absorbing cane handle spliced into the blade. His 'springy' handle set a pattern that has survived, and been improved over the years by the insertion of other materials such as gutta-percha, whalebone, cork and rubber for even greater comfort and resilience. The blade arrived at its present shape, straight-sided with a bulge known as the 'meat' about two-thirds of the way down the back, by around 1775, but subtle variations of that shape have been and still are the province of the bat-makers, each with his own theory of what constitutes perfection.

The maker has a free hand within maximum dimensions fixed as long ago as 1835; the bat must be no more than $4\frac{1}{4}$ inches wide and 38 inches long.

There are many varieties of willow but few suitable for making cricket bats. Of these the best is *Salix alba caerulea*, which can grow up to 100 feet tall. It is close-grained, resilient and, when seasoned, resistant to splitting. The bat-maker quite often cultivates his own willow; otherwise he buys it from a willow plantation owner or timber merchant.

Bat willows are grown from cuttings known as 'setts'. They are selected for cultivation when they are 12 feet high and must be perfectly free from knots and blemishes. In their first years they may need to be protected from damage by cattle and wild animals, and the trunk is kept free from branches for its first 10 feet by rubbing off shoots and buds. They grow fast—one giant willow felled at Boreham, Essex, in 1888 was 111 feet tall, weighed 11 tons and was fifty-three years old. It made 1,179 bats, each one 'sound as a bell'. The normal age of a tree considered large enough for bat-making is ten to twelve years.

Handles are made from Sarawak cane. The long canes are all $\frac{1}{2}-\frac{5}{8}$ of an inch in diameter. When needed, they are cut into sections of varying sizes, according to the length of the handles required. Then they are

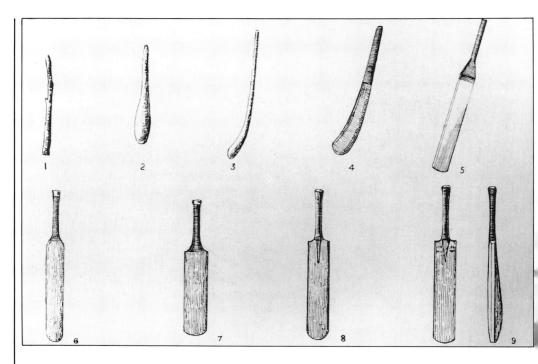

The evolution of THE BAT.

1. Piece of stick	6. Skyscraper
2. Club	7. Shouldered bat
3. Battes	8. Spliced bat
4. Curved bat	9. Present-day bat
5. Batten bat	

carefully sorted and put through a cane-splitting machine, which also planes them into squared sections. Each handle is made up from twelve to sixteen of these sections, with 'springs' of resilient, shock-absorbing material inserted. They are glued together then turned to shape on a special lathe which gives them a slightly oval, rather than round, section for better grip. The fitting of the handle to the bat and the final finishing processes are completed by highly skilled craftsmen.

Cricket Ball Manufacture

Over the years, craftsmen responsible for the manufacture of traditional cricket balls have come from generation after generation of the same families in the west of Kent. Several of the terms used in cricket ball manufacture originated in other leather-working crafts. The closer—a name borrowed from the shoe-making trade—makes covers from prepared strips of white cowhide cut into quarters, then he sews up two quarters into half covers. The turner stretches the halves and glues 'false quarters' of leather on the insides as reinforcement. He bangs out the ridge where the quarters were stitched together and stamps the halves to the right size and shape around moulds in a hydraulic press. Surplus leather is trimmed off under a turning press. Years ago only knives and hand-presses were used. The few machines that are used today, however, do little more than speed up what is still very much a handcraft.

By this stage the centres have already been made. Only a few years ago the 'quilts'—a term borrowed from the saddler's craft—were made by hand, but today they are

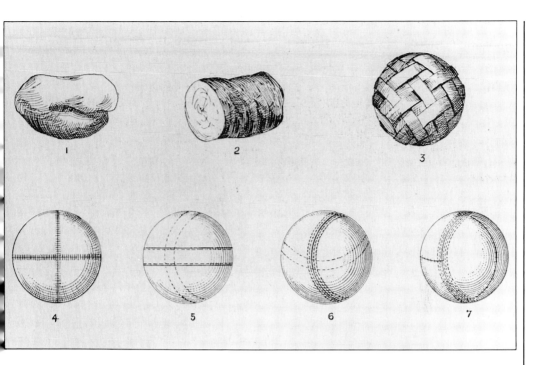

The evolution of THE BALL.
1. A stone
2. Piece of wood
3. Hidebound ball
4. Small's ball
5 & 6. Other improved balls
7. Present-day ball

mostly machine-moulded. This is the only radical departure from traditional methods of manufacture. The quilt-maker used to take a 1-inch cube of cork and wind up to eight alternate layers of worsted and cork strips around it. Since the worsted was worked wet, it tightened around the cork as it dried out and shrank. It was this process that gave the ball its bounce. Occasionally the quilt was hammered in a mould to make it spherical, but the quilt-makers only other tools were a gauge and an experienced eye. With these, a skilled craftsman could transform the cube into a perfectly round ball in about a quarter of an hour.

Machine-moulds can now produce sixty identical centres in the same time. A tapered strip of material, consisting of a layer of cork and terylene fibre and a layer of rubber, is wrapped around a rubber core. This is then moulded into a ball in a press.

After a fitter has weighed the centre and matched it up with the cover, a seamer places it inside the two halves which he then stitches up. The ball is held in a seamer's vice so that the seam stands proud; this stretches the leather to ensure a tight fit and makes the seam easier to sew. Depending on the quality of the ball, the seamer sews exactly eighty, seventy or sixty stitches into the seam. He has nothing to guide him but his eye.

In the finishing department, the balls are stamped with gold leaf and moulded for up to twenty minutes in screw-presses until they are perfectly shaped. They are then tested by eye, feel, and also on gauges and scales. Finally, they are polished. Each craftsman—closer, turner, fitter, seamer and stitcher—has left his own mark on the ball in the form of a letter, a figure or a collection of dots. If anything is wrong, the ball can be sent back to the man responsible.

In 1950 there were seven factories producing handmade cricket balls in West Kent. Appropriately, it is the area in which the origins of cricket were first discovered. In all, they employed more than two hundred craftsmen. Today, there is nothing like that number, but as long as first-class cricket is played in England there will be a need for craftsmen to produce the finest leather balls.

Having said this, we must remember that only a very small part of cricket played in the country comes under the heading of 'first-class'. So let us accept that only in certain sections of the game is it necessary to retain all the traditional materials. Of course, it is marvellous to play with the highest quality English-made leather cricket ball, but is it really necessary for practice and junior cricket when the cost of such a ball is so high? Manufacturers, and there are few left, have some good alternatives to offer.

John Reader the grandson of Alfred Reader (one of the traditional ball manufacturers in Kent) is a great innovator and now produces a variety of cricket balls, still in the old factory, still with care, that will satisfy even the most discerning customer. 'Value for money' needs to be the watchword in buying cricket balls as in everything else—and remember that hard balls break soft expensive bats. So choose carefully.

THE CRICKET GROUND

One of the many attractions of cricket is the variety of grounds on which the game is played—several thousand of them all over the world, all different, many beautiful in their surroundings, others less so.

Years ago, as a young man, I had the privilege of playing cricket on some of the most spectacular grounds: Sydney, Australia's palladium of cricket, with the barrackers on 'the Hill' at their most inventive; Calcutta, hot and spicy, with the music of India swelling above the noise of an 80,000 crowd just before play, taking me into another world. In a similar vein, Karachi on the edge of the Sind desert and a wicket to match, at least in colour, on which Steve Davis might easily make a hundred. When we played at Bridgetown in Barbados, the wicket there, appeared to have been polished, such was the shine on it. Two days later it showed no change other than the fact that the late and much loved Frank Worrell, (later Sir Frank) together with his equally revered fellow knight of today, Sir Garfield Sobers, had put together a stand of 399 for the fourth wicket. Heady days indeed, but returning as I did to the county game in such places as Taunton and Trent Bridge, Bradford and Bath, I was conscious that though the accents changed, the feeling did not. How different they all are, these homes of cricket, from Test match arena to village green, but how real is their welcome, as they stand at the start of play, trim and prepared, wickets set, umpires out, all ready for the match to commence.

The Playing Surface

'The state of the wicket' is cricket's eternal talking point and as much as any of the many oddities in cricket, the discussion, argument, assessment, condemnation, mythology, speculation, you name it, has all been said before. We do not even agree as to what the playing surface is really called. Officially, it is the pitch, but most cricketers call the pitch the wicket. I take either as being satisfactory and I hope the reader will also. I know at least one colleague of mine who will not let me get away with such a bland statement, but if I am not going to take up too much time on the matter, let it rest there.

What about the other uses of the terms 'pitch' and 'wicket'? Each has more than one description. 'Pitch' can mean the point at which a thrown or bowled ball first lands after its flight. 'Wicket' can be the term for the three stumps surmounted by two bails. When the bails are removed in an attempt, successful or otherwise, to dismiss a batsman during a match, the wicket is broken. But for the purpose of this writing, I shall be as most cricketers, and use the word 'wicket' to describe the playing surface.

In considering the wicket it would be very easy to move into the specialised subject of groundsmanship as we talk about top soil and sub-base and such things, but again, I will attempt to keep it simple. Most cricketers like to play on a dry surface with a reasonable bounce from a good length (not much more than stump height). If the surface (generally soil) is dry and has been well drained and flattened by plenty of heavy rolling, it is likely to bounce evenly and with more pace, depending upon the hardness of the surface. Providing also the grass roots bind the soil, it will form a firm playing surface, particularly if it contains a high percentage of clay. This type of wicket will be termed 'fast' and good to bat on, whilst giving a fast bowler a chance of success if he bowls accurately and a spin

PERTH, WESTERN AUSTRALIA, one of the world's fastest wickets in the Eighties. The end of the Australia v. England Test match, 1982.

bowler a similar chance of success if he can really spin the ball.

Should the surface be very well grassed, wet, or cracked and dusty, so the wicket will be less pleasant to bat upon, as very often the bowler can make the ball move laterally off the wicket as it pitches. This lateral (sideways) movement can be obtained by a pronounced vertical seam hitting the ground in such a way that it causes deviation. Another form of lateral movement (spin) can be obtained by rotating or spinning the ball at right angles, or near enough, to its line of flight so that deviation occurs on landing because of the ball spinning around a horizontal axis. A loose, dusty surface enables greater deviation to be obtained through the ball (and seam of the ball) gripping the loose surface. A wet, drying surface,

causing the soil to be 'tacky', allows an even greater degree of spin from the wicket. This is very often referred to as a 'sticky wicket', and is generally acknowledged to be most suitable for spin bowling. So the wicket or the state of it complicates cricket discussion—but it is a part of cricket lore and as such has a definite, even vital role to play. Some of the most experienced groundsmen are great disciples of the heavy roller on well-drained ground.

The Outfield

The wicket obviously takes up much preparation time, very often to the detriment of the ground as a whole. The outfield is as important as the wicket, for its state can easily affect the enjoyment of a cricket match. If the grass is left long and unrolled, the outfield is slow and runs are difficult to score. The game can easily become equally slow and boring. Outfields should have as fast a surface as possible. This ensures that instead of singles, boundaries (fours) are scored and the whole tempo of the game is lifted. Fielding can also be so much more sure and spectacular, again for the enjoyment of all. I have always thought that in some areas of cricket, even Test matches, a non-turf outfield makes good sense, particularly in the English climate.

If a club is lucky enough to have the opportunity of constructing a new pavilion, it is worth taking some care in its location. Building the pavilion higher than the rest of the ground gives spectators a better overall view of the game, and somehow the action in the middle seems nearer when viewed from above. A good position for the pavilion viewing area on the compass can be facing south-south-east which will ensure sunshine on the front of the pavilion all day (with luck). This is assuming the ground allows the wickets to be pitched north/south, avoiding the setting sun in the West disturbing the batsman's vision.

Fig. 52 SUGGESTED LOCATION OF THE PAVILION AND PITCH DIRECTION

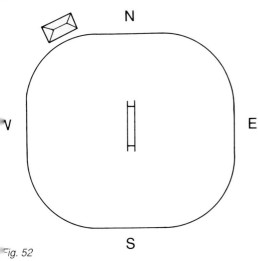

Fig. 52

The Groundsman

Cricket groundsmen, some say, are a dying breed. I hope not, as they are special men of the game. The true cricket groundsman has a feeling for his ground and is worth his weight in gold. Sadly, and maybe too late, the value of the good groundsman is only just becoming recognised. Cricket people are funny: we turn up, play and enjoy the game and, with the crowd if there is one, complain about the conditions at the drop of a hat.

It is surely time we looked at our priorities! Is it so difficult, when we can put a man on the moon, to produce twenty-two yards of soil on which a leather ball will bounce consistently to a reasonable height? Do you not think we should give our groundsmen more credibility and more help?

Drainage is All Important

If a cricket square/ground has a light subsoil of a sandy or gravel texture, artificial drainage may not be needed. If the subsoil is heavy (clay etc.), artificial drainage is essential. Labour on a cricket ground is important, voluntary work by many hands can help an overworked groundsman—but no matter how much time is put into the making of a good ground, the basic ingredients are the most important, and so, if your ground or your wicket is not what it should be to produce good cricket, consult an expert; it will be well worthwhile.

The Non-Turf (Artificial) Wicket

Some of the best and most enjoyable matches I have seen in recent years have been played on non-turf wickets. Economically and very often from a playing point of view, they can be far and away ahead of the traditional wicket. I feel something of a heretic in saying that, but one has to be realistic. In some areas of this country where cricket can give so much to the population, it is hardly likely that we will be able to engage the quality of groundsman that is needed to produce a good natural turf wicket, more's the pity!

A non-turf wicket is a commercially produced top surface laid on a sub-base, commercial or natural, to reproduce conditions for cricket that may be compared to those obtained from the very best turf wickets. Different materials are used, but in general a mat (which could be synthetic turf, rubberised pad or a carpet-like material) is laid on a a prepared base of either solid (concrete-type) or hard porous material. In certain circumstances a mat can be laid directly on to a prepared ground surface. It is essential that time is taken to:

1) Identify the type of pitch required.
2) Select the correct base.
3) Select the top surface to meet the requirements of the situation.

Indoors a solid base is likely to be used, whereas outdoors a hard porous base is used with a synthetic turf or carpet-type material. Whilst non-turf pitches are excellent in practice nets, they are equally effective when used adjacent to the square for junior/senior matches on the main cricket ground.

CHAPTER SIX

Enjoying Cricket Off the Field

FAVOURITE WRITINGS and AUTHORS

I have never really been sure as to whether I prefer to play cricket, watch cricket or read about cricket. Playing can be more than frustrating, as we all know: a first baller, a 'green' wicket when you are a spin bowler or vice versa, or standing at first slip without an edge all day. Even wicket-keeping has its frustrations, especially on a slow but true batting wicket, when hardly a ball beats the bat.

Watching can be similarly disappointing, especially when your hero gets out first ball, or, should he be a bowler, pulls a muscle in his first over; and nothing is worse than watching a poor fielding side badly captained. Even if all is well with your team there is always the vagaries of weather that can depress the most avid watcher of the game.

With reading, however, one can have it always. You can pick your captain (author) and your team, decide on whether to bat, even select your favourite batsman and his best innings. The most attractive grounds are at your disposal and after a real match one can very quickly read every possible different version of it. On another front, from a practical book it is very easy to learn how to play every stroke and bowl with the most classical action—you simply need to mentally absorb the skills described. When some fiercely controversial point is being contested, specific reading can come in very handy, especially as marathon volumes of statistical information abound these days in cricket literature. No wonder cricket quizzes are the 'in thing' for cricket lovers on winter evenings.

What of biographies? Not to be confused with autobiographies or travelogues as they are sometimes called when concerned with cricket. Of course, a good, well-researched biography can be the most stimulating read and a number of classics have been written over the years. Nothing is worse though, than the hastily put together story of some young phenomenon's life up to the age of twenty, when you read within the first few pages that the hero's mother was entirely responsible for his masterly late cut (in more than one sense of the word)!

So to my desert island choice of cricket books.

AN EYE FOR CRICKET by Patrick Eagar and John Arlott (published by Hodder and Stoughton in 1979)

This book, through its photographs, makes moments in cricket live in such a way that even the brilliant words of John Arlott for once take second place, and I am sure he will not mind me saying this. Patrick Eagar's favourite pictures remind me, and I hope you, of our good fortune in being able to not only see, but somehow feel so many of cricket's very special moments. My selfish complaint is that the book is not twice the size with each black and white photograph also reproduced in colour!

THE ART OF CRICKET by Robin Simon and Alistair Smart (published by Secker and Warburg in 1983)

This is a book that tells the story of art in cricket or cricket in art, whichever way you want it. What I like about it is that through meticulous research the authors have brought to life a section of cricket history that normally would only be appreciated by the cricket art enthusiast. With great respect this book deserves the widest possible audience. An unhurried journey through its pages will give great pleasure to any cricket lover uninitiated into this field of cricket history.

AS I SAID AT THE TIME A Lifetime of Cricket by E.W. Swanton (published by Collins Willow in 1983)

Whilst I have not always agreed with the technical content of Jim Swanton's cricket reports I cannot help but admire the charm of his writings. This is a cricket book by a great author who obviously loves his subject.

BARCLAY'S WORLD OF CRICKET 1986 Edition. General Editor—E.W. Swanton, Assistant Editor—John Woodcock (published by Collins Ltd in association with Barclay's Bank International)

When thumbing through this giant of cricket literature, brilliantly brought together by Jim Swanton and John Woodcock and possibly influenced by the late and great Harry Altham in his *History of Cricket*, I am severely tempted to change my mind about *The Cricketer's Companion* being my number one choice of book. In approximately three quarters of a million words contained in large and beautifully produced pages, a myriad of contributors ensure that the title is fully justified and that includes the subtitle, *The A to Z of Cricket*. If there ever was an A to Z of cricket, this is it. Of all the books I have ever read, none have contained such a volume of detailed information. Whilst statistics are an essential part of the book, never at any time are they put forward in anything but a concise and interesting style. It truly is A WORLD OF CRICKET and a magnificent and beautiful book. It is also excellent value for money.

BEYOND A BOUNDARY by C.L.R. James (published by Hutchinson in 1963)

This is more than a book on cricket—it is the classic story of one man's life and his love affair with the game. It could only have been written by a West Indian.

BRIGHTLY FADES THE DON by Jack Fingleton (published by Collins in 1949)

Some books are very well written by authors who are far removed from their subjects, but this can hardly be possible for the great books. Certainly in terms of a biography it must be almost an essential for the author to have a close association with the subject, if only through the most exhaustive and thorough research. So it is with Jack Fingleton and Don Bradman in this classic Australian cricket book. In 1977, during the Centenary match, I had the pleasure and privilege of walking from the Windsor Hotel in Melbourne, down to the famous MCG (Melbourne Cricket Ground) with Jack Fingleton, following an evening reception. Joe Hardstaff was with us which added to my fascination. Jack told me, in his slow Australian drawl, of the times he had made that very same walk (sometimes with The Don), on Test match mornings in the Thirties. It was easy from Jack's words and the pictures already in my mind to capture the atmosphere of those days. It seemed to me that Jack Fingleton was obsessed with Bradman and somehow in this book one can sense the strength of this feeling. It is an unusual book, and that is why it is so good. It projects the feeling of actually being in the Australian team of the day, as of course Fingleton was. Even so, the personality of Bradman comes through very strongly, suggesting a remoteness and insularity almost cultivated to achieve the single-mindedness of the greatest run-scorer in the history of the game.

THE CRICKETER'S COMPANION edited by Alan Ross (published by Eyre and Spottiswoode in 1960)

Divided into five sections—Cricket Stories

182

Great Matches, Great Players, Men and Moments, The Poetry of Cricket. If I had to settle for one book only, this would be it. From some of cricket's greatest scribes, Alan Ross has put together an unsurpassed treasure trove. If the reader cannot find the heart of cricket in this book it is more than sad. In musical terms it can be likened to the greatest of concerts, thankfully recorded for cricketing life. The virtuosity of its contributors touches every feeling one can have for cricket. To mention but one of them might take away from the reader that sense of pleasant surprise ripening into pure delight that comes from the discovery of sentence after sentence of the most compelling lines and verses that stir the memory of games and players gone by. After closing the pages of *The Cricketer's Companion*, I could easily throw my pen away—but I press on stoically. . . .

ENGLAND versus AUSTRALIA—a Pictorial History of Test Matches since 1877 by David Frith (published by Butterworth Press in 1981)

I can think of no better way to extol the excellence of this book than to quote from some of its reviews:

> 'A rare publication. . . .a royal feast for a cricket buff. . . .a unique kaleidoscope of pictorial drama.' *Australian Cricket*
> 'A genuine collector's piece, a work to be read, looked at and admired again and again.' *The Financial Times*
> 'David Frith has done a marvellous job. . . .some of his photographs are so sensational that one wonders where he ever found them.' *The Spectator*

David Frith is perhaps the foremost cricket historian of this or any other generation. The breadth of his research is well identified in the preceding comment from *The Spectator*. On Anglo-Australian issues, he understandably has an Australian bias but this is healthy enough to only partially redress a deluge of written comment from the other side.

PRO by Bruce Hamilton (first published by the Cresset Press in 1946)

Out of print and not easy to obtain, this book is the sad story of a county professional (who never quite made it, or did he?) in the early years of this century. It is not the most literary book in the world, but whoever Bruce Hamilton is, he had a feeling for the times and an in-depth knowledge of a county cricketer's lot in those years. He certainly gives the reader a feeling of what it must have been like to be an average county cricketer living on the razor's edge of his next one-year contract in the hard times before and between the wars. I suspect the author himself at some time experienced the vagaries of a selection committee! For years it has been my intention to contact David Puttnam who could make the most marvellous film of *PRO, à la Chariots of Fire*.

WISDEN CRICKETERS' ALMANACK (published annually by Sporting Handbooks Ltd. on behalf of John Wisden and Co. Ltd.)

WISDEN—unique amongst books concerned with cricket—has been published annually since 1864. Each year this chunky bible of cricket, records everything of significance that has occurred in cricket throughout the world. Records and accounts of all first-class matches, player's records, the laws of the game, historical data, school's records, births and deaths of cricketers, articles of topical interest by the game's foremost writers, Wisden's Five Cricketers of the Year (selected by the Editor and one of the greatest honours that can be bestowed on a player), and so much more.

The older editions contained the most fascinating dialogue, with asides that bring alive not only the cricket but many other aspects of life at the time. For the uninitiated, just another book of statistics, but for the cricket lover a companion whose pages can conjure up pictures of cricketing days, of cricketing people, of incidents and controversies, of unforgettable moments in the continuing saga of a way of life that means the same in Manchester as it does in Melbourne. There are those lucky enough to own a whole set of Wisdens, one of which brought over £10,000 at auction in 1987, but their value in cricketing terms must be much more.

John Wisden was born at Brighton in 1826 and played his first match for Sussex in 1845. He was a cricketer of repute, in fact one of the finest in England in the mid-nineteenth century. Playing for the North against the South in 1850 at Lord's, he clean bowled ten batsmen in the second innings. Neither was he a bad batsman, scoring centuries on occasions in a time when they were not common. He was also a very successful entrepreneur, as, together with a Sussex colleague, James Dean, he was responsible for forming the United England XI, a wandering XI that more than rivalled William Clarke's team of the day.

John Wisden, through his business, John Wisden & Co, first published his *Cricketer's Almanack* in 1864 at the price of one shilling. He died twenty years later, little realising the immense contributions his *Almanack* was destined to make to cricket.

I cannot imagine a selection of cricket literature without Cardus. All his books are so superbly written that we are spoilt for choice. Try any one of these: *Days in the Sun, The Summer Game, Good Days, Australian Summer, Cricket, Autobiography, Second Innings, Close of Play, Full Score.* What joy lies ahead for those who have not yet shared with the immortal writer his life and love of cricket, born on the hard benches of Old Trafford in the Twenties and moulded through the pageant of characters that passed his way on the cricket grounds of England for nigh on fifty years.

Neither would I wish to be without the warmth of A.A. Thompson, the versatility of R.C. Robertson-Glasgow or the lovely humour of Arthur Mailey who for me ranks with Fingleton as Australia's best.

The problem with reading about cricket is that there is so much written one can easily miss or be late in sampling some very good works. Only because of my closeness to the art of wicket-keeping did I come into contact with David Lemmon who endeared himself to the 'club' by writing *The Great Wicket-Keepers.* After this pleasure, I was attracted to read the *Benson and Hedges Cricket Year,* edited by David and published by Pelham— and what a treasure trove it is. Every single detail of the previous year's cricket, including some marvellous photographs, is produced in the most readable style. This series must surely be a collector's item.

Of the younger writers, I am particularly fond of Tony Lewis. Many people will know him for his MCC Bi-Centenary book, *Double Century,* which is a marvellous documentary, if a little restricting in that it subdues the humorous and compassionate style of his other cricket writings.

I also like the refreshing revelations of Frances Edmonds. I hope she gives full rein to her undoubted talent and spreads her wings into fields other than cricket. If she does, I for one will be a subscriber.

I do not suppose we will be able to classify Mike Brearley as a future Cardus, but his writings are superbly incisive. For those who like to delve into the depths of the game of cricket, his book *The Art of Captaincy,* will make compulsive reading. It is already a classic. Maybe he will find time to give us more?

Quite rightly you may say, 'What about John Arlott?' Indeed, on the odd occasion when I want to put my book down and

JOHN ARLOTT in the commentary box during the Centenary Match at Lord's in 1980; his last Test match commentary. KEITH MILLER and TREVOR BAILEY keep him company.

'listen' to cricket, who better to listen to than the legendary John Arlott, whose voice of cricket will live for ever.

Finally, in my world of reading about our superb game I may surprise some by hoping that Ian Wooldridge of the *Daily Mail* will one day put all his cricket articles into a book. If he does, open-minded cricket folk will have a lot of fun. I may even suggest that alternate chapters of Wooldridge and E.W. Swanton would be the best of all—a cricket cocktail to suit all tastes? Perhaps, if spiced with a good slice of Matthew Engel!

WATCHING CRICKET

Whilst to some extent, with tongue in cheek, I have previously extolled the pleasures of reading about cricket as against playing and watching, on reflection there can be nothing quite like 'being there', playing if you are lucky, watching if you cannot play. The great advantage in watching is that there is a choice of whom you watch and where. Not so wide, of course, as for the reader, or so convenient, but far more than for the player whose role needs to be one of commitment to a single, if stimulating, game.

Particularly enjoyable for the cricket watcher is the sense of anticipation days and weeks before a game. It may be a Test match on one of the great grounds or just a village match in the peace of the English countryside. A common sight these days is the very competitive junior cricket played at clubs throughout the country. The enthusiasm and ability of these youngsters shines through and gives the lie to those uninformed critics who belittle the role of those in schools and clubs who encourage youngsters and work so hard for the game. Some of the most enjoyable watching is to be had from these junior games—every one a 'Test' match to its players. If you have not partaken of the hurly-burly of a Northern League match or the more relaxed but equally entertaining skills that can be seen on the friendly wickets of the South, your view of cricket will not be complete.

Mostly, but not always, it is worthwhile to plan your watching. Fixture lists and relevant maps and train timetables etc. are important. A good quality 'cool bag' has its obvious uses also. Whilst all committed cricket watchers follow their favourites and visit the grounds they know, they should not be averse to trying something new. There really are some delightful cricket grounds all over England and kindred spirits are always so helpful when you give them a chance. Being one, I shall take the liberty of making a few recommendations.

There is nothing quite like the first day of any Lord's Test. If you really want to do the job in style and you have a couple of days to spare, I recommend you to book in at a nearby hotel the night before or perhaps at a country inn not too far from London. The object of this is to visit Lord's before the match when not too many people are around. You will be able to visit the nets and see players of both sides in close-up action. Lunch is obtainable to suit anyone's taste, either in the Lord's Tavern or in some other nearby hostelry. A worthwhile part of this practice day can be a visit to the museum where all the treasures of two hundred years of cricket are housed. Of course, you will need to make special arrangements for this but I have never found MCC anything but accommodating to a genuine cricket lover. Another 'must' is the Lord's shop with its host of souvenirs, the most complete cricket book section you could ever wish for and many other 'goodies'. You will notice other things about Lord's, not least the beauty of the gardens and the quiet civility of the gatemen and match attendants. One can always feel the air of expectancy as countless people, some far removed from the game itself, strive to make sure that when the Grace Gates open at 9 a.m. on the day of the match everything is as it should be.

Be sure to get to the ground early, for there is much atmosphere to be soaked up and many personalities to come through the Grace Gates, some trying to look inconspicuous, others less so. After all, it is a social occasion as much as a cricket match! Incidentally, what about seats? Most seats are good with the Father Time side of the ground having the best of the day's sunshine, should such a phenomenon occur. I cannot speak for the Mound stand, not having been a spectator there, but the new 'Far Pavilions' are just magnificent and a sight worth seeing. Whatever you do, however, and no matter how much you are enjoying your day always be certain to make a couple of tours of the ground. The first should be just before the start of the game or it is equally enjoyable, and probably more useful physically, just after lunch. Make arrangements to meet friends at some appropiate venue at about five o'clock. This is the perfect time to appreciate the atmosphere of this unique place and put the cricket world to rights before the close of play. I have done this for years with my lifelong friend Lewis McGibbon and it finishes off the day's cricket very nicely. So much for watching a Lord's Test match. It is a special cricketing experience.

However, there is as much to offer from all the Test match grounds. I am biased, but Old Trafford is not far behind Lord's in every respect and boasts the finest Ladies Stand in the world. Leeds, Edgbaston and Trent Bridge each have their special features. The comments of a Yorkshire crowd always make fascinating cricket lore. The views of the game and the facilities at Edgbaston are unsurpassed, and Trent Bridge is, as it always must have been, the friendliest cricket ground in England, with a scoreboard that tells you everything you want to know about the match progress. The Oval is the home of every season's final Test and as such has produced one or two epic encounters. Here again the facilities are continually being improved with a budget of millions of pounds devoted to the cricket watchers of the future.

Where else may a keen watcher go? What about Hove? All the pleasures of the seaside and the lovely feeling of cricket that somehow belongs to the past are with you as you walk up to the ground from the promenade.

There has always been great batsmanship at Hove, from C.B. Fry and Ranji right through to Dexter and more recently Imran Khan. You can do worse than a trip to Brighton in early summer and if Sussex are not at their best, over the years the sea air has had the effect of inspiring the visiting batsmen.

Alongside Sussex I bracket Scarborough, for the Festival in September, a cricket holiday if ever there was one, although one day will hardly suffice. One of the many interesting features of the Scarborough Festival is the close proximity of the players' dressing-rooms to the passing throng. It is a particularly fascinating experience for any cricket lover to take a stroll in that direction early in the day, but please remember that it is a Festival and players will not necessarily have gone to bed before eleven as they would in the serious day-to-day grind of championship cricket! Do not be surprised if you bump into a few ghosts, some of them strangely alive! The intrepid cricket watcher will also enjoy the predominantly Yorkshire crowd. Take care to sit on the opposite side to the pavilion. That is where the real 'knowledge' congregates and has done for a hundred years and more.

The town of Scarborough is delightful. There are donkeys on the sands and Peasholme Park in which to stroll, plus a sandy beach for young families to play their own form of cricket. There is a northern and very warm atmosphere at Scarborough. Great cricketers will always come there—it is their beginning and their end and a stage free from the confines of the more serious duels they have to fight. Their names are a kaleidoscope of cricket and watching them play at the close of another summer provides memories that are treasured forever.

For a change of atmosphere I recommend any watchers who enjoy their lunch-time picnic in the most tranquil of surroundings to visit either of the two University grounds, Fenners at Cambridge, The Parks at Oxford.

There is an air of nostalgia about both these beautiful grounds where some of the finest players have initially graced the first-class game. University cricket was first played at The Parks in 1881, at Fenners in 1848. Great names such as C.B. Fry, Douglas Jardine (of Bodyline fame) and Colin Cowdrey for Oxford; Prince Ranjitsinhji, Freddie Brown and more recently Peter May, Ted Dexter and Mike Brearley for Cambridge, are just a few in the roll-call of talent that have somehow left their mark in the historic environs of both grounds. One can still see the occasional batsman of the very highest potential, thriving on the magnificent batting wickets that are a part of the varsity traditions.

In the same mood, in terms of the tranquillity that seems to grow from the academic atmosphere, one can conveniently reach the cricket ground of Cheltenham College where Gloucestershire's relaxed cricket is always worth watching. Bath, also in this lively West Country scene, always has good cricket, or, better still, why not go up to Worcester where in addition to the beauty of the cathedral background these days there is a young man called Hick, who is surely at the beginning of what can only be a great player's destiny.

So the journey is endless from Canterbury in England to Christchurch in New Zealand—and on to the vast arenas of Australia,

(*Opposite above*) SYDNEY CRICKET GROUND, 1982—The famous Hill; the home of cricket's most famous barrackers.

(*Opposite below*) SYDNEY CRICKET GROUND, 1984—Now with Mitsubishi's view of the game.

(*Below*) WEST INDIAN CRICKET—On the beach.

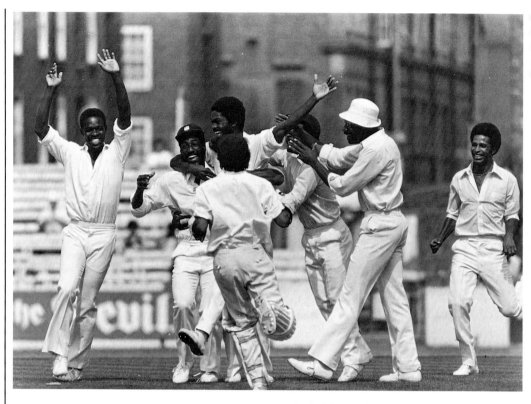

WEST INDIAN CRICKET in a Test match; this marvellous picture says it all.

India and Pakistan where crowds of up to a hundred thousand are in stark contrast to the homes of cricket we mostly know.

In terms of watching cricket in the most enjoyable of surroundings with sunshine practically guaranteed, we must finally look briefly to the West Indies. Again, as in all cricketing countries, each ground has its individual atmosphere. In Barbados the West Indies opposition must feel something like the football teams that take on Liverpool at Anfield. But in Trinidad, at Queens Park Oval on the most beautiful of West Indian grounds, the cricket is more cosmopolitan. Wherever you go in the Caribbean, there is a feeling for cricket, and watching cricket can only be the most delightful of occupations—especially if you can fit it in between a swim or two in the bluest of blue seas, whilst occasionally partaking of the most delightful refreshments.

Even in the writing of these few words, I find the prospect more appealing as my mind's eye brings forward visions of cricketing occasions as yet unsavoured.

CHAPTER SEVEN

Umpiring, Scoring and the Laws of Cricket

UMPIRING

At the heart of cricket there are very many special people, most of whom go unrecognised and unsung. Umpires, scorers, groundsmen, tea ladies, helpers of all kinds, from the little boys who help to pull the roller and sometimes sit on it to the senior citizens who so willingly sell the score-cards. Week in, week out they do a marvellous job for cricket and the community and whilst I am not qualified to discuss the merits of Yorkshire fruit cakes against those from southern climes, I can at least extol the virtues of good umpiring and scoring; especially as they are more than relevant to the very considerable and unique dialogue that follows—the official Laws of Cricket.

In my life in cricket, I have played in over four hundred first-class matches and countless other games at all levels. You can imagine how many times, as a wicket-keeper, I have appealed to many different umpires with various degrees of commitment, or should I say hope. You know, I can honestly say I have never had a cross word with any of them and sometimes they have been wrong. But so what? Give and take, there was a bond between us. Of all the people respected in the game, umpires somehow seem to represent all that is best. They are the non-pretenders who know the game and the players, and they are all 'characters', from village green to Test match.

It is said that umpiring at its best is hardly noticed but these days, in Test cricket at least, umpires are more often than not centre stage with the sometimes cruel eye of the television camera watching every move they make. What Frank Chester, Syd Buller and

(*Opposite*) 'DICKIE' BIRD AND DAVID SHEPHERD considering the light without caps!

Alec Skelding would have made of it all I cannot imagine, although I can visualise Alec's famous close of play performance on the television screen, as he removed the bails with a loud 'Time, gentlemen please.' There is no doubt that Alec and many of the others would have made very marketable television. Alec's white boots would have become even more famous than Harold (Dickie) Bird's white cap. It is in watching the television replays that the difficulty of the umpire's job can really be appreciated. How on earth are they so often right in those split second run-out decisions? Every time there is a replay of a controversial decision, umpires are put on the spot to such a degree that they deserve a fee from the television company for the instant drama provided at their expense. Less sympathy should be expended on those stupid batsmen who stand at the wicket pretending they have not nicked the ball, when they and everyone else knows they have knocked the cover off it. Ridiculing the umpire, cheating—call it what you like—the game does not need it. After all, umpires rightly give the batsmen the benefit of the doubt if there is one.

I read in Tom Smith's writings about his twenty-five years as Secretary of ACU, that the word umpire was first used in sport in 1714. It is apparently a development of the old English word 'numpere', meaning 'man above all', and so he should be on the field of play.

For those readers of this book, who, having reached this far, must be keen lovers of the game, I feel there should be some advice as to how they may take up umpiring if they so desire. Many will be ex-players, or they may be those who for some reason or another are physically unable to play the game. I suggest they simply contact the Secretary of a local cricket club who will put them in touch with the local umpires' association. From there, starting in the simplest way, an enthusiast can learn the job and enjoy being part of cricket life.

The Umpire's Lament by Alec Skelding

Portrayed by most cartoonists as a
  'Snoozer',
With red proboscis claiming him a
  'Boozer',
And a mien most dejected,
As if spinally affected,
Whom the tossed coin makes an
  everlasting loser.

Six hours a day—if there's actual play—
He stands as in thought, clad in white
  array;
Confident, though in purgatory,
Prepared for all emergency,
A martyr to the game—but for his pay!

Some of the time he stands to be shot at;
An immobile creature for mankind to pot at;
But you can disturb his conscience,
Should he hear such utter nonsense
As whisperings that he's likely to be 'got
  at'.

'How was it, How is it, How's this, How's
  that?'
Appeals required to be answered 'hand
  pat',
Some frantic and fierce, some pleading;
With gestures that could be misleading;
He must decide—laws provide no time for
  chat.

He can no question make of 'ayes or noes',
Deciding whether batsman stays or goes;
For 'tis ordered his decision
Must be prompt, and with precision,
For he's s'posed to be the only one who
  knows.

To be correct and please both sides he
  aims,
Suffering sleepless nights for his pains,
A-worrying over rumours
Of LBW bloomers
And departure times of home-returning
  trains.

So, when a batsman's making runs galore,
Amassing near a century in score,
'Tis hoped he will not linger
When he sees the index finger
Raised against him in accordance with the
  law.

Each year his club sends in his nomination,
Accompanied by MO's examination
As to eyesight, health and hearing,
And it must at least be cheering,
To have a chance at all for application.

Beginneth then his winter's discontent,
With eight months o'er his errors to
  lament;
And he may be re-elected,
When his record is inspected,
Or he may not—so he tries to be content.

'Twould need Aladdin's Lamp to aid the
  Umpire Gent
To run and wish, as down the pitch a ball is
  sent;
To help achieve the miracle,
He needs to reach the pinnacle
Of points award—a century per cent.

So now, you willow wielders,
And you volley-catching fielders;
You who stand there at the wicket,
Injured innocence—'Didn't snick it';
Bowlers who are apt to squeal
At a negative appeal;
Think of umpire Jack, or Jim;
Think kindly, please—and pity him!

SCORING

Whilst umpiring and scoring go together like bread and butter they usually attract quite different personalities to their ranks. The umpire is generally more of an extrovert and more sociable in outlook. Scorers tend to be quieter types with a fondness for statistics. Scoring can be a fascinating occupation if the scorer is dedicated. Many scorers produce the most interesting and useful statistics and records from the game. For years Bill Frindall of radio fame has been the most famous of scorers, 'the Bearded Wonder' as the delightfully ageless Brian Johnston has called him in countless Test match commentaries. Bill has developed scoring into an art form, inventing new ways of presenting the complex data that originates from a cricket match. His work has persuaded thousands of other enthusiasts to look again at their hobby and such items as batsmen's scoring charts are not now so rare as they were when the legendary Australian scorer 'Fergie' first charted the feats of Don Bradman.

Unfortunately, not all teams have the benefit of a dedicated scorer and on many occasions players are required to fulfil the scorer's vital role. Many young cricketers learn to score as part of their cricket educa-

BILL FRINDALL—Cricket's most famous scorer.

tion and it is encouraging that women are involving themselves in cricket club life very often these days by becoming the team scorer. Many television viewers will have seen the name Wendy Wimbush—Scorer, on the credits of the Test match cricket programmes.

Law 4 in the Laws of Cricket provides for the appointment of scorers and details their joint duties with the umpires. Generally one scorer is appointed for each side. Whilst methods of scoring vary, it makes sense if both scorers use similar methods as the necessary checks can be made so much easier. Usually before the commencement of a match the home team scorer will arrange a meeting with the other scorer and the umpires so that the match regulations are known and agreed.

Items for consideration are:
Hours of play
The timepiece to follow
Boundaries
New ball management
Competition rules
Time and over restrictions
The method of determining a result in
    special circumstances, i.e. inclement
    weather, light, etc.

Brian Johnston's eightieth birthday bronze portrait by Neale Andrew.

Scorebook

Scorers should make sure they have enough sharp pencils (and a sharpener) and a good eraser. Experience will very soon determine what other items will be necessary to do the job properly. A watch is important, of course, and a copy of the Laws is essential.

The umpires are responsible for the correctness of the scores, but to ensure that mistakes are not made scorers should constantly check and double-check their entries in the scorebook. A simple method at the end of each over is to ensure that the total runs made by all the batsmen plus extras equals the total runs scored off the bowlers plus extras. The running total section should give an extra check on the score.

Scorers should be well versed in the Laws of Cricket and any local rules appertaining to the match in which they are involved. It is, of course, vital that the scorer is fully conversant with all the umpire's signals. As in all aspects of the game, scoring should be practised, then it will give those who become involved many hours of pleasure in the most sporting of environments.

THE LAWS OF CRICKET

Law 1 THE PLAYERS

1. Number of Players and Captain A match is played between two sides each of eleven Players, one of whom shall be Captain. In the event of the Captain not being available at any time a Deputy shall act for him.

2. Nomination of Players Before the toss for innings, the Captain shall nominate his Players who may not thereafter be changed without the consent of the opposing Captain.

NOTES
(a) More or Less than Eleven Players a Side
A match may be played by agreement between sides of more or less than eleven players but not more than eleven players may field.

Law 2 SUBSTITUTES AND RUNNERS: BATSMAN OR FIELDSMAN LEAVING THE FIELD: BATSMAN RETIRING: BATSMAN COMMENCING INNINGS

1. Substitutes Substitutes shall be allowed by right to field for any player who during the match is incapacitated by illness or injury. The consent of the opposing Captain must be obtained for the use of a Substitute if any player is prevented from fielding for any other reason.

2. Objection to Substitutes The opposing Captain shall have no right of objection to any player acting as Substitute in the field, nor as to where he shall field, although he may object to the Substitute acting as Wicket-Keeper.

3. Substitute Not to Bat or Bowl A Substitute shall not be allowed to bat or bowl.

4. A Player for whom a Substitute has acted A player may bat, bowl or field even though a Substitute has acted for him.

5. Runner A Runner shall be allowed for a Batsman who during the match is incapacitated by illness or injury. The player acting as Runner shall be a member of the batting side and shall, if possible, have already batted in that innings.

6. Runner's Equipment The player acting as Runner for an injured Batsman shall wear batting gloves and pads if the injured Batsman is so equipped.

7. Transgression of the Laws by an Injured Batsman or Runner An injured Batsman may be out should his Runner break any one of Laws 33. (Handled the Ball), 37. (Obstructing the Field) or 38. (Run Out). As Striker he remains himself subject to the Laws. Furthermore, should he be out of his ground for any purpose and the wicket at the Wicket-Keeper's end be put down he shall be out under Law 38. (Run Out) or Law 39. (Stumped) irrespective of the position of the other Batsman or the Runner and no runs shall be scored.

When not the Striker, the injured Batsman is out of the game and shall stand where he does not interfere with the play. Should he bring himself into the game in any way then he shall suffer the penalties that any transgression of the Laws demands.

8. Fieldsman Leaving the Field No Fieldsman shall leave the field or return during a session of play without the consent of the Umpire at the Bowler's end. The Umpire's consent is also necessary if a Substitute is required for a Fieldsman, when his side returns to the field after an interval. If a member of the fielding side leaves the field or fails to return after an interval and is absent from the field for longer than 15 minutes, he shall not be permitted to bowl after his return until he has been on the field for at least that length of playing time for which he was absent. This restriction shall not apply at the start of a new day's play.

9. Batsman leaving the Field or Retiring A Batsman may leave the field or retire at any time owing to illness, injury or other unavoidable cause, having previously notified the Umpire at the Bowler's end. He may resume his innings at the fall of a wicket, which for the purposes of this Law shall include the retirement of another Batsman.

If he leaves the field or retires for any other reason he may only resume his innings with the consent of the opposing Captain.

When a Batsman has left the field or retired and is unable to return owing to illness, injury or other unavoidable cause, his innings is to be recorded as 'retired, not out'. Otherwise it is to be recorded as 'retired, out'.

10. Commencement of a Batsman's Innings A Batsman shall be considered to have commenced his innings once he has stepped on to the field of play.

NOTES
(a) Substitutes and Runners
For the purpose of these Laws allowable illnesses or injuries are those which occur at any time after the nomination by the Captains of their teams.

Law 3 THE UMPIRES

1. Appointment Before the toss for innings two Umpires shall be appointed, one for each end, to control the game with absolute impartiality as required by the Laws.

2. Change of Umpire No Umpire shall be changed during a match without the consent of both Captains.

3. Special Conditions Before the toss for innings, the Umpires shall agree with both Captains on any special conditions affecting the conduct of the match.

4. The Wickets The Umpires shall satisfy themselves before the start of the match that the wickets are properly pitched.

5. Clock or Watch The Umpires shall agree between themselves and inform both Captains before the start of the match on the watch or clock to be followed during the match.

6. Conduct and Implements Before and during a match the Umpires shall ensure that the conduct of the game and the implements used are strictly in accordance with the Laws.

7. Fair and Unfair Play The Umpires shall be the sole judges of fair and unfair play.

8. Fitness of Ground, Weather and Light
(a) The Umpires shall be the sole judges of the fitness of the ground, weather and light for play.
  (i) However, before deciding to suspend play or not to start play or not to resume play after an interval or stoppage, the Umpires shall establish whether both Captains (the Batsmen at the wicket may deputise for their Captain) wish to commence or to continue in the prevailing conditions; if so, their wishes shall be met.

(ii) In addition, if during the play, the Umpires decide that the light is unfit, only the batting side shall have the option of continuing play. After agreeing to continue to play in unfit light conditions, the Captain of the batting side (or a Batsman at the wicket) may appeal against the light to the Umpires, who shall uphold the appeal only if, in their opinion, the light has deteriorated since the agreement to continue was made.

(b) After any suspension of play, the Umpires, unaccompanied by any of the Players or Officials shall, on their own initiative, carry out an inspection immediately the conditions improve and shall continue to inspect at intervals. Immediately the Umpires decide that play is possible they shall call upon the Players to resume the game.

9. Exceptional Circumstances In exceptional circumstances, other than those of weather, ground or light, the Umpires may decide to suspend or abandon play. Before making such a decision the Umpires shall establish, if the circumstances allow, whether both Captains (the Batsmen at the wicket may deputise for their Captain) wish to continue in the prevailing conditions: if so their wishes shall be met.

10. Position of Umpires The Umpires shall stand where they can best see any act upon which their decision may be required.

Subject to this over-riding consideration the Umpire at the Bowler's end shall stand where he does not interfere with either the Bowler's run up or the Striker's view.

The Umpire at the Striker's end may elect to stand on the off instead of the leg side of the pitch, provided he informs the Captain of the fielding side and the Striker of his intention to do so.

11. Umpires Changing Ends The Umpires shall change ends after each side has had one innings.

12. Disputes All disputes shall be determined by the Umpires and if they disagree the actual state of things shall continue.

13. Signals The following code of signals shall be used by Umpires who will wait until a signal has been answered by a Scorer before allowing the game to proceed.

Boundary 4	by waving the arm from side to side.
Boundary 6	by raising both arms above the head.
Bye	by raising an open hand above the head.
Dead Ball	by crossing and re-crossing the wrists below the waist.
Leg Bye	by touching a raised knee with the hand.
No Ball	by extending one arm horizontally.
Out	by raising the index finger above the head. If not out the Umpire shall call 'not out'.
Short Run	by bending the arm upwards and by touching the nearer shoulder with the tips of the fingers.
Wide	by extending both arms horizontally.

(see illustrations on pages 200 and 201)

14. Correctness of Scores The Umpires shall be responsible for satisfying themselves on the correctness of the scores throughout and at the conclusion of the match. See Law 21.6. (Correctness of Result).

NOTES
(a) Attendance of Umpires
The Umpires should be present on the ground and report to the Ground Executive or the equivalent at least 30 minutes before the start of a day's play.
(b) Consultation Between Umpires and Scorers
Consultation between Umpires and Scorers over doubtful points is essential.
(c) Fitness of Ground
The Umpires shall consider the ground as unfit for play when it is so wet or slippery as to deprive the Bowlers of a reasonable foothold, the Fieldsmen, other than the deep-fielders, of the power of free movement, or the Batsmen the ability to play their strokes or to run between the wickets. Play should not be suspended merely because the grass and the ball are wet and slippery.
(d) Fitness of Weather and Light
The Umpires should only suspend play when they consider that the conditions are so bad that it is unreasonable or dangerous to continue.

Law 4 THE SCORERS

1. Recording Runs All runs scored shall be recorded by Scorers appointed for the purpose. Where there are two Scorers they shall frequently check to ensure that the score sheets agree.

2. Acknowledging Signals The Scorers shall accept and immediately acknowledge all instructions and signals given to them by the Umpires.

UMPIRING SIGNALS.
A Boundary 4
B Boundary 6
C Bye
D Dead ball
E Leg bye
F No ball
G Out
H Short run
I Wide

Law 5 THE BALL

1. Weight and Size The ball, when new, shall weigh not less than $5\frac{1}{2}$ ounces/155.9g., nor more than $5\frac{3}{4}$ ounces/163g.: and shall measure not less than $8.\frac{13}{16}$ inches/22.4 cm., nor more than 9 inches/22.9 cm. in circumference.

2. Approval of Balls All balls used in matches shall be approved by the Umpires and Captains before the start of the match.

3. New Ball Subject to agreement to the contrary, having been made before the toss, either Captain may demand a new ball at the start of each innings.

4. New Ball in Match of 3 or more Days Duration In a match of 3 or more days duration, the Captain of the fielding side may demand a new ball after the prescribed number of overs has been bowled with the old one. The Governing Body for cricket in the country concerned shall decide the number of overs applicable in that country which shall be not less than 75 six-ball overs (55 eight-ball overs).

5. Ball Lost or Becoming Unfit for Play In the event of a ball during play being lost or, in the opinion of the Umpires, becoming unfit for play, the Umpires shall allow it to be replaced by one that in their opinion has had a similar amount of wear. If a ball is to be replaced, the Umpires shall inform the Batsmen.

NOTES
(a) Specifications
The specifications, as described in 1. above shall apply to top-grade balls only. The following degrees of tolerance will be acceptable for other grades of ball.
  (i) Men's Grades 2–4
    Weight: $5\frac{5}{16}$ ounces/150g. to $5\frac{13}{16}$ ounces/165g.
    Size: $8\frac{11}{16}$ inches/22.0cm. to $9\frac{1}{16}$ inches/23.0cm.
  (ii) Women's
    Weight: $4\frac{15}{16}$ ounces/140g. to $5\frac{5}{16}$ ounces/150g.
    Size: $8\frac{1}{4}$ inches/21.0cm. to $8\frac{7}{8}$ inches/22.5cm.
  (iii) Junior
    Weight: $4\frac{5}{16}$ ounces/133g. to $5\frac{1}{16}$ ounces/143g.
    Size: $8\frac{1}{16}$ inches/20.5cm. to $8\frac{11}{16}$ inches/22.0cm.

Law 6 THE BAT

1. Width and Length The bat overall shall not be more than 38 inches/96.5 cm. in length; the blade of the bat shall be made of wood and shall not exceed $4\frac{1}{4}$ inches/10.8 cm. at the widest part.

NOTES
(a) *The blade of the bat may be covered with material for protection, strengthening or repair. Such material shall not exceed $\frac{1}{16}$ inches/1.56 mm. in thickness.*

Law 7 THE PITCH

1. Area of Pitch The pitch is the area between the bowling creases—see Law 9. (The Bowling, Popping and Return Creases). It shall measure 5 ft./1.52m. in width on either side of a line joining the centre of the middle stumps of the wickets—see Law 8. (The Wickets).

2. Selection and Preparation Before the toss for innings, the Executive of the Ground shall be responsible for the selection and preparation of the pitch; thereafter the Umpires shall control its use and maintenance.

3. Changing Pitch The pitch shall not be changed during a match unless it becomes unfit for play, and then only with the consent of both Captains.

4. Non-Turf Pitches In the event of a non-turf pitch being used, the following shall apply:
(a) LENGTH: That of the playing surface to a minimum of 58ft. (17.68 m.)
(b) WIDTH: That of the playing surface to a minimum of 6ft. (1.83 m.)
See Law 10. (Rolling, Sweeping, Mowing, Watering the Pitch and Re-marking of Creases) Note (a).

Law 8 THE WICKETS

1. Width and Pitching Two sets of wickets, each 9 inches/22.86 cm. wide, and consisting of three wooden stumps with two wooden bails upon the top, shall be pitched opposite and parallel to each other at a distance of 22 yards/20.12m. between the centres of the two middle stumps.

2. Size of Stumps The stumps shall be of equal and sufficient size to prevent the ball from passing between them. Their tops shall be 28 inches/71.1cm. above the ground, and shall be dome-shaped except for the bail grooves.

3. Size of Bails The bails shall be each $4\frac{3}{8}$ inches/ 11.1cm. in length and when in position on the top of the stumps shall not project more than $\frac{1}{2}$ inch/1.3cm. above them.

NOTES
(a) Dispensing with Bails
In a high wind the Umpires may decide to dispense with the use of bails.
(b) Junior Cricket
For Junior Cricket, as defined by the local Governing Body, the following measurements for the Wickets shall apply:

Width	*8 inches/20.32 cm.*
Pitched	*21 yards/19.20 m.*
Height	*27 inches/68.58 cm.*
Bails	*each $3\frac{7}{8}$ inches/9.84 cm. in length and should not project more than $\frac{1}{2}$ inch/ 1.3cm. above them.*

Law 9 THE BOWLING, POPPING AND RETURN CREASES

1. The Bowling Crease The bowling crease shall be marked in line with the stumps at each end and shall be 8 ft. 8 inches/2.64 m. in length, with the stumps in the centre.

2. The Popping Crease The popping crease, which is the back edge of the crease marking, shall be in front of and parallel with the bowling crease. It shall have the back edge of the crease marking 4 ft./1.22 m. from the centre of the stumps and shall extend to a minimum of 6 ft./ 1.83 m. on either side of the line of the wicket.
The popping crease shall be considered to be unlimited in length.

3. The Return Crease The return crease marking, of which the inside edge is the crease, shall be at each end of the bowling crease and at right angles to it. The return crease shall be marked to a minimum of 4 ft./1.22 m. behind the wicket and shall be considered to be unlimited in length. A forward extension shall be marked to the popping crease.

Fig. 53 PITCH MARKINGS AND DIMENSIONS

Law 10 ROLLING, SWEEPING, MOWING, WATERING THE PITCH AND RE-MARKING OF CREASES

1. Rolling During the match the pitch may be rolled at the request of the Captain of the batting side, for a period of not more than 7 minutes before the start of each innings, other than the first innings of the match, and before the start of each day's play. In addition, if, after the toss and before the first innings of the match, the start is delayed, the Captain of the batting side shall have the right to have the pitch rolled for not more than 7 minutes.
The pitch shall not otherwise be rolled during the match.
The 7 minutes rolling permitted before the start of a day's play shall take place not earlier than half an hour before the start of play and the Captain of the batting side may delay such rolling until 10

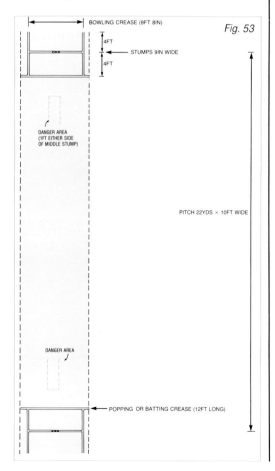

Fig. 53

BOWLING CREASE (8FT 8IN)
4FT
STUMPS 9IN WIDE
4FT
DANGER AREA
(1FT EITHER SIDE
OF MIDDLE STUMP)
PITCH 22YDS × 10FT WIDE
DANGER AREA
POPPING OR BATTING CREASE (12FT LONG)

minutes before the start of play should he so desire.

If a Captain declares an innings closed less than 15 minutes before the resumption of play, and the other Captain is thereby prevented from exercising his option of 7 minutes rolling or if he is so prevented for any other reason the time for rolling shall be taken out of the normal playing time.

2. Sweeping Such sweeping of the pitch as is necessary during the match shall be done so that the 7 minutes allowed for rolling the pitch provided for in 1. above is not affected.

3. Mowing
(a) **Responsibilities of Ground Authority and of Umpires** All mowings which are carried out before the toss for innings shall be the responsibility of the Ground Authority. Thereafter they shall be carried out under the supervision of the Umpires, see Law 7.2. (Selection and Preparation).
(b) **Initial Mowing** The pitch shall be mown before play begins on the day the match is scheduled to start or in the case of a delayed start on the day the match is expected to start. See 3(a) above. (Responsibilities of Ground Authority and of Umpires).
(c) **Subsequent Mowings in a Match of 2 or More Days' Duration** In a match of two or more days' duration, the pitch shall be mown daily before play begins. Should this mowing not take place because of weather conditions, rest days or other reasons the pitch shall be mown on the first day on which the match is resumed.
(d) **Mowing of the Outfield in a Match of 2 or More Days' Duration** In order to ensure that conditions are as similar as possible for both sides, the outfield shall normally be mown before the commencement of play on each day of the match, if ground and weather conditions allow. See Note (b) to this Law.

4. Watering The pitch shall not be watered during a match.

5. Re-Marking Creases Whenever possible the creases shall be re-marked.

6. Maintenance of Foot Holes In wet weather, the Umpires shall ensure that the holes made by the Bowlers and Batsmen are cleaned out and dried whenever necessary to facilitate play. In matches of 2 or more days' duration, the Umpires shall allow, if necessary, the re-turfing of foot holes made by the Bowler in his delivery stride, or the

use of quick-setting fillings for the same purpose, before the start of each day's play.

7. Securing of Footholds and Maintenance of Pitch During play, the Umpires shall allow either Batsman to beat the pitch with his bat and players to secure their footholds by the use of sawdust, provided that no damage to the pitch is so caused, and Law 42. (Unfair Play) is not contravened.

NOTES
(a) Non-Turf Pitches
The above Law 10 applies to turf pitches.
The game is played on non-turf pitches in many countries at various levels. Whilst the conduct of the game on these surfaces should always be in accordance with the Laws of Cricket, it is recognised that it may sometimes be necessary for Governing Bodies to lay down special playing conditions to suit the type of non-turf pitch used in their country.
In matches played against Touring Teams, any special playing conditions should be agreed in advance by both parties.
(b) Mowing of the Outfield in a Match of 2 or More Days' Duration
If, for reasons other than ground and weather conditions, daily and complete mowing is not possible, the Ground Authority shall notify the Captains and Umpires, before the toss for innings, of the procedure to be adopted for such mowing during the match.
(c) Choice of Roller
If there is more than one roller available the Captain of the batting side shall have a choice.

Law 11 COVERING THE PITCH

1. Before the Start of a Match Before the start of a match complete covering of the pitch shall be allowed.

2. During a Match The pitch shall not be completely covered during a match unless prior arrangement or regulations so provide.

3. Covering Bowlers' Run-Up Whenever possible, the Bowlers' run-up shall be covered, but the covers so used shall not extend further than 4 ft. 1.22 m. in front of the popping crease.

NOTES

(a) Removal of Covers
The covers should be removed as promptly as possible whenever the weather permits.

Law 12 INNINGS

1. Number of Innings A match shall be of one or two innings of each side according to agreement reached before the start of play.

2. Alternate Innings In a two innings match each side shall take their innings alternately except in the case provided for in Law 13. (The Follow-On).

3. The Toss The Captains shall toss for the choice of innings on the field of play not later than 15 minutes before the time scheduled for the match to start, or before the time agreed upon for play to start.

4. Choice of Innings The winner of the toss shall notify his decision to bat or to field to the opposing Captain not later than 10 minutes before the time scheduled for the match to start, or before the time agreed upon for play to start. The decision shall not thereafter be altered.

5. Continuation After One Innings of Each Side Despite the terms of 1. above, in a one innings match, when a result has been reached on the first innings the Captains may agree to the continuation of play if, in their opinion, there is a prospect of carrying the game to a further issue in the time left. See Law 21. (Result).

NOTES

(a) Limited Innings—One Innings Match
In a one innings match, each innings may, by agreement, be limited by a number of overs or by a period of time.

(b) Limited Innings—Two Innings Match
In a two innings match, the first innings of each side may, by agreement, be limited to a number of overs or by a period of time.

Law 13 THE FOLLOW-ON

1. Lead on First Innings In a two innings match the side which bats first and leads by 200 runs in a match of five days or more, by 150 runs in a three-day or four-day match, by 100 runs in a two-day match, or by 75 runs in a one-day match, shall have the option of requiring the other side to follow their innings.

2. Day's Play Lost If no play takes place on the first day of a match of 2 or more days' duration, 1. above shall apply in accordance with the number of days' play remaining from the actual start of the match.

Law 14 DECLARATIONS

1. Time of Declaration The Captain of the batting side may declare an innings closed at any time during a match irrespective of its duration.

2. Forfeiture of Second Innings A Captain may forfeit his second innings, provided his decision to do so is notified to the opposing Captain and Umpires in sufficient time to allow 7 minutes rolling of the pitch. See Law 10. (Rolling, Sweeping, Mowing, Watering the Pitch and Re-Marking of Creases). The normal 10 minute interval between innings shall be applied.

Law 15 START OF PLAY

1. Call of Play At the start of each innings and of each day's play and on the resumption of play after any interval or interruption the Umpire at the Bowler's end shall call 'play'.

2. Practice on the Field At no time on any day of the match shall there be any bowling or batting practice on the pitch.

No practice may take place on the field if, in the opinion of the Umpires, it could result in a waste of time.

3. Trial Run-Up No Bowler shall have a trial run-up after 'play' has been called in any session of play, except at the fall of a wicket when an Umpire may allow such a trial run-up if he is satisfied that it will not cause any waste of time.

Law 16 INTERVALS

1. Length The Umpire shall allow such intervals as have been agreed upon for meals, and 10 minutes between each innings.

2. Luncheon Interval—Innings Ending or Stoppage within 10 Minutes of Interval If an innings ends or there is a stoppage caused by weather or bad light within 10 minutes of the agreed time for the luncheon interval, the interval shall be taken immediately.

The time remaining in the session of play shall be added to the agreed length of the interval but no extra allowance shall be made for the 10 minutes interval between innings.

3. Tea Interval—Innings Ending or Stoppage within 30 Minutes of Interval If an innings ends or there is a stoppage caused by weather or bad light within 30 minutes of the agreed time for the tea interval, the interval shall be taken immediately.

The interval shall be of the agreed length and, if applicable, shall include the 10 minute interval between innings.

4. Tea Interval—Continuation of Play If at the agreed time for the tea interval, nine wickets are down, play shall continue for a period not exceeding 30 minutes or until the innings is concluded.

5. Tea Interval—Agreement to Forego At any time during the match, the Captains may agree to forego a tea interval.

6. Intervals for Drinks If both Captains agree before the start of a match that intervals for drinks may be taken, the option to take such intervals shall be available to either side. These intervals shall be restricted to one per session, shall be kept as short as possible, shall not be taken in the last hour of the match and in any case shall not exceed 5 minutes.

The agreed times for these intervals shall be strictly adhered to except that if a wicket falls within 5 minutes of the agreed time then drinks shall be taken out immediately.

If an innings ends or there is a stoppage caused by weather or bad light within 30 minutes of the agreed time for a drinks interval, there will be no interval for drinks in that session.

At any time during the match the Captains may agree to forego any such drinks interval.

NOTES

(a) Tea Interval—One-Day Match
In a one-day match, a specific time for the tea interval need not necessarily be arranged, and it may be agreed to take this interval between the innings of a one-innings match.

(b) Changing the Agreed Time of Intervals
In the event of the ground, weather or light conditions causing a suspension of play, the Umpires, after consultation with the Captains, may decide in the interests of time-saving, to bring forward the time of the luncheon or tea interval.

Law 17 CESSATION OF PLAY

1. Call of Time The Umpire at the Bowler's end shall call 'time' on the cessation of play before any interval or interruption of play, at the end of each day's play, and at the conclusion of the match. See Law 27. (Appeals).

2. Removal of Bails After the call of 'time', the Umpires shall remove the bails from both wickets.

3. Starting a Last Over The last over before an interval or the close of play shall be started provided the Umpire, after walking at his normal pace, has arrived at his position behind the stumps at the Bowler's end before time has been reached.

4. Completion of the Last Over of a Session The last over before an interval or the close of play shall be completed unless a Batsman is out or retires during that over within 2 minutes of the interval or the close of play or unless the Players have occasion to leave the field.

5. Completion of the Last Over of a Match An over in progress at the close of play on the final day of a match shall be completed at the request of either Captain even if a wicket falls after time has been reached.

If during the last over the Players have occasion to leave the field the Umpires shall call 'time' and there shall be no resumption of play and the match shall be at an end.

6. Last Hour of Match—Number of Overs The Umpires shall indicate when one hour of playing time of the match remains according to the agreed hours of play. The next over after that moment shall be the first of a minimum of 20 6-ball overs, (15 8-ball overs), provided a result is not reached earlier or there is no interval or interruption of play.

7. Last Hour of Match—Intervals Between Innings and Interruptions of Play If, at the commencement of the last hour of the match, an interval or interruption of play is in progress or if, during the last hour there is an interval between innings or an interruption of play, the minimum number of overs to be bowled on the resumption of play shall be reduced in proportion to the duration, within the last hour of the match, of any such interval or interruption.

The minimum number of overs to be bowled after a resumption of play shall be calculated as follows:

(a) In the case of an interval or interruption of play

being in progress at the commencement of the last hour of the match, or in the case of a first interval or interruption a deduction shall be made from the minimum of 20 6-ball overs (or 15 8-ball overs).

(b) If there is a later interval or interruption a further deduction shall be made from the minimum number of overs which should have been bowled following the last resumption of play.

(c) These deductions shall be based on the following factors:

(i) the number of overs already bowled in the last hour of the match or, in the case of a later interval or interruption in the last session of play.

(ii) the number of overs lost as a result of the interval or interruption allowing one 6-ball over for every full three minutes (or one 8-ball over for every full four minutes) of interval or interruption.

(iii) any over left uncompleted at the end of an innings to be excluded from these calculations.

(iv) any over left uncompleted at the start of an interruption of play to be completed when play is resumed and to count as one over bowled.

(v) an interval to start with the end of an innings and to end 10 minutes later; an interruption to start on the call of 'time' and to end on the call of 'play'.

(d) In the event of an innings being completed and a new innings commencing during the last hour of the match, the number of overs to be bowled in the new innings shall be calculated on the basis of one 6-ball over for every three minutes or part thereof remaining for play (or one 8-ball over for every four minutes or part thereof remaining for play); or alternatively on the basis that sufficient overs be bowled to enable the full minimum quota of overs to be completed under circumstances governed by (a), (b) and (c) above. In all such cases the alternative which allows the greater number of overs shall be employed.

8. Bowler Unable to Complete an Over During Last Hour of the Match If, for any reason, a Bowler is unable to complete an over during the period of play referred to in 6. above, Law 22.7. (Bowler Incapacitated or Suspended during an Over) shall apply.

Law 18 SCORING

1. A Run The score shall be reckoned by runs. A run is scored:

(a) So often as the Batsmen, after a hit or at any time while the ball is in play, shall have crossed and made good their ground from end to end.

(b) When a boundary is scored. See Law 19. (Boundaries).

(c) When penalty runs are awarded. See 6. below.

2. Short Runs

(a) If either Batsman runs a short run, the Umpire shall call and signal 'one short' as soon as the ball becomes dead and that run shall not be scored. A run is short if a Batsman fails to make good his ground on turning for a further run.

(b) Although a short run shortens the succeeding one, the latter, if completed shall count.

(c) If either or both Batsmen deliberately run short the Umpire shall, as soon as he sees that the fielding side have no chance of dismissing either Batsman, call and signal 'dead ball' and disallow any runs attempted or previously scored. The Batsmen shall return to their original ends.

(d) If both Batsmen run short in one and the same run, only one run shall be deducted.

(e) Only if three or more runs are attempted can more than one be short and then, subject to (c) and (d) above, all runs so called shall be disallowed. If there has been more than one short run the Umpires shall instruct the Scorers as to the number of runs disallowed.

3. Striker Caught If the Striker is Caught, no run shall be scored.

4. Batsman Run Out If a Batsman is Run Out, only that run which was being attempted shall not be scored. If, however, an injured Striker himself is run out no runs shall be scored. See Law 2.7. (Transgression of the Laws by an Injured Batsman or Runner).

5. Batsman Obstructing the Field If a Batsman is out Obstructing the Field, any runs completed before the obstruction occurs shall be scored unless such obstruction prevents a catch being made in which case no runs shall be scored.

6. Runs Scored for Penalties Runs shall be scored for penalties under Laws 20. (Lost Ball), 24. (No Ball), 25. (Wide Ball), 41.1. (Fielding the Ball) and for boundary allowances under Law 19. (Boundaries).

7. Batsman Returning to Wicket he has Left If, while the ball is in play, the Batsmen have crossed in running, neither shall return to the wicket he has left even though a short run has been called or no run has been scored as in the case of a catch. Batsmen, however, shall return to the wickets they originally left in the cases of a boundary and of any disallowance of runs and of an injured Batsman being, himself, run out. See Law 2.7. (Transgression of the Laws by an Injured Batsman or Runner).

NOTES
(a) Short Run
A Striker taking stance in front of his popping crease may run from that point without penalty.

Law 19 BOUNDARIES

1. The Boundary of the Playing Area Before the toss for innings, the Umpires shall agree with both Captains on the boundary of the playing area. The boundary shall, if possible, be marked by a white line, a rope laid on the ground, or a fence. If flags or posts only are used to mark a boundary, the imaginary line joining such points shall be regarded as the boundary. An obstacle, or person, within the playing area shall not be regarded as a boundary unless so decided by the Umpires before the toss for innings. Sight-screens within, or partially within, the playing area shall be regarded as the boundary and when the ball strikes or passes within or under or directly over any part of the screen, a boundary shall be scored.

2. Runs Scored for Boundaries Before the toss for innings, the Umpires shall agree with both Captains the runs to be allowed for boundaries, and in deciding the allowance for them, the Umpires and Captains shall be guided by the prevailing custom of the ground. The allowance for a boundary shall normally be 4 runs, and 6 runs for all hits pitching over and clear of the boundary line or fence, even though the ball has been previously touched by a Fieldsman. 6 runs shall also be scored if a Fieldsman, after catching a ball, carries it over the boundary. See Law 32. (Caught) Note (a). 6 runs shall not be scored when a ball struck by the Striker hits a sightscreen full pitch if the screen is within, or partially within, the playing area, but if the ball is struck directly over a sightscreen so situated, 6 runs shall be scored.

3. A Boundary A boundary shall be scored and signalled by the Umpire at the Bowler's end whenever, in his opinion:

(a) A ball in play touches or crosses the boundary, however marked.
(b) A Fieldsman with ball in hand touches or grounds any part of his person on or over a boundary line.
(c) A Fieldsman with ball in hand grounds any part of his person over a boundary fence or board. This allows the Fieldsman to touch or lean on or over a boundary fence or board in preventing a boundary.

4. Runs Exceeding Boundary Allowance The runs completed at the instant the ball reaches the boundary shall count if they exceed the boundary allowance.

5. Overthrows or Wilful Act of a Fieldsman If the boundary results from an overthrow or from the wilful act of a Fieldsman, any runs already completed and the allowance shall be added to the score. The run in progress shall count provided that the Batsmen have crossed at the instant of the throw or act.

NOTES
(a) Position of Sight-Screens
Sight-screens should, if possible, be positioned wholly outside the playing area, as near as possible to the boundary line.

Law 20 LOST BALL

1. Runs Scored If a ball in play cannot be found or recovered any fieldsman may call 'lost ball' when 6 runs shall be added to the score; but if more than 6 have been run before 'lost ball' is called, as many runs as have been completed shall be scored. The run in progress shall count provided that the Batsmen have crossed at the instant of the call of 'lost ball'.

2. How Scored The runs shall be added to the score of the Striker if the ball has been struck, but otherwise to the score of byes, leg-byes, no-balls or wides as the case may be.

Law 21 THE RESULT

1. A Win—Two Innings Matches The side which has scored a total of runs in excess of that scored by the opposing side in its two completed innings shall be the winners.

2. A Win—One Innings Matches

(a) One innings matches, unless played out as in 1. above, shall be decided on the first innings, but see Law 12.5. (Continuation After One Innings of Each Side).

(b) If the Captains agree to continue play after the completion of one innings of each side in accordance with Law 12.5. (Continuation After One Innings of Each Side) and a result is not achieved on the second innings, the first innings result shall stand.

3. Umpires Awarding a Match

(a) A match shall be lost by a side which, during the match,
  (i) refuses to play, or
  (ii) concedes defeat,
and the Umpires shall award the match to the other side.

(b) Should both Batsmen at the wickets or the fielding side leave the field at any time without the agreement of the Umpires, this shall constitute a refusal to play and, on appeal, the Umpires shall award the match to the other side in accordance with (a) above.

4. A Tie

The result of a match shall be a tie when the scores are equal at the conclusion of play, but only if the side batting last has completed its innings.

If the scores of the completed first innings of a one-day match are equal, it shall be a tie but only if the match has not been played out to a further conclusion.

5. A Draw

A match not determined in any of the ways as in 1, 2, 3 and 4 above shall count as a draw.

6. Correctness of Result

Any decision as to the correctness of the scores shall be the responsibility of the Umpires. See Law 3.14. (Correctness of Scores).

If, after the Umpires and Players have left the field, in the belief that the match has been concluded, the Umpires decide that a mistake in scoring has occurred, which affects the result, and provided time has not been reached, they shall order play to resume and to continue until the agreed finishing time unless a result is reached earlier.

If the Umpires decide that a mistake has occurred and time has been reached, the Umpires shall immediately inform both Captains of the necessary corrections to the scores and, if applicable, to the result.

7. Acceptance of Result

In accepting the scores as notified by the scorers and agreed by the Umpires, the Captains of both sides thereby accept the result.

NOTES

(a) Statement of Results

The result of a finished match is stated as a win by runs, except in the case of a win by the side batting last when it is by the number of wickets still left then to fall.

(b) Winning Hit or Extras

As soon as the side has won, see 1. and 2. above, the Umpire shall call 'time', the match is finished, and nothing that happens thereafter other than as a result of a mistake in scoring, see 6. above, shall be regarded as part of the match.

However, if a boundary constitutes the winning hit—or extras—and the boundary allowance exceeds the number of runs required to win the match, such runs scored shall be credited to the side's total and, in the case of a hit to the Striker's score.

Law 22 THE OVER

1. Number of Balls

The ball shall be bowled from each wicket alternately in overs of either 6 or 8 balls according to agreement before the match.

2. Call of 'Over'

When the agreed number of balls has been bowled, and as the ball becomes dead or when it becomes clear to the Umpire at the Bowler's end that both the fielding side and the Batsmen at the wicket have ceased to regard the ball as in play, the Umpire shall call 'over' before leaving the wicket.

3. No Ball or Wide Ball

Neither a no ball nor a wide ball shall be reckoned as one of the over.

4. Umpire Miscounting

If an Umpire miscounts the number of balls, the over as counted by the Umpire shall stand.

5. Bowler Changing Ends

A Bowler shall be allowed to change ends as often as desired provided only that he does not bowl two overs consecutively in an innings.

6. The Bowler Finishing an Over

A Bowler shall finish an over in progress unless he be incapacitated or be suspended under Law 42.8. (The

Bowling of Fast Short Pitched Balls), 42.9. (The Bowling of Fast High Full Pitches), 42.10. (Time Wasting) and 42.11. (Players Damaging the Pitch). If an over is left incomplete for any reason at the start of an interval or interruption of play, it shall be finished on the resumption of play.

7. Bowler Incapacitated or Suspended During an Over If, for any reason, a Bowler is incapacitated while running up to bowl the first ball of an over, or is incapacitated or suspended during an over, the Umpire shall call and signal 'dead ball' and another Bowler shall be allowed to bowl or complete the over from the same end, provided only that he shall not bowl two overs, or part thereof, consecutively in one innings.

8. Position of Non-Striker The Batsman at the Bowler's end shall normally stand on the opposite side of the wicket to that from which the ball is being delivered, unless a request to do otherwise is granted by the Umpire.

Law 23 DEAD BALL

1. The Ball Becomes Dead, when:
(a) It is finally settled in the hands of the Wicket-Keeper or the Bowler.
(b) It reaches or pitches over the boundary.
(c) A Batsman is out.
(d) Whether played or not, it lodges in the clothing or equipment of a Batsman or the clothing of an Umpire.
(e) A ball lodges in a protective helmet worn by a member of the fielding side.
(f) A penalty is awarded under Law 20. (Lost Ball) or Law 41.1. (Fielding the Ball).
(g) The Umpire calls 'over' or 'time'.

2. Either Umpire Shall Call and Signal 'Dead Ball', when:
(a) He intervenes in a case of unfair play.
(b) A serious injury to a Player or Umpire occurs.
(c) He is satisfied that, for an adequate reason, the Striker is not ready to receive the ball and makes no attempt to play it.
(d) The Bowler drops the ball accidentally before delivery, or the ball does not leave his hand for any reason.
(e) One or both bails fall from the Striker's wicket before he receives delivery.
(f) He leaves his normal position for consultation.
(g) He is required to do so under Laws 26.3. (Disallowance of Leg-Byes), etc.

3. The Ball Ceases to be Dead, when:
(a) The Bowler starts his run up or bowling action.

4. The Ball is Not Dead, when:
(a) It strikes an Umpire (unless it lodges in his dress).
(b) The wicket is broken or struck down (unless a Batsman is out thereby).
(c) An unsuccessful appeal is made.
(d) The wicket is broken accidentally either by the Bowler during his delivery or by a Batsman in running.
(e) The Umpire has called 'no ball' or 'wide'.

NOTES
(a) Ball Finally Settled
Whether the ball is finally settled or not—see 1 (a) above—must be a question for the Umpires alone to decide.
(b) Action on Call of 'Dead Ball'
(i) If 'dead ball' is called prior to the Striker receiving a delivery the Bowler shall be allowed an additional ball.
(ii) If 'dead ball' is called after the Striker receives a delivery the Bowler shall not be allowed an additional ball, unless a 'no-ball' or 'wide' has been called.

Law 24 NO BALL

1. Mode of Delivery The Umpire shall indicate to the Striker whether the Bowler intends to bowl over or round the wicket, overarm or underarm, or right or left-handed. Failure on the part of the Bowler to indicate in advance a change in his mode of delivery is unfair and the Umpire shall call and signal 'no ball'.

2. Fair Delivery—The Arm For a delivery to be fair the ball must be bowled not thrown—see Note (a) below. If either Umpire is not entirely satisfied with the absolute fairness of a delivery in this respect he shall call and signal 'no ball' instantly upon delivery.

3. Fair Delivery—The Feet The Umpire at the bowler's wicket shall call and signal 'no ball' if he is not satisfied that in the delivery stride:
(a) the Bowler's back foot has landed within and not touching the return crease or its forward extension
or
(b) some part of the front foot whether grounded or raised was behind the popping crease.

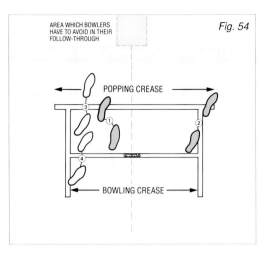

Fig. 54

Fig. 54 NO BALL SITUATIONS. Foot positions 1 and 2 are fair deliveries, but 3 and 4 are no balls.

4. Bowler Throwing at Striker's Wicket Before Delivery If the Bowler, before delivering the ball, throws it at the Striker's wicket in an attempt to run him out, the Umpire shall call and signal 'no ball'. See Law 42.12. (Batsman Unfairly Stealing a Run) and Law 38. (Run Out).

5. Bowler Attempting to Run Out Non-Striker Before Delivery If the Bowler, before delivering the ball, attempts to run out the non-Striker, any runs which result shall be allowed and shall be scored as no balls. Such an attempt shall not count as a ball in the over. The Umpire shall not call 'no ball'. See Law 42.12. (Batsman Unfairly Stealing a Run).

6. Infringement of Laws by a Wicket-Keeper or a Fieldsman The Umpire shall call and signal 'no ball' in the event of the Wicket-Keeper infringing Law 40.1. (Position of Wicket-Keeper) or a Fieldsman infringing Law 41.2. (Limitation of On-side Fieldsmen) or Law 41.3. (Position of Fieldsmen).

7. Revoking a Call An Umpire shall revoke the call 'no ball' if the ball does not leave the Bowler's hand for any reason. See Law 23.2. (Either Umpire Shall Call and Signal 'Dead Ball').

8. Penalty A penalty of one run for a no ball shall be scored if no runs are made otherwise.

9. Runs From a No Ball The Striker may hit a no ball and whatever runs result shall be added to his

score. Runs made otherwise from a no ball shall be scored no balls.

10. Out From a No Ball The Striker shall be out from a no ball if he breaks Law 34. (Hit the Ball Twice) and either Batsman may be Run Out or shall be given out if either breaks Law 33. (Handled the Ball) or Law 37. (Obstructing the Field).

11. Batsman Given Out Off a No Ball Should a Batsman be given out off a no ball the penalty for bowling it shall stand unless runs are otherwise scored.

NOTES
(a) Definition of a Throw
A ball shall be deemed to have been thrown if, in the opinion of either Umpire, the process of straightening the bowling arm, whether it be partial or complete, takes place during that part of the delivery swing which directly precedes the ball leaving the hand. This definition shall not debar a Bowler from the use of the wrist in the delivery swing.
(b) No Ball not Counting in Over
A no ball shall not be reckoned as one of the over. See Law 22.3. (No Ball or Wide Ball).

Law 25 WIDE BALL

1. Judging a Wide If the Bowler bowls the ball so high over or so wide of the wicket that, in the opinion of the Umpire it passes out of reach of the Striker, standing in a normal guard position, the Umpire shall call and signal 'wide ball' as soon as it has passed the line of the Striker's wicket.
    The Umpire shall not adjudge a ball as being a wide if:
(a) The Striker, by moving from his guard position, causes the ball to pass out of his reach.
(b) The Striker moves and thus brings the ball within his reach.

2. Penalty A penalty of one run for a wide shall be scored if no runs are made otherwise.

3. Ball Coming to Rest in Front of the Striker If a ball which the Umpire considers to have been delivered comes to rest in front of the line of the Striker's wicket, 'wide' shall not be called. The Striker has a right, without interference from the fielding side, to make one attempt to hit the ball. If the fielding side interfere, the Umpire shall replace the ball where it came to rest and shall order the Fieldsmen to resume the places they occupied in the field before the ball was delivered.

The Umpire shall call and signal 'dead ball' as soon as it is clear that the Striker does not intend to hit the ball, or after the Striker has made one unsuccessful attempt to hit the ball.

4. Revoking a Call The Umpire shall revoke the call if the Striker hits a ball which has been called 'wide'.

5. Ball Not Dead The ball does not become dead on the call of 'wide ball'—see Law 23.4. (The Ball is Not Dead).

6. Runs Resulting from a Wide All runs which are run or result from a wide ball which is not a no ball shall be scored wide balls, or if no runs are made one shall be scored.

7. Out from a Wide The Striker shall be out from a wide ball if he breaks Law 35. (Hit Wicket) or Law 39. (Stumped). Either Batsman may be Run Out and shall be out if he breaks Law 33. (Handled the Ball) or Law 37. (Obstructing the Field).

8. Batsman Given Out Off a Wide Should a Batsman be given out off a wide, the penalty for bowling it shall stand unless runs are otherwise made.

NOTES
(a) Wide Ball not Counting in Over
A wide ball shall not be reckoned as one of the over—see Law 22.3. (No Ball or Wide Ball).

Law 26 BYE AND LEG-BYE

1. Byes If the ball, not having been called 'wide' or 'no ball' passes the Striker without touching his bat or person, and any runs are obtained, the Umpire shall signal 'bye' and the run or runs shall be credited as such to the batting side.

2. Leg-Byes If the ball, not having been called 'wide' or 'no ball' is unintentionally deflected by the Striker's dress or person, except a hand holding the bat, and any runs are obtained the Umpire shall signal 'leg-bye' and the run or runs so scored shall be credited as such to the batting side.

Such leg-byes shall only be scored if, in the opinion of the Umpire, the Striker has:
(a) attempted to play the ball with his bat, or
(b) tried to avoid being hit by the ball.

3. Disallowance of Leg-Byes In the case of a deflection by the Striker's person, other than in 2(a) and (b) above, the Umpire shall call and signal 'dead ball' as soon as one run has been completed or when it is clear that a run is not being attempted or the ball has reached the boundary.

On the call and signal of 'dead ball' the Batsmen shall return to their original ends and no runs shall be allowed.

Law 27 APPEALS

1. Time of Appeals The Umpires shall not give a Batsman out unless appealed to by the other side which shall be done prior to the Bowler beginning his run-up or bowling action to deliver the next ball. Under Law 23.1.(g) (The Ball Becomes Dead) the ball is dead on 'over' being called; this does not, however, invalidate an appeal made prior to the first ball of the following over provided 'time' has not been called. See Law 17.1. (Call of Time).

2. An Appeal 'How's That?' An appeal 'How's That?' shall cover all ways of being out.

3. Answering Appeals The Umpire at the Bowler's wicket shall answer appeals before the other Umpire in all cases except those arising out of Law 35. (Hit Wicket) or Law 39. (Stumped) or Law 38. (Run Out) when this occurs at the Striker's wicket.

When either Umpire has given a Batsman not out, the other Umpire shall, within his jurisdiction, answer the appeal or a further appeal, provided it is made in time in accordance with 1. above (Time of Appeals).

4. Consultation by Umpires An Umpire may consult with the other Umpire on a point of fact which the latter may have been in a better position to see and shall then give his decision. If, after consultation, there is still doubt remaining the decision shall be in favour of the Batsman.

5. Batsman Leaving his Wicket under a Misapprehension The Umpires shall intervene if satisfied that a Batsman, not having been given out, has left his wicket under a misapprehension that he has been dismissed.

6. Umpire's Decision The Umpire's decision is final. He may alter his decision, provided that such alteration is made promptly.

7. Withdrawal of an Appeal In exceptional circumstances the Captain of the fielding side may seek permission of the Umpire to withdraw an appeal providing the outgoing Batsman has not left the playing area. If this is allowed, the Umpire shall cancel his decision.

Law 28 THE WICKET IS DOWN

1. Wicket Down The wicket is down if:
(a) Either the ball or the Striker's bat or person completely removes either bail from the top of the stumps. A disturbance of a bail, whether temporary or not, shall not constitute a complete removal, but the wicket is down if a bail in falling lodges between two of the stumps.
(b) Any player completely removes with his hand or arm a bail from the top of the stumps, providing that the ball is held in that hand or in the hand of the arm so used.
(c) When both bails are off, a stump is struck out of the ground by the ball, or a player strikes or pulls a stump out of the ground, providing that the ball is held in the hand(s) or in the hand of the arm so used.

2. One Bail Off If one bail is off, it shall be sufficient for the purpose of putting the wicket down to remove the remaining bail, or to strike or pull any of the three stumps out of the ground in any of the ways stated in 1. above.

3. All the Stumps Out of the Ground If all the stumps are out of the ground, the fielding side shall be allowed to put back one or more stumps in order to have an opportunity of putting the wicket down.

4. Dispensing with Bails If owing to the strength of the wind, it has been agreed to dispense with the bails in accordance with Law 8. (Note (a) (Dispensing with Bails) the decision as to when the wicket is down is one for the Umpires to decide on the facts before them. In such circumstances and if the Umpires so decide the wicket shall be held to be down even though a stump has not been struck out of the ground.

NOTES
(a) Remaking the Wicket
If the wicket is broken while the ball is in play, it is not the Umpire's duty to remake the wicket until the ball has become dead—see Law 23. (Dead Ball). A member of the fielding side, however, may remake the wicket in such circumstances.

Law 29 BATSMAN OUT OF HIS GROUND

1. When out of his Ground A Batsman shall be considered to be out of his ground unless some part of his bat in his hand or of his person is grounded behind the line of the popping crease.

Law 30 BOWLED

1. Out Bowled The Striker shall be out bowled if:
(a) His wicket is bowled down, even if the ball first touches his bat or person.
(b) He breaks his wicket by hitting or kicking the ball on to it before the completion of a stroke, or as a result of attempting to guard his wicket. See Law 34.1. (Out—Hit the Ball Twice).

NOTES
(a) Out Bowled—Not L.B.W.
The Striker is out Bowled if the ball is deflected on to his wicket even though a decision against him would be justified under Law 36. (Leg Before Wicket).

Law 31 TIMED OUT

1. Out Timed Out An incoming Batsman shall be out Timed Out if he wilfully takes more than two minutes to come in—the two minutes being timed from the moment a wicket falls until the new batsman steps on to the field of play.

If this is not complied with and if the Umpire is satisfied that the delay was wilful and if an appeal is made, the new Batsman shall be given out by the Umpire at the Bowler's end.

2. Time to be Added The time taken by the Umpires to investigate the cause of the delay shall be added at the normal close of play.

NOTES
(a) Entry in Score Book
The correct entry in the score book when a Batsman is given out under this Law is 'timed out', and the Bowler does not get credit for the wicket.
(b) Batsmen Crossing on the Field of Play
It is an essential duty of the Captains to ensure that the in-going Batsman passes the out-going one before the latter leaves the field of play.

Law 32 CAUGHT

1. Out Caught The Striker shall be out Caught if

the ball touches his bat or if it touches below the wrist his hand or glove, holding the bat, and is subsequently held by a Fieldsman before it touches the ground.

2. A Fair Catch A catch shall be considered to have been fairly made if:
(a) The Fieldsman is within the field of play throughout the act of making the catch.
(i) The act of making the catch shall start from the time when the Fieldsman first handles the ball and shall end when he both retains complete control over the further disposal of the ball and remains within the field of play.
(ii) In order to be within the field of play, the Fieldsman may not touch or ground any part of his person on or over a boundary line. When the boundary is marked by a fence or board the Fieldsman may not ground any part of his person over the boundary fence or board, but may touch or lean over the boundary fence or board in completing the catch.
(b) The ball is hugged to the body of the catcher or accidentally lodges in his dress or, in the case of the Wicket-Keeper, in his pads. However, a Striker may not be caught if a ball lodges in a protective helmet worn by a Fieldsman, in which case the Umpire shall call and signal 'dead ball'. See Law 23. (Dead Ball.)
(c) The ball does not touch the ground even though a hand holding it does so in effecting the catch.
(d) A Fieldsman catches the ball, after it has been lawfully played a second time by the Striker, but only if the ball has not touched the ground since being first struck.
(e) A Fieldsman catches the ball after it has touched an Umpire, another Fieldsman or the other Batsman. However a Striker may not be caught if a ball has touched a protective helmet worn by a Fieldsman.
(f) The ball is caught off an obstruction within the boundary provided it has not previously been agreed to regard the obstruction as a boundary.

3. Scoring of Runs If a Striker is caught, no runs shall be scored.

NOTES
(a) Scoring from an Attempted Catch
When a Fieldsman carrying the ball touches or grounds any part of his person on or over a boundary marked by a line, 6 runs shall be scored.
(b) Ball Still in Play
If a Fieldsman releases the ball before he crosses the

boundary, the ball will be considered to be still in play and it may be caught by another Fieldsman. However, if the original Fieldsman returns to the field of play and handles the ball, a catch may not be made.

Law 33 HANDLED THE BALL

1. Out Handled the Ball Either Batsman on appeal shall be out Handled the Ball if he wilfully touches the ball while in play with the hand not holding the bat unless he does so with the consent of the opposite side.

NOTES
(a) Entry in Score Book
The correct entry in the score book when a Batsman is given out under this Law is 'handled the ball', and the Bowler does not get credit for the wicket.

Law 34 HIT THE BALL TWICE

1. Out Hit the Ball Twice The Striker, on appeal, shall be out Hit the Ball Twice if, after the ball is struck or is stopped by any part of his person, he wilfully strikes it again with his bat or person except for the sole purpose of guarding his wicket: this he may do with his bat or any part of his person other than his hands, but see Law 37.2. (Obstructing a Ball From Being Caught).
For the purpose of this Law, a hand holding the bat shall be regarded as part of the bat.

2. Returning the Ball to a Fieldsman The Striker, on appeal, shall be out under this Law, if, without the consent of the opposite site, he uses his bat or person to return the ball to any of the fielding side.

3. Runs from Ball Lawfully Struck Twice No runs except those which result from an overthrow or penalty, see Law 41. (The Fieldsman), shall be scored from a ball lawfully struck twice.

NOTES
(a) Entry in Score Book
The correct entry in the score book when the Striker is given out under this Law is 'hit the ball twice' and the Bowler does not get credit for the wicket.
(b) Runs Credited to the Batsman
Any runs awarded under 3. above as a result of an overthrow or penalty shall be credited to the Striker, provided the ball in the first instance has touched the bat, or, if otherwise as extras.

Law 35 HIT WICKET

1. Out Hit Wicket The Striker shall be out Hit Wicket if, while the ball is in play.
(a) His wicket is broken with any part of his person, dress, or equipment as a result of any action taken by him in preparing to receive or in receiving a delivery, or in setting off for his first run, immediately after playing, or playing at, the ball.
(b) He hits down his wicket whilst lawfully making a second stroke for the purpose of guarding his wicket within the provisions of Law 34.1. (Out Hit the Ball Twice).

NOTES
(a) Not Out Hit Wicket
A Batsman is not out under this Law should his wicket be broken in any of the ways referred to in 1(a) above if:
   (i) It occurs while he is in the act of running, other than in setting off for his first run immediately after playing at the ball, or while he is avoiding being run out or stumped.
   (ii) The Bowler after starting his run-up or bowling action does not deliver the ball; in which case the Umpire shall immediately call and signal 'dead ball'.
   (iii) It occurs whilst he is avoiding a throw-in at any time.

Law 36 LEG BEFORE WICKET

1. Out L.B.W. The Striker shall be out L.B.W. in the circumstances set out below:
(a) **Striker Attempting to Play the Ball**
The Striker shall be out L.B.W. if he first intercepts with any part of his person, dress or equipment a fair ball which would have hit the wicket and which has not previously touched his bat or a hand holding the bat, provided that:
   (i) The ball pitched, in a straight line between wicket and wicket or on the off side of the Striker's wicket, or in the case of a ball intercepted full pitch would have pitched in a straight line between wicket and wicket.
   and
   (ii) the point of impact is in a straight line between wicket and wicket, even if above the level of the bails.
(b) **Striker Making No Attempt to Play the Ball**
The Striker shall be out L.B.W. even if the ball is intercepted outside the line of the off-stump, if, in the opinion of the Umpire, he has made no

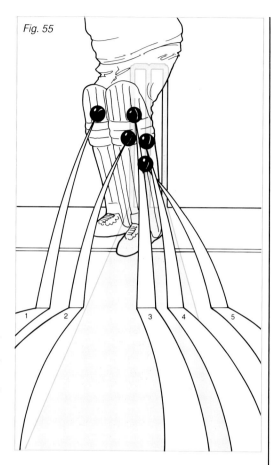

Fig. 55

Fig. 55 L.B.W. 1. Not out. 2. Probably out, but the umpire may rule not out if he thinks the ball was turning sharply enough to have missed the stumps altogether. 3. Probably out, but the umpire may rule not out if he thinks the ball was still rising sharply. 4. Probably out, but the umpire may rule not out if he thinks the ball was turning so sharply that it would have missed off-stump. 5. Not out.

genuine attempt to play the ball with his bat, but has intercepted the ball with some part of his person and if the circumstances set out in (a) above apply.

Law 37 OBSTRUCTING THE FIELD

1. Wilful Obstruction Either Batsman, on appeal, shall be out Obstructing the Field if he wilfully obstructs the opposite side by word or action.

215

2. Obstructing a Ball from Being Caught The Striker, on appeal, shall be out should wilful obstruction by either Batsman prevent a catch being made.

This shall apply even though the Striker causes the obstruction in lawfully guarding his wicket under the provisions of Law 34. See Law 34.1. (Out Hit the Ball Twice).

NOTES
(a) Accidental Obstruction
The Umpires must decide whether the obstruction was wilful or not. The accidental interception of a throw-in by a Batsman while running does not break this Law.
(b) Entry in Score Book
The correct entry in the score book when a Batsman is given out under this Law is 'obstructing the field', and the bowler does not get credit for the wicket.

Law 38 RUN OUT

1. Out Run Out Either Batsman shall be out Run Out if in running or at any time while the ball is in play—except in the circumstances described in Law 39. (Stumped)—he is out of his ground and his wicket is put down by the opposite side. If, however, a Batsman in running makes good his ground he shall not be out Run Out, if he subsequently leaves his ground, in order to avoid injury, and the wicket is put down.

2. 'No Ball' Called If a no ball has been called, the Striker shall not be given Run Out unless he attempts to run.

3. Which Batsman is Out If the Batsmen have crossed in running, he who runs for the wicket which is put down shall be out; if they have not crossed, he who has left the wicket which is put down shall be out. If a Batsman remains in his ground or returns to his ground and the other Batsman joins him there, the latter shall be out if his wicket is put down.

4. Scoring of Runs If a Batsman is run out, only that run which is being attempted shall not be scored. If however an injured Striker himself is run out, no runs shall be scored. See Law 2.7. (Transgression of the Laws by an Injured Batsman or Runner).

NOTES
(a) Ball Played on to Opposite Wicket
If the ball is played on to the opposite wicket neither

Batsman is liable to be Run Out unless the ball has been touched by a Fieldsman before the wicket is broken.
(b) Entry in Score Book
The correct entry in the score book when the Striker is given out under this Law is 'run out', and the Bowler does not get credit for the wicket.

Law 39 STUMPED

1. Out Stumped The Striker shall be out Stumped if, in receiving a ball, not being a no-ball, he is out of his ground otherwise than in attempting a run and the wicket is put down by the Wicket-Keeper without the intervention of another Fieldsman.

2. Action by the Wicket-Keeper The Wicket-Keeper may take the ball in front of the wicket in an attempt to Stump the Striker only if the ball has touched the bat or person of the Striker.

NOTES
(a) Ball Rebounding from Wicket-Keeper's Person
The Striker may be out Stumped if in the circumstances stated in 1. above, the wicket is broken by a ball rebounding from the Wicket-Keeper's person or equipment or is kicked or thrown by the Wicket-Keeper on to the wicket.

Law 40 THE WICKET-KEEPER

1. Position of Wicket-Keeper The Wicket-Keeper shall remain wholly behind the wicket until a ball delivered by the Bowler touches the bat or person of the Striker, or passes the wicket, or until the Striker attempts a run.
In the event of the Wicket-Keeper contravening this Law, the Umpire at the Striker's end shall call and signal 'no ball' at the instant of delivery or as soon as possible thereafter.

2. Restriction on Actions of the Wicket-Keeper If the Wicket-Keeper interferes with the Striker's right to play the ball and to guard his wicket, the Striker shall not be out, except under Laws 33 (Handled the Ball), 34. (Hit the Ball Twice), 37 (Obstructing the Field) and 38. (Run Out).

3. Interference with the Wicket-Keeper by the Striker If in the legitimate defence of his wicket the Striker interferes with the Wicket-Keeper, he shall not be out, except as provided for in Law 37.2. (Obstructing a Ball From Being Caught).

Law 41 THE FIELDSMAN

1. Fielding the Ball The Fieldsman may stop the ball with any part of his person, but if he wilfully stops it otherwise, 5 runs shall be added to the run or runs already scored; if no run has been scored 5 penalty runs shall be awarded. The run in progress shall count provided that the Batsmen have crossed at the instant of the act. If the ball has been struck, the penalty shall be added to the score of the Striker, but otherwise to the score of byes, leg-byes, no balls or wides as the case may be.

2. Limitation of On-Side Fieldsmen The number of on-side Fielsdmen behind the popping crease at the instant of the Bowler's delivery shall not exceed two. In the event of infringement by the fielding side the Umpire at the Striker's end shall call and signal 'no ball' at the instant of delivery or as soon as possible thereafter.

3. Position of Fieldsmen Whilst the ball is in play and until the ball has made contact with the bat or the Striker's person or has passed his bat, no Fieldsman, other than the Bowler, may stand on or have any part of his person extended over the pitch (measuring 22 yards/20.12 m. × 10 ft./ 3.05 m.). In the event of a Fieldsman contravening this Law, the Umpire at the bowler's end shall call and signal 'no ball' at the instant of delivery or as soon as possible thereafter. See Law 40.1. (Position of Wicket-Keeper).

NOTES
(a) Batsmen Changing Ends
The 5 runs referred to in 1. above are a penalty and the Batsmen do not change ends solely by reason of this penalty.

Law 42 UNFAIR PLAY

1. Responsibility of Captains The Captains are responsible at all times for ensuring that play is conducted within the spirit of the game as well as within the Laws.

2. Responsibility of Umpires The Umpires are the sole judges of fair and unfair play.

3. Intervention by the Umpire The Umpires shall intervene without appeal by calling and signalling 'dead ball' in the case of unfair play, but should not otherwise interfere with the progress of the game except as required to do so by the Laws.

4. Lifting the Seam A Player shall not lift the seam of the ball for any reason. Should this be done, the Umpires shall change the ball for one of similar condition to that in use prior to the contravention. See Note (a).

5. Changing the Condition of the Ball Any member of the fielding side may polish the ball provided that such polishing wastes no time and that no artificial substance is used. No-one shall rub the ball on the ground or use any artificial substance or take any other action to alter the condition of the ball.

In the event of a contravention of this Law, the Umpires, after consultation, shall change the ball for one of similar condition to that in use prior to the contravention.

This Law does not prevent a member of the fielding side from drying a wet ball, or removing mud from the ball. See Note (b).

6. Incommoding the Striker An Umpire is justified in intervening under this Law and shall call and signal 'dead ball' if, in his opinion, any Player of the fielding side incommodes the Striker by any noise or action while he is receiving a ball.

7. Obstruction of a Batsman in Running It shall be considered unfair if any Fieldsman wilfully obstructs a Batsman in running. In these circumstances the Umpire shall call and signal 'dead ball' and allow any completed runs and the run in progress or alternatively any boundary scored.

8. The Bowling of Fast Short Pitched Balls The bowling of fast short pitched balls is unfair if, in the opinion of the Umpire at the Bowler's end, it constitutes an attempt to intimidate the Striker. See Note (d).

Umpires shall consider intimidation to be the deliberate bowling of fast short pitched balls which by their length, height and direction are intended or likely to inflict physical injury on the Striker. The relative skill of the Striker shall also be taken into consideration.

In the event of such unfair bowling, the Umpire at the Bowler's end shall adopt the following procedure:
(a) In the first instance the Umpire shall call and signal 'no ball', caution the Bowler and inform the other Umpire, the Captain of the fielding side and the Batsmen of what has occurred.
(b) If this caution is ineffective, he shall repeat the above procedure and indicate to the Bowler that this is a final warning.

(c) Both the above caution and final warning shall continue to apply even though the Bowler may later change ends.

(d) Should the above warnings prove ineffective the Umpire at the Bowler's end shall:

(i) At the first repetition call and signal 'no ball' and when the ball is dead direct the Captain to take the Bowler off forthwith and to complete the over with another Bowler, provided that the Bowler does not bowl two overs or part thereof consecutively. See Law 22.7. (Bowler Incapacitated or Suspended during an Over).

(ii) Not allow the Bowler, thus taken off, to bowl again in the same innings.

(iii) Report the occurrence to the Captain of the batting side as soon as the Players leave the field for an interval.

(iv) Report the occurrence to the Executive of the fielding side and to any governing body responsible for the match who shall take any further action which is considered to be appropriate against the Bowler concerned.

9. The Bowling of Fast High Full Pitches The bowling of fast high full pitches is unfair. See Note (e). In the event of such unfair bowling the Umpire at the Bowler's end shall adopt the procedures of caution, final warning, action against the Bowler and reporting as set out in 8. above.

10. Time Wasting Any form of time wasting is unfair.

(a) In the event of the Captain of the fielding side wasting time or allowing any member of his side to waste time, the Umpire at the Bowler's end shall adopt the following procedure:

(i) In the first instance he shall caution the Captain of the fielding side and inform the other Umpire of what has occurred.

(ii) If this caution is ineffective he shall repeat the above procedure and indicate to the Captain that this is a final warning.

(iii) The Umpire shall report the occurrence to the Captain of the batting side as soon as the Players leave the field for an interval.

(iv) Should the above procedure prove ineffective the Umpire shall report the occurrence to the Executive of the fielding side and to any governing body responsible for that match who shall take appropriate action against the Captain and the Players concerned.

(b) In the event of a Bowler taking unnecessarily long to bowl an over the Umpire at the Bowler's end shall adopt the procedures, other than the calling of 'no-ball', of caution, final warning,

action against the Bowler and reporting.

(c) In the event of a Batsman wasting time (See Note (f)) other than in the manner described in Law 31. (Timed Out), the Umpire at the Bowler's end shall adopt the following procedure:

(i) In the first instance he shall caution the Batsman and inform the other Umpire at once, and the Captain of the batting side, as soon as the Players leave the field for an interval, of what has occurred.

(ii) If this proves ineffective, he shall repeat the caution, indicate to the Batsman that this is a final warning and inform the other Umpire.

(iii) The Umpire shall report the occurrence to both Captains as soon as the Players leave the field for an interval.

(iv) Should the above procedure prove ineffective, the Umpire shall report the occurrence to the Executive of the batting side and to any governing body responsible for that match who shall take appropriate action against the Player concerned.

11. Players Damaging the Pitch The Umpires shall intervene and prevent Players from causing damage to the pitch which may assist the Bowlers of either side. See Note (c).

(a) In the event of any member of the fielding side damaging the pitch the Umpire shall follow the procedure of caution, final warning and reporting as set out in 10(a) above.

(b) In the event of a Bowler contravening this Law by running down the pitch after delivering the ball, the Umpire at the Bowler's end shall first caution the Bowler. If this caution is ineffective the Umpire shall adopt the procedures, other than the calling of 'no-ball', of final warning, action against the Bowler and reporting.

(c) In the event of a Batsman damaging the pitch the Umpire at the Bowler's end shall follow the procedures of caution, final warning and reporting as set out in 10(c) above.

12. Batsman Unfairly Stealing a Run Any attempt by the Batsman to steal a run during the Bowler's run-up is unfair. Unless the Bowler attempts to run out either Batsman—see Law 24.4. (Bowler Throwing at Striker's Wicket Before Delivery) and Law 24.5. (Bowler Attempting to Run Out Non-Striker Before Delivery)—the Umpire shall call and signal 'dead ball' as soon as the Batsmen cross in any such attempt to run. The Batsmen shall then return to their original wickets.

13. Players' Conduct In the event of a player

failing to comply with the instructions of an Umpire, criticising his decisions by word or action, or showing dissent, or generally behaving in a manner which might bring the game into disrepute, the Umpire concerned shall, in the first place report the matter to the other Umpire and to the Player's Captain requesting the latter to take action. If this proves ineffective, the Umpire shall report the incident as soon as possible to the Executive of the Player's team and to any Governing Body responsible for the match, who shall take any further action which is considered appropriate against the Player or Players concerned.

NOTES

(a) The Condition of the Ball

Umpires shall make frequent and irregular inspections of the condition of the ball.

(b) Drying of a Wet Ball

A wet ball may be dried on a towel or with sawdust.

(c) Danger Area

The danger area on the pitch, which must be protected from damage by a Bowler, shall be regarded by the Umpires as the area contained by an imaginary line 4 ft./1.22 m. from the popping crease, and parallel to it, and within two imaginary and parallel lines drawn down the pitch from points on that line 1 ft./30.48 cm. on either side of the middle stump.

(d) Fast Short Pitched Balls

As a guide, a fast short pitched ball is one which pitches short and passes, or would have passed, above the shoulder height of the Striker standing in a normal batting stance at the crease.

(e) The Bowling of Fast Full Pitches

The bowling of one fast, high full pitch shall be considered to be unfair if, in the opinion of the Umpire, it is deliberate, bowled at the Striker, and if it passes or would have passed above the shoulder height of the Striker when standing in a normal batting stance at the crease.

(f) Time Wasting by Batsmen

Other than in exceptional circumstances, the Batsman should always be ready to take strike when the Bowler is ready to start his run-up.

Glossary and Index

GLOSSARY OF CRICKETING TERMS

ALL-ROUNDER—A player with the ability to contribute to the game more than a single skill. A batsman who can also bowl to a reasonable standard or vice versa. Sir Garfield Sobers (see page 50) is arguably the greatest all-rounder ever, being able to bat, bowl in different styles, field in all positions and even keep wicket.

ANALYSIS—A summary of performance usually in writing. A bowler's analysis could be 20 overs, 5 maidens, 50 runs, 5 wickets.

ARTIFICIAL SURFACES—A playing surface or outfield made of something other than turf (see page 177).

AVERAGE—The expected number of runs per innings (over a period) of a batsman or runs per wicket of a bowler. A batting average would be 50 if a batsman, in 10 innings, made 500 runs.

AWAY-SWINGER—A ball that, in its flight towards the stumps, swerves in the direction of the off-side (the slips).

BACK UP—In batting, to make ground down the pitch, when at the non-striker's end, as the ball leaves the bowler's hand, in order to shorten the distance of a potential run.

In the field it involves any action by a fielder to prevent overthrows.

BAILS—The two cross pieces each of $4\frac{3}{8}$ ins long that rest on top of the stumps. At least one part must be dislodged for the wicket to be broken.

BLOCK—The mark made by the batsman when taking guard from the umpire. This enables the batsman to know his position in relation to the wicket when in the stance position.

A 'BLUE'—A player who has represented either Cambridge or Oxford in a match between the two universities.

'BOSIE'—The Australian name for a googly (see entry below). Named after B.J.T. Bosanquet, its originator.

BOX—The shield designed to protect the genitals

from injury. Batsman and wicket-keeper should always wear a box.

BREAK—The deviation of the ball on pitching. Off break deviates from off to leg.

BUMP BALL—What at first appears to be a legitimate catch by a fielder but in fact has been hit 'into' the ground and rebounded.

BUTTER FINGERS—The name often directed at a fielder who has dropped a simple catch.

'CARRIED HIS BAT'—The term used when a batsman who has opened the innings remains 'not out' when the rest of the team have been dismissed.

COW SHOT—A wild 'swipe' to leg.

CRICKETANA—A collection of cricket relics.

CROSS BAT—A stroke played across the line of the ball, not necessarily a bad stroke. The pull stroke is a cross bat stroke.

DECLARE—A captain can 'declare' by bringing his team's innings to a close, whilst wickets are still standing.

DEEP—The area in the outfield next to the boundary.

DONKEY DROP—An old-fashioned term for a high full toss aimed to land on top of the stumps.

A DUCK—A score of 0.

FAST-FOOTED BATSMAN—A batsman who is reluctant to use his feet to make strokes.

FLY SLIP—The position of a slip fielder half way to the boundary, anticipating a catch from a top-edged attacking stroke.

FULL PITCH—A ball that can be hit by the batsman before it bounces.

GOOGLY—An off-break bowled with a leg-break type action to fool a right-handed batsman. (*See* page 21.)

HALF-COCK—A 'half' stroke, usually forward, i.e. incomplete and therefore not getting towards the pitch of the ball.

'HOW'S THAT?'—The traditional appeal to the umpire from the bowler and wicket-keeper and very often other fielders, when asking for a decision to be given against the batsman.

THE LAP—What may be termed an 'agricultural' sweep stroke.

LEG TRAP—A ring of close fielders behind the wicket on the leg-side.

LENGTH—The point where the ball pitches in relation to the batsman. A good length is one which causes the batsman doubt as to whether to play back or forward.

LONG STOP—Originally a fielding position on the boundary directly behind the wicket-keeper. Now obsolete.

MAIDEN
An over from which no runs have been scored from the bat.

NELSON—The score 111. 222 is 'double Nelson'.

NIGHT WATCHMAN—A late order batsman, promoted in the hope that he will stay at the wicket for a short period before the close of play, thus saving the more recognised batsman till the following day.

OVERTHROW—As the name implies, this is a throw at either wicket by a fielder, which is not collected and results in an extra run or runs being taken.

A PAIR—Two scores of 0 in the same match. A King Pair is two scores of 0 in the same match, each being a first ball dismissal.

PITCH (OF A BALL)—The point at which the bowled ball hits the ground.

PLUMB—A word expressing a positive opinion on the question of batsman being out. Usually applied to LBW.

RUBBER—A series of matches.

SHOOTER—A ball that shoots along the ground on pitching.

SIGHT SCREEN—Screens, usually white and positioned behind the bowler's arm on the boundary edge, thus enabling the batsman to have a better sight of the ball as it is delivered.

SILLY—A prefix to a number of often dangerously close fielding positions, i.e. silly mid-off, silly point.

SKY—To top edge the ball very high in the air—a skyer.

STICKY WICKET—A pitch made soft by rain and drying quickly in the sun or wind. Very difficult to bat upon.

STONE-WALL—To block the ball, making no attempt to score. To simply stay at the wicket.

TAIL ENDER—A batsman, usually a specialist bowler, in one of the last three places in the team's batting order.

WRONG'UN—Another expression for the googly.

WALK—Over the years but less so in recent times, some batsmen have 'walked' (giving themselves out) when they have 'nicked' the ball to the wicket-keeper, saving the umpire the task of making a decision.

Index

Page numbers in *italic* refer to the illustrations